THE MYTHS

of

HAPPINESS

ALSO BY SONJA LYUBOMIRSKY

The How of Happiness

THE MYTHS

of

HAPPINESS

What Should Make You Happy, but Doesn't

What Shouldn't Make You Happy, but Does

SONJA LYUBOMIRSKY

THE PENGUIN PRESS | NEW YORK | 2013

THE PENGUIN PRESS
Published by the Penguin Group
Penguin Group (USA) Inc., 375 Hudson Street, New York, New York 10014, USA •
Penguin Group (Canada), 90 Eglinton Avenue East, Suite 700, Toronto, Ontario M4P 2Y3,
Canada (a division of Pearson Penguin Canada Inc.) • Penguin Books Ltd, 80 Strand, London
WC2R 0RL, England • Penguin Ireland, 25 St Stephen's Green, Dublin 2, Ireland (a division
of Penguin Books Ltd) • Penguin Group (Australia), 707 Collins Street, Melbourne, Victoria
3008, Australia (a division of Pearson Australia Group Pty Ltd) • Penguin Books India Pvt
Ltd, 11 Community Centre, Panchsheel Park, New Delhi–110 017, India • Penguin Group
(NZ), 67 Apollo Drive, Rosedale, Auckland 0632, New Zealand (a division of Pearson
New Zealand Ltd) • Penguin Books (South Africa), Rosebank Office Park, 181 Jan Smuts
Avenue, Parktown North 2193, South Africa • Penguin China, B7 Jiaming Center,
27 East Third Ring Road North, Chaoyang District, Beijing 100020, China

Penguin Books Ltd., Registered Offices:
80 Strand, London WC2R 0RL, England

First published in 2013 by The Penguin Press,
a member of Penguin Group (USA) Inc.

1   3   5   7   9   10   8   6   4   2

LIBRARY OF CONGRESS CATALOGING IN PUBLICATION DATA

Lyubomirsky, Sonja.
The myths of happiness : what should make you happy but doesn't, what shouldn't make you
happy but does / Sonja Lyubomirsky.
     p.   cm.
Includes bibliographical references and index.
ISBN 978-1-59420-437-1
1. Happiness.   I. Title.
BF575.H27L983   2013
152.4'2—dc23   2012030936

Printed in the United States of America

Designed by Gretchen Achilles

TO ISABELLA

Contents

CHAPTER 10

I Can't Be Happy When . . .
the Best Years of My Life Are Over   *233*

"Life is so constructed, that the event does not, cannot, will not, match the expectation."

—CHARLOTTE BRONTË

"He who is not contented with what he has, would not be contented with what he would like to have."

—SOCRATES

"Chance favors the prepared mind."

—LOUIS PASTEUR

THE MYTHS
of
HAPPINESS

INTRODUCTION

The Myths of Happiness

Nearly all of us buy into what I call the myths of happiness—beliefs that certain adult achievements (marriage, kids, jobs, wealth) will make us forever happy and that certain adult failures or adversities (health problems, not having a life partner, having little money) will make us forever unhappy. This reductive understanding of happiness is culturally reinforced and continues to endure, despite overwhelming evidence that our well-being does not operate according to such black-and-white principles.[1]

One such happiness myth is the notion that "I'll be happy *when* ____ (fill in the blank)." I'll be happy when I net that promotion, when I say "I do," when I have a baby, when I'm rich, and so on. The false promise is not that achieving those dreams won't make us happy. They almost certainly will. The problem is that these achievements—even when initially perfectly satisfying—will not make us as intensely happy (or for as long) as we believe they will. Hence, when fulfilling these goals doesn't make us as happy as we expected, we feel there must be something wrong with us or we must be the only ones to feel this way.

The flip side is an equally pervasive, and equally toxic, happiness myth. This is the belief that "I *can't* be happy when ____ (fill in the blank)." When a negative change of fortune befalls us, our reaction is often supersized. We feel that we can never be happy again, that our life as we know it is now over.

My relationship is in trouble. I've achieved my dreams but feel emptier than ever. My work isn't what it used to be. The test results were positive. I have huge regrets. What I hope this book will make singularly clear is that although it may appear that some of these major challenges will definitively and permanently change our lives for better or for worse, it is really our responses to them that govern their repercussions. Indeed, it is our initial reactions that make these turns of events into crisis points in the first place, instead of the foreseeable and even ordinary passages of life that they actually are. Unfortunately, our initial reactions compel us to choose dramatic (and often devastating) response paths. For example, whereas our first response to the realization that our job no longer brings satisfaction might be to conclude that there is something wrong with the job and immediately begin looking for a position elsewhere, the solution with more long-term rewards may be to try instead to reshape and reconsider our job—to revisit and revise our present-day thoughts and feelings.

This book covers ten different adult crisis points—beginning with relationships (marriage, singlehood, kids), moving on to money and work (job malaise, financial success and ruin)—and ending with problems inherent to middle age and beyond (health issues, aging, regrets). Feel free to begin with the crisis points that you most connect to or are most curious about. I expect that all of us will identify with a good portion of the particular challenges and transitions that I describe here, as some of them may represent a part of ourselves as we were yesterday, are today, and will be tomorrow. With age, responsibilities and losses pile up, and life becomes more complicated, more challenging, and sometimes more confusing. Before things start cascading, it's valuable to take a long and thoughtful look at the major passages and touchstones of our lives, and what motivates our reactions to them.

Instead of being frightening or depressing, your crisis points can be opportunities for renewal, growth, or meaningful change. However, how you greet them really matters: Science shows that chance does favor the prepared mind. I draw on research from several related fields—including positive psychology, social psychology, personality psychology, and clinical psychology—to help those of you facing consequential turning points to choose wisely. The science I describe will offer you a broader perspective—essentially a birds-eye-view of your unique situation—and push you beyond your expectations. I can't tell you which path to take, but I can help provide the tools so that you can make healthier and more informed decisions on your own. I can help you achieve that prepared mind, the one that knows where happiness really lies and where it doesn't.

Our crisis points—times when in an instant we feel our lives will never be the same, when we come to a realization or take in a weighty piece of news—are key moments in our lives. They are the moments that we remember and pivot on, the ones we need to consider and respond to. This is true not just because such moments are "big," but because even seemingly devastating crossroads can be gateways to positive changes in our lives. Recent research reveals that people who have experienced *some* adversity (for example, several negative events or life-changing moments) are ultimately happier (and less distressed, traumatized, stressed, or impaired) than those who have experienced no adversity at all.[2] Having a history of enduring several devastating moments "toughens us up" and makes us better prepared to manage later challenges and traumas, big and small. In addition to fostering resilience in general, researchers have shown that making sense of our life's challenges helps us define and anchor our identities, which bolsters optimism about our futures and fosters more effective coping with ongoing sources of stress.[3] Finally, the experience of negative emotions like grief, worry, and anger during our crisis points—when these emotions are not chronic or severe—can be extremely valuable, as such emotions alert us to threats, wrongs, and problems that require our attention. In summary, learning to look beyond the expectations that accompany the myths of happiness may be uncomfortable and even painful in the beginning, but it has the potential to lead to flourishing and to growth.

Many consequential turning points can be viewed as crossroads from which we can pursue two or more paths. How we react to these moments—which may seem at the time like "points of no return"—will in part determine how their outcomes will unfold. If we understand how the myths of happiness drive our responses, we are more likely to respond wisely. Indeed, failing to grasp the impact of the "I'll be happy *when* [I have a partner, job, money, kids]" fallacy may lead us to make very poor decisions—for example, leaving perfectly good jobs and marriages, harming our relationships with our children, squandering our money, and wounding our self-esteem. And, if we continue to believe "I *can't* be happy when [I don't have a partner, money, youth, accomplishments]," we may unwittingly create a self-fulfilling prophecy, such that those turning points end up poisoning our happiness and contaminating the still satisfying aspects of our lives.

How we respond to crisis moments—whether we keep our heads down when we should lift them up, or stay put when we should act—may have cascading effects across our lives. In these moments, we choose the future.

Once upon a time, an old farmer lived in a poor country village. His neighbors considered him well-to-do because he owned a horse, which he used for many years to work his crops. One day his beloved horse ran away. Upon hearing the news, his neighbors gathered to commiserate with him. "Such bad luck," they said sympathetically. "May be," the farmer replied. The next morning the horse returned, but brought with it six wild horses. "How wonderful," the neighbors rejoiced. "May be," replied the old man. The following day, his son tried to saddle and ride one of the untamed horses, was thrown, and broke his leg. Again, the neighbors visited the farmer to offer their sympathy on his misfortune. "May be," said the farmer. The day after that, conscription officers came to the village to draft young men into the army. Seeing that the farmer's son had a broken leg, they passed him by. The neighbors congratulated the farmer on how well things had turned out. "May be," the farmer replied.

"Joy and woe are woven fine." William Blake's line from the poem "Auguries of Innocence" elegantly and simply extracts the kernel of wisdom from this story. It also helps answer the question of why the myths of happiness are wrongheaded. We may think we know whether a particular turning point should make us laugh or cry, but the truth is that positive and negative events are often entwined, rendering predictions about consequences—which may cascade in unexpected ways—exceedingly complex. Similarly, when we consider the single best thing that has happened to us during past years—and the single worst thing—we may be surprised to learn that they are often one and the same. Perhaps we had our hearts broken, but then being single solidified our identity and led us to meet a more ideal mate. Perhaps we were laid off from a longstanding career, but the event prompted us to make the transition to a more exciting field. Or, perhaps we were thrilled after we sold our company for a great deal of money, but now deem it one of the biggest mistakes of our lives.[4] In sum, which events are life changing, and in what ways, is often not immediately knowable. Sometimes an unassailably positive event—winning the lottery, getting promoted, having a child—sets into motion a crisis or deep disappointment, because our less-than-joyful reactions to them violate our notions of what should make us happy. And other times a misfortune—losing a job, a dream, or a life partner—is a gateway to something wonderful, in part because we realize that we were wrong to believe that such events would permanently damage us.

In a series of elegant experiments, University of Virginia professor Tim Wilson and Harvard University professor Dan Gilbert and their colleagues have shown that our key error is that we overestimate how long and how intensely a particular negative life event (such as a diagnosis of HIV or being fired from a cherished job) will throw us into despair, and how long and how intensely a particular positive event (earning lifetime tenure or having our marriage proposal accepted) will throw us over the moon.[5] The primary reason that we do this is neatly summed up by the fortune-cookie maxim: "Nothing in life is as important as you think it is while you are thinking about it." In other words, we exaggerate the effect a life change will have upon our happiness because we cannot foresee that we won't always be thinking about it.

For example, when we try to predict how dejected we will feel after our romance dissolves or how blissful we will feel after we finally have the money to buy the long-dreamed-of beach house, we neglect to consider that during the days, weeks, and months after the event in question, many other events will intervene, thus serving to temper our pleasure or mitigate our pain. Daily hassles (like being stuck in traffic or overhearing a catty comment) and daily uplifts (like running into an old friend) are likely to toy with our emotions to a significant degree and thus buffer the misery of a breakup or dilute the joy of a new home.

Two other forces are at work that conspire to lead us astray in predicting our future feelings. The first is simply our failure to imagine accurately the impact of the transition point we are predicting. For example, for many of us, images of a future marriage comprise romantic picnics for two, drinking champagne by the fire, sex as often as we want, harmonious collaboration on all difficult life decisions, and a cherubic infant sleeping in our arms, with our spouse offering to make all the diaper changes. We don't tend to visualize the stresses, ups and downs, waning passions, disagreements, misunderstandings, and disappointments of long-term love—all of the things that connive to short-circuit a marriage's honeymoon period. Similarly, the pictures in our minds of what it would be like to experience joblessness or deep regrets or being single are unduly dark and pessimistic.

The second factor that helps foil our predictions is that we underestimate the strength of what Gilbert and Wilson call our "psychological immune system." Much as our immune cells protect us from pathogens and disease, it turns out that we have a host of skills and talents that we underappreciate or fail to foresee—from our knack for rationalizing our failures to our capacity to rise to the occasion—that protect us from buckling in the face of adversity or stress. People are quite resilient, and are quick to discount, explain away, or block out negative experiences or transform them into something positive. When we imagine how we would feel after learning that our work hours have been seriously slashed, we don't appreciate that the initial despondency and self-doubt that we will experience will be softened by our improved fitness (from those extra hours in the gym), our increased closeness with our kids (from those extra hours at the playground), our realization that we never really wanted to be a broker anyway (from late-night tête-à-têtes with our partner), and our sense of growth (from appreciating how the setback has revealed to us strengths that we didn't even know we had). Don't get me wrong: The initial wretchedness after a rejection or job loss is unlikely to metamorphose into delight, but studies show that the distress is very likely to be cushioned by our psychological immune system.[6]

Notably, our psychological immune system operates after positive events as well. As I discuss in detail in chapters 2, 6, and 8, human beings have a tremendous capacity to adapt to new relationships, jobs, and wealth, with the result that even such rewarding life changes yield fewer and fewer rewards with time. This phenomenon, which is called "hedonic adaptation," is an important theme of the book, because our tendency to get used to almost everything positive that happens to us is a formidable obstacle to our happiness. After all, if we ultimately take for granted our new jobs, new loves, new homes, and new successes, then how can our joy and satisfaction from these things ever endure? To this question, I offer evidence-based recommendations for how to head off or rise above this obstacle and find our way to flourishing and fulfillment.

My argument is that once we understand the misconceptions and biases motivating our reactions, we will understand that no matter how clear the way forward seems, there is no one direct, apposite path or one way of regarding our situation. Instead, there are multiple routes. I hope that reading this book will guide us toward a better understanding of our own unique paths. There is much risk and there is much at risk, for whichever path we choose will have cascading effects for years to come—no do-overs allowed. "For whatever we do," wrote James Salter in *Light Years*, his novel about marriage, "even whatever we do not do prevents us from doing the opposite. Acts demolish their alternatives, that is the paradox."[7]

In his best-selling book *Blink: The Power of Thinking Without Thinking*, Malcolm Gladwell advanced the idea that decisions made in the blink of an eye—based on little information, on pure emotion and instinct—are often better than carefully reasoned and considered ones.[8] The broader culture, fueled by media reports, has picked up this feel-good idea with gusto. After all, the notion of relying on intuition to make important decisions and judgments—of not having to do *any* work!—is incredibly appealing, especially to American minds yearning for quick fixes.

In this book, I argue that the second—or even third—thought may be the best thought. My approach is, "Think, don't blink."

The debate over whether the first thought versus the second (or *n*th) thought is the best thought has a very long history. Beginning with Plato and Aristotle, philosophers, writers, and, in the last decades, social and cognitive psychologists have distinguished between two different tracks on which our brains run when making judgments and decisions.[9] The first track (with the uncatchy name of System 1; I'll call it *intuitive*) is the one that Gladwell described in *Blink*. When we rely on our intuitions, gut instincts, or on-the-spot emotions to decide whether we should walk away from our job, we rely on our intuitive system. Such decisions are made so quickly and automatically that we are not aware of what precisely influenced them. In these pages, I will illuminate the misconceptions about our happiness that serve as the influences on each of these first thoughts.

The second track on which our minds operate (labeled by scientists as System 2, but what I'll call *rational*) is much more deliberate. When we rely on reason or rational thought to decide whether to throw over our employer for a new one, we muster energy and effort, we take our time, we systematically and critically analyze, and we may make use of particular principles or rules. This is precisely what this book will call on you—and help you—to do.

During the past half century, a huge literature in psychology has documented the many errors and biases that lead human beings to make poor decisions based on their intuitions.[10] To be sure, we often

make costly mistakes when making choices. This is because our intuitive system—which many of us put great trust in—typically re-
lies on quick-and-dirty mental shortcuts or rules of thumb ("Did
you hear about the shooting at the movie theater? I better watch
TV instead"), which often lead us astray. Yet, despite the pitfalls
inherent in the intuitive system, our intuitive first thoughts are usually far more compelling than our well-thought-through second and
third ones. Indeed, because intuitive judgments often seem to
emerge spontaneously, automatically, and unsolicited, we experience
them almost like a "given" or an established fact.[11] Thus, when we
have a strong sense that we must take our job and shove it, even
though that sense is rooted in myths about happiness, we accord
that intuition extra meaning and import because it "just feels right."
Indeed, we tend to prefer gut instincts even when they are obviously
irrational.

I don't mean to imply that thinking twice or thrice is *always*
the optimal approach, especially when our heads and hearts offer
us conflicting advice. But the truth is that our initial reactions (or
first thoughts) to crisis points (e.g., "My life is going downhill" or
"I'll never find love again") are tainted by our biases and governed
by fallacies we buy into about what should and shouldn't bring us
happiness. My goal is to lay bare and dismantle these biases and
fallacies.

The challenge, of course, is how to do this—how to shift your
habitual reactions to major life changes or epiphanies from a purely
intuitive approach rooted in misinformation about happiness to a
more reasoned one. After you understand the assumptions govern-
ing your reactions, you must decide how to act or whether (and how)
to change your perspective. In this way, you will replace reliance on
the myths of happiness with a prepared mind—a mind equipped to

make a better, reason-based decision and to think instead of blink. Consider the case that I focus on in chapter 1—that you are feeling bored in your marriage. Your first thought may be, "I don't want my husband as much as I used to, so our marriage must not be working, or he must no longer be right for me." Drawing on theoretical and empirical evidence, I will unmask the fallacy behind your thinking— the notion that marriage is permanently satisfying—and offer recommendations about how to address, remedy, or cope with your situation. How then do you make the decision about next steps in circumstances like these? Psychologists offer several evidence-backed practical suggestions.[12]

First, make a mental note of your initial intuitions or gut reactions about the path you should be taking—perhaps even write them down—and then shelve them for a while. After you spend time thinking through your situation systematically, you may reconsider the initial gut reaction in light of new information or insights. Second, seek the opinion of an outsider (impartial friend or counselor) or simply make an effort to take an objective observer's perspective. The key is to liberate yourself from the nitty-gritty details of your particular problem (say, that you're currently experiencing a loss of passion) and try to consider the broader class of problems to which yours belongs (say, the course of physical attraction in a long-term relationship). Third, consider the *opposite* of whatever your gut instinct is telling you to do, and systematically play through the consequences in your mind. And, finally, when your crossroads involves multiple decisions (as opposed to just one), weigh all your options simultaneously rather than separately. Research reveals that such "joint" decision making is more successful and less prone to bias than "separate" decision making.

Although these four recommendations are not panaceas, they

have the potential to launch us in the direction of better decisions about the road to take in the face of life's challenges and turning points. However, we should be vigilant that our thoughtful, systematic analysis doesn't devolve into rumination or overthinking about our life choices; rumination is a dangerous habit that is likely to trigger a vicious cycle of increased worry, gloom, hopelessness, and "paralysis by analysis." If our second and third thoughts are repeating themselves or going around in circles, then we are ruminating, not analyzing.

In sum, when we are facing an epiphany or a major life change, it's natural to want to act quickly and instinctively. But there is great value to waiting and thinking, and not rushing to conclusions. Our first thought will only get us so far. Although it isn't easy to identify an optimal course of action, we can begin by rejecting our first thoughts, and, instead, leaving ourselves open to multiple potential responses to life's crisis points.

I can't counsel each individual to follow a particular trajectory. Each of us must choose and fashion our own unique path. Depending on our personal histories, our social-support networks, and our personalities, goals, and resources, particular roads or detours may be more or less appropriate, beneficial, or rewarding. Researchers have shown that when people behave in ways that fit their personalities, interests, and values, they are more satisfied, more confident, more successful, more engaged in what they are doing, and feel "right" about it.[13] Instead, the goal of *The Myths of Happiness* is to draw on the latest scientific research to expand readers' perspectives about the crisis points they are confronting, dismantle the false beliefs about happiness driving their initial reactions, and introduce the tools that they can use to draw their own verdicts and develop new skills and habits of mind. Fortified with counterintuitive wisdom and instructive distance from their problems, their next crisis point will be met with a prepared mind.

Although our crisis points may initially feel disappointing or confusing or even tragic, they are opportunities to change our lives or, at the very least, to achieve a clearer vision. With new understanding, we will be better able to use major challenges to make major strides. The message of *The Myths of Happiness* is that, ultimately, we each can identify the steps to take to forge our way to a fulfilling life and help ourselves reach and exceed our happiness potentials.

PART I

CONNECTIONS

THE challenges central to this section of the book—about the pain of having or not having intimate relationships—are particularly agonizing for many of us. As just one case in point, an especially evocative description I've heard of the stress of divorce is that it's equivalent to the stress of experiencing a car crash every day over six months. The time might come when we ask ourselves, should I stay with my partner or should I leave? Should I be optimistic about marriage or give up hope of finding a soul mate? The answers to these questions are complicated, but, fortunately, a great deal of psychological science illuminates why we arrive at such crisis moments in the first place and the nature of the paths to which those moments can lead. When we find ourselves acutely troubled by our love lives or our family lives, it's critical that before we act, we examine our culturally prescribed expectations about finding a lifetime partner and having children. Because most of us deeply share and embrace these expectations, we feel certain that meeting relationship-relevant milestones (finding Mr. Right or becoming a parent) will make us forever happy and that failing to meet such milestones (not finding a partner, or Mr. Right turning out to be Mr. Wrong) will leave us forever unhappy. In this section, I hope to push all of us to confront these expectations and assumptions and to consider the persuasive research showing in which ways we may be wrong. For example, studies show that people adapt remarkably well to challenges, like being or becoming single or enduring the trials and tribulations of parenting. On the flip side, however, we are also remarkably swift to habituate to positive circumstantial changes, such as new marriages and jobs. My laboratory and those of other social psychologists and behavioral economists have been systematically investigating the phenomenon of how we take our own lives for granted and, importantly, how we can avert or slow down that habituation when we find ourselves bored, for example, with our marriages and our sex lives. The lessons from this work may steer us to some unexpected insights and decisions.

I will offer a number of ideas for how you can become happier and more fulfilled by combating this insidious habituation and, ultimately, by determining at what point you should persist at reclaiming your former happiness, improving the status quo, or, instead, take a step toward radical change. Although I cannot tell you what to do, I can arm you with the latest findings illuminating the likely paths you'll face, while introducing the tools that you can use to develop an appropriate response—or, rather, a response that's right for you. Fortunately, plenty of new research on close relationships can expose the fallacies underlying your reactions to a miserable marriage or divorce or parenting or singlehood, and your new understanding will open up a world of possible trajectories available to you. Everyone will recognize themselves somewhere in the findings and implications from this new science. After you stop regarding your situation in black-and-white terms ("I must stay" or "I must leave"), your options about what steps to take will increase exponentially.

I'll Be Happy When . . .
I'm Married to the Right Person

I f you've been in a marriage or committed relationship for some length of time, you may be experiencing something that you are reluctant to share even with your closest family and friends—boredom. Although this may seem like a paltry or self-indulgent problem, it can begin with petty misgivings and complaints and ultimately snowball into dissatisfactions and breakup daydreams that plague you and poison your relationship. Your first instinct may be to end the marriage, but you don't know whether you should or how to go about it. Instead, you may be hurting, consumed with guilt, ruminating about your feelings, making excuses, and oscillating between paralysis and panic.

Before you take a single step, it's critical to consider the happiness myth that is likely driving those first instincts. This is the assumption that "I'll be happy when . . . I'm married to the right person."[14] You may have devoted a great deal of time, energy, and consideration to finding a fitting or ideal partner, and you applied yourself to caring for your marriage. Yet despite your efforts and good fortune, you are now beginning to realize that your marriage is not giving you the satisfaction that you thought it would or that it once had. This is a determining moment, as it calls for you to understand whether your expectations are realistic and whether you are asking too much of your marriage. As I describe below, even the happiest marriages cannot maintain their initial satisfaction level, and only with a great deal of energy and commitment can you approach that initial level.

This chapter is about the choices and insights available if you find yourself in a marriage or long-term relationship that has ceased to satisfy. You can continue to be tormented by your thoughts and hope that they will fade with time, or you can strive to understand their source and act to resolve or attenuate them. The approaches I describe teach you and your partner how to reinvest in your relationship. After all, the promise of new, fulfilling, positive directions is at stake.

I'M BORED WITH MY MARRIAGE, OR, GETTING USED TO YOUR SPOUSE

As I mentioned earlier, one of my primary scientific interests is in the area of hedonic adaptation—namely, the fact that human beings have the remarkable capacity to grow habituated or inured to most life changes.[15] A hot topic today in the fields of psychology and economics, hedonic adaptation explains why both the thrill of victory and the agony of defeat abate with time.[16] What is particularly fascinating about this phenomenon, however, is that it is most pronounced with respect to positive experiences. Indeed, it turns out that we are prone to take for granted pretty much everything positive that happens to us. When we move into a beautiful new loft with a grand view, when we partake of plastic surgery, when we purchase a fancy new automobile or nth-generation smartphone, when we earn the corner office and a raise at work, when we become immersed in a new hobby, and even when we wed, we obtain an immediate boost of happiness from the improved situation; but the thrill only lasts for a short time. Over the coming days, weeks, and months, we find our expectations ramping upward and we begin taking our new improved circumstances for granted. We are left with "felicific stagnation."[17] I will discuss the implications of hedonic adaptation to our jobs and to our incomes in chapters 5 and 7, but I focus on adaptation to marriage here.

In my view, marrying my husband was the best thing that ever happened to me—an event that brought me immense joy, which reverberates to this day, and which has given rise to multiple and wonderful downstream repercussions in my life. The most famous study exploring this issue, however, found that although the average person picks up a sizable boost in happiness when he or she gets married, this boost only lasts about two years, after which the former newlywed reverts back to his or her happiness level before the engagement.[18]

When you were newly in love, you probably had the capacity to be happy while being stuck in traffic or getting your teeth cleaned. But this phase didn't last very long. So, if you find yourself less euphoric and less amorous than at the beginning of your relationship, you are experiencing what most other humans have experienced before you,[19] and any friends of yours who claim otherwise (with rare exceptions) are probably lying to you or to themselves.

Marital bliss, like new job bliss or new car bliss, is highly prone to hedonic adaptation, but infatuation, passion, and electric attraction carry the added liability of having an even shorter half-life. When we first fall in love, if we are lucky, we experience what researchers call passionate love, but over the years, this type of love usually turns into companionate love.[20] Passionate love is a state of intense longing, desire, and attraction, whereas companionate love is composed more of deep affection, connection, and liking. If you are wondering what kind of love you are experiencing now—or had in the past—judge the extent to which you agree with statements like the ones below.[21] For passionate love:

- I find it hard to work because I'm always thinking about my partner.

- I am so involved with my partner that I could not even be slightly interested in someone else.

- I am terribly afraid that my partner might reject me.

For companionate love:

- My partner is one of the most likable people I know.

- My partner is the sort of person that I would like to be.

- I have great confidence in my partner's good judgment.

There are evolutionary, physiological, and practical reasons for why passionate love cannot endure for very long. I hazard to say that if we continued to obsess about our partners and to have sex multiple times a day—every day—we would not be very productive at work or attentive to our children, our friends, or our health. To quote a line from the 2004 film *Before Sunset*, about two former lovers who chance to meet again after a decade, if passion did not fade, "we would end up doing nothing at all with our lives."[22] Indeed, being madly in love shares some key characteristics with addiction and narcissism, and if unabated, would eventually take its toll. In any event, the heightened passion and chemical attraction evident at the beginning of a love affair have been found to fade to neutral in a couple of years,[23] after the love affair turns into a solid, committed relationship or marriage.[24] Furthermore, this shift in feelings is often accompanied by a decline in overall satisfaction, as the fun and leisure typical of the honeymoon phase turn to domestic drudgery, and as partners stop being on their best behavior and relax their efforts to be constantly responsive and considerate toward each other.[25]

Fortunately, as evolutionary psychologists might tell it, both passionate and companionate love are essential for human beings to survive and reproduce. While passionate love is necessary to galvanize us to pair up and direct all our energies into building a new relationship, companionate love appears to be critical for nourishing a committed, stable partnership long enough to reproduce our genes (i.e., have children) and ensure they survive and flourish. It should be said that both types of love bring their own unique brand of happiness—one more exciting, perhaps, and the other more meaningful.

In light of the naturally occurring decay of the passion and joy experienced early in marriage, we seem to be perverse in our expectations that our long-term relationships should continue to serve as vehicles for our desires and wish fulfillments. Indeed, I would argue even more strongly that our romance with the idea of romance has led us to misunderstand the function, complexity, and typical life course of marriage, leaving us disappointed when our marriages don't constantly fulfill our longings for passion, satisfaction, intimacy, and permanence. As we reflect on our experiences of boredom or waning passion or petty dissatisfaction in our current partnerships, we should reexamine these assumptions and establish the extent to which our experiences may simply be manifestations of an extraordinarily ordinary process.

Research from my lab and that of several colleagues suggests several secrets to overcoming, forestalling, or at least slowing down hedonic adaptation to committed relationships. The first recommendation is one you have already begun to follow simply by reading this, and that is to learn about the ordinariness of this phenomenon and to acknowledge the creeping normalcy in your own relationship. By recognizing the happiness myth that is underlying your dismay and discontent, you can begin to understand and exculpate your experiences and take steps to elevate them. Next comes the difficult part, as slowing down the process by which you take your partner (and other things in your life) more and more for granted demands dedicated effort—effort that may be required every week of your married life. Indeed, if we are to successfully resolve the crisis point at the heart of this chapter, the process of resisting adaptation should ideally begin long before that crisis point ever comes.

WHY YOU ADAPT TO THE GOOD STUFF

I met Keith eight years ago, at a Fourth of July barbecue. I tagged along with my housemate, not having any other plans and it being too hot to stay at home. The people there were all nice enough, but I didn't know them, and found myself ambling through the air-conditioned house, thumbing through the novels on the shelves. Then Keith walked in, wearing his Harry Potter glasses. He was wiry and very tall, with shaggy brown hair very much in need of a haircut, and an open face. He smiled at me, and I felt that the whole world was smiling.

Thus began the most exciting and vibrant time in my life. Keith pursued me with a single mind and I was falling in love. Every day, every week, there was something to look forward to—something fun or exciting or surprising. Time went by lightning fast. I had trouble focusing on my job. We were like two peas in a pod.

We had candlelit dinners and Keith made curry from scratch. Once in a while, we skipped out on work during an afternoon and met to make love at one of our apartments—and once even in a fancy hotel.

We shared private thoughts, discussed our adolescent traumas, and, with time, fantasized out loud about what we'd name our kids and which of our favorite houses (that we'd seen on drives) we'd live in. Oh, and we danced. We loved, loved, loved to dance. I felt stronger, happier, prettier, more confident about myself in every way. Keith is not an extrovert but he has tons of friends who are devoted to him, so I met lots of people. My best girlfriend today is someone I got to know during that time.

Of course, there were many firsts. Our first kiss, the first time Keith said, "I love you," our first trip together (to Vegas). The problem with firsts, of course, is that they can only happen once. The second kiss, the seventh time he said "I love you," and every subsequent vacation together were not as special and joy-inducing as the first. With time, and as our relationship progressed, the wonderful things didn't happen as frequently or as intensely. He stopped saying, "I love you" several times a day; we had fewer feverish conversations about our future life together, and the frequency with which I spontaneously smiled at the thought of kissing him or deemed myself incredibly lucky inevitably waned.

Before too long, I became used to the idea of being in a loving relationship, to the amount of time we spent together in the evenings and on the weekends, and to the pride I felt when I reported all about Keith to my family and friends. Never mind that Keith loved me and was faithful to me; now I began to wish he'd propose that we move in together. And after he did propose that and we decorated our rented house, I began to want even more—marriage, kids.

Today, there's nothing really wrong with my life with Keith and our sons. Nothing except that it stings that we can never bring back the early days. Back then we had a lot of free time, time we spent getting coffee and seeing movies and taking trips; today we have a lot of responsibilities and chores. Sometimes a week goes by without us really talking, and we find ourselves passing each other in the kitchen. We disappoint each other sometimes now and are not always as attentive or generous as we used to be. We've lost steam. One time Keith told me that he went to an overnight comic book convention and I realized that I didn't remember that he had ever gone and I had no idea that he even liked comic books. It's like we've turned into different people without even noticing, and it kills me. I see his eyes wandering to an attractive woman and I don't even feel jealous, because I look, too, and because I'm secure that he'll never leave us. So, how exciting can we be to one another? How much is there to look forward to now?

Jennifer, 35, freelance children's photographer[26]

Jennifer's experience is devilishly common. Nearly all of us eventually become accustomed to our marriages and to our partners, and the science of adaptation explains why. Although some of its implications are unwelcome, they also reveal ways we can grapple with this near-universal problem. Just as understanding a disease yields insight into how to treat it, the benefits of understanding a psychological phenomenon is that we gain insight into how we can manipulate it. To this end, my collaborator Ken Sheldon and I developed a theory of how to thwart, resist, and slow down adaptation.[27] Below, I describe a number of practical strategies suggested by our theory, which will be valuable when we say to ourselves, "After finding the right person, I thought I'd be happy for a long time, but now I find myself dissatisfied and bored."

THE IMPORTANCE OF APPRECIATING

One of the clues that lets you know you've adapted to your partner is that you've ceased to appreciate her. Truly appreciating someone means valuing her, being grateful for her, savoring your time with her, and remaining keenly aware of the goodness she has brought into your life. When you first got married, for example, the shift in your circumstances was captivating and novel. You delighted in using the words *husband* and *wife*, and you couldn't help but be conscious and grateful for all the fringe benefits that marriage brings. You may have savored your spouse and thought about her frequently, if not constantly. In due time, however, being married—being called husband or wife, sitting at the kitchen table with your spouse, greeting her passionately at the end of the day—stopped being novel or surprising. After all, your daily life is undoubtedly replete with uplifts and hassles wholly unrelated to your being married—frustration at work, car problems, a successful exercise program, a surprise visit from a high-school friend. Such everyday events elicit their own emotional reactions, making you feel stressed, amused, jubilant, or relieved, and they may eventually overshadow the fact of your new marital status, compelling it to fade into the background of your life.[28] However, the lesson is that if we continue to be grateful, appreciative, and aware of our new spouse—if she frequently pops into our minds and inspires strong emotional reactions in us—we will be able to resist taking her for granted. Several studies support this notion, including one from our very own lab, which revealed that people who persist at appreciating a good turn in their lives are less likely to adapt to it.[29]

Appreciation is vitally important for several reasons. First, appreciating our relationship compels us to extract the maximum possible satisfaction from it and helps us to be grateful for it, relish it, savor it, and not take it for granted. Second, we come to feel more positively about ourselves and to feel more connected to others.[30] Third, our expression of appreciation motivates both us and our partners to bolster efforts to take care of the relationship.[31] And, finally, appreciation helps prevent us from getting too "spoiled" and from paying too much attention to social comparisons ("My friend Kelly's husband, unlike mine, does all the cooking!") and experiencing envy. In other words, pausing to appreciate the positives in our relationships and to reevaluate them as gifts or "blessings" prompts us to focus on what we have today, rather than heeding what our friends and neighbors have or what we wish we had.

Numerous experiments from my own and my colleagues' laboratories have demonstrated that people who regularly practice appreciation or gratitude—who, for example, "count their blessings" once a week over the course of one to twelve consecutive weeks or pen appreciation letters to people who've been kind and meaningful—become reliably happier and healthier, and remain happier for as long as six months after the experiment is over.[32] This is persuasive evidence that appreciating a positive circumstance (like marriage) may help us defy adaptation to it. Simple exercises involving writing down what you appreciate about your partner or your marriage, or writing a gratitude letter to your partner (and not even necessarily sharing it) have been shown to be highly effective.

Another way to truly appreciate and relish our relationship is to imagine *subtracting* it from our lives.[33] What if we had never been introduced to our husband? In that case, a multitude of good things about our lives today may not have come to pass. When not taken to an extreme (which could leave us feeling undeserving about our lives or anxious about losing everything), this "subtraction" strategy can be even more effective than direct attempts at gratitude.[34]

In sum, appreciation exercises will help us bask in the overlooked positives within our relationship by savoring the here and now and by maintaining a positive and optimistic perspective. When we relish our partner's strengths, mentally transport ourselves to days when we felt closest, or truly appreciate the present moment, we are not taking our relationship for granted.

THE IMPORTANCE OF VARIETY

Not all life changes are equally subject to hedonic adaptation. In my work with Ken Sheldon, we have found that our participants are much less likely to become accustomed to changes in their lives that involve variable, dynamic, and effortful engagement (for example, taking a language class or making a new friend) than those that are relatively static and unchangeable (moving to a more desirable apartment or securing a much-needed loan).[35] Furthermore, dynamic changes seem to exert a sustained impact on people's happiness. After making a dynamic change, the participants in our studies are *still* happier six to twelve weeks or longer. After making a static change, our participants appear to be already emotionally accustomed to it six to twelve weeks later.[36] We were also interested to find that if our participants told us that a particular life change added variety to their lives (e.g., led them to meet new people on a regular basis) and if they reported that they remained appreciative of that life change, then they were even more likely to reap the greatest amount of happiness from that change.

The lesson is that ensuring that our marriages are spiced with plentiful variety is critical if we want to stave off adaptation. Indeed, by definition, adaptation happens when we face something constant or repeated[37]—when every weekend date night involves dinner and a movie, or when the intimacy or commitment we feel with our partner has reached an unchanging equilibrium. There is something about variety—variety in our thoughts, our feelings, and our behaviors—that is innately stimulating and rewarding.[38] Indeed, being exposed to variety and novelty appears to have similar affects on our brains—specifically, on activity involving the neurotransmitter dopamine[39]—as do pharmacological "highs," positive emotions, and reward-seeking behavior.[40] Hence, we can maximize and help sustain (at least in part) the happiness of our marriages and the excitement of our time together by mixing things up—by varying what we do with our partners, by changing our minds, and by being spontaneous. This might seem trite advice, but variety can truly permit our relationships and our loves to remain fresh, meaningful, and positive. As a very simple analogy, consider an experiment that my students and I conducted, in which we instructed our participants to do several acts of kindness each week for a period of ten weeks.[41] Some were instructed to vary their acts of kindness (e.g., give their pet a special treat one day and make breakfast for their partner the next day), whereas others were instructed to do similar things each time (e.g., make breakfast for their partner again and again). Not surprisingly, the only ones who got happier were those who varied their generosities.

THE IMPORTANCE OF SURPRISE

Another pivotal factor in the pursuit of sustained marital bliss (and the prevention of hedonic adaptation) is the element of surprise. Although variety and surprise seem like very similar concepts—and, to be sure, they often go together—they are in fact distinct. For example, a series of events (like the movies you might see in a single summer) can be varied but not surprising, and, although a single event (like an unexpected confession) can be surprising, by definition, a single event cannot be variable.

The beginnings of relationships hold a million surprises for us: How will she react when I tell her about my interest in magic? Does she like to be touched in this way or that way? I wonder if she wants to have kids as badly as I do? Is he funny at dinner parties? What are his friends and family really like? In short, new relationships, like new jobs, hobbies, and travels, have the property of yielding many surprising experiences, challenges, fascinations, and novel opportunities. Furthermore, new relationships possess what researchers call "the lure of ambiguity": When we don't know our partners very well, we read into them what we wish to see.[42] However, with time, our partners become altogether known, we fall into a routine, and the number of surprises decreases, even dwindling to zero. During our first year together, our partners may reveal a side of themselves that we never knew. During the tenth year, such an experience is a great deal less likely. At some point, we may feel that we have learned everything there is to learn about our spouse and there are no more surprises left.

What's so special about surprise? When we perceive something novel in our environments ("I never noticed how considerate he is to strangers"), we stand to attention and hence are more likely to appreciate it, to contemplate it, and remember it.[43] We are less likely to take our marriage for granted when it continues to deliver strong emotional reactions in us. (It's worth noting that this argument applies to negative reactions as well, but, of course, I am talking about positive emotions here.) Furthermore, uncertainty in and of itself can enhance the pleasure of positive events. For example, a series of studies showed that people experience longer bursts of happiness when they receive an unexpected act of kindness and remain uncertain about who did it and why.[44] Such reactions are even mirrored in our brains. In one experiment, when thirsty participants were informed that they would finally be able to drink, those who didn't know what they were going to get (i.e., water versus a more attractive beverage) showed more activity in the parts of their brains linked to positive emotions.[45] So, our goal should be to create more unexpected moments and unpredictable pleasures in our relationship—surprises that fire and delight. This may be easier said than done, but several strategies have been found to be successful.

A PINCH OF NOVELTY AND A SOUPÇON OF SURPRISE

The advice that we should be more spontaneous strikes many as a little bit perverse. The same may be said about recommendations to intentionally create surprise and variety in our lives. I agree, in principle, yet following such recommendations is more feasible than we might think. Of course, sitting around and willing surprise, mystery, and randomness to come into our lives won't work. What's more effective is to partake of activities known to yield varied and surprising experiences. Traveling to novel places with our partners—by definition, an activity in which we are no longer slaves to daily routines, have more time to relax and reflect, and are prone to chance experiences—is a no-brainer. So is opening up our socializing to a wider set of acquaintances and friends, or being receptive to new opportunities and adventures. When you and your live-in boyfriend are invited to an intriguing fund-raiser by someone you met at the gym, you go. When the two of you learn about a funky restaurant in a dodgy part of town, you try it. When your spouse develops a new interest in art or Spain or cycling or massively multiplayer online games, you join her on an odyssey to learn more.

Some researchers propose that injecting novelty requires a direct approach—namely, mustering effort to literally notice new things about your partner. For example, every day next week, charge yourself with detecting one way in which your partner is different that day. This extremely simple exercise may render him or her more compelling and appealing. Although every time you read the Sunday paper together and every time you kiss and every time you make *pasta e fagioli* seems indistinguishable from the previous time, try to observe ways in which each occasion is actually different. Supporting this idea, one study asked people to select an activity that they disliked (such as vacuuming or commuting or watching *American*

Idol) and then instructed them to pay heed to three novel or unfamiliar qualities of the activity while they were engaging in it ("The hum of the vacuum cleaner brings me back to second grade" or "I never noticed how short Ryan Seacrest is"). Those asked to hunt for novelty ended up liking the activity more and were more likely to repeat it on their own.[46]

Another technique to prevent ourselves from getting used to something or someone involves shaking up our routines. An intriguing line of research has found that interrupting positive experiences renders them more enjoyable. The argument seems counterintuitive at first. When your spouse is giving you a rather good massage or you are listening together to your favorite album or watching a hilarious movie or relishing a hike through the canyon during perfect weather, the last thing you want is to suspend what you are doing. However, it turns out that people enjoy massages more when they are interrupted with a twenty-minute break, enjoy television programs more when they are interrupted with commercials, and enjoy songs they like more when they are interrupted with a twenty-second gap.[47]

The key to understanding these findings is to recognize that we can adapt to a short-term positive experience like watching a movie or getting a massage in much the same way we adapt to a major life change like getting married or moving to Florida. The moderately pleasant experience of watching a comedy yields us slightly less delight and satisfaction as it runs—not because we enjoy it less, but because we gradually get used to the pleasant feeling (or amusement or cleverness or suspense), so much so that it becomes our new norm or standard. At that point, an even more pleasant jolt would be needed to evoke a stronger emotional response from us. What interruptions are able to accomplish is essentially to disrupt this process of relaxing into our experience and "reset" it to a higher intensity of enjoyment.[48] For example, a break during a massage or a gripping conversation may magnify our anticipation for their resumption and provide us with an opportunity to savor what is still to follow. William James, who advised people to enliven dull activities with "ruptures of routine," would have wholeheartedly agreed.[49]

A leading authority on love, SUNY–Stony Brook professor Art Aron argues that in order to fend off boredom in a marriage, couples should mutually engage in what he calls "expanding" activities—that is, novel activities that are stimulating, yield new experiences, and teach new skills—and challenge each other to grow. In a classic experiment, upper-middle-class middle-aged couples were presented with a list of activities that both members had reported doing infrequently and had agreed were either "pleasant" (such as creative cooking, visiting friends, or seeing a movie) or "exciting" (skiing, dancing, or attending concerts).[50] Then, over the course of the next ten weeks, they were instructed to select one of these activities each week and to spend ninety minutes doing it together. Those couples that engaged in the "exciting" activities reported being more satisfied with their marriages at the end of the ten weeks than those that simply did "pleasant" or enjoyable things together.

Aron obtained similar results when he instructed couples to visit his laboratory and complete a very brief (seven-minute) task that was either neutral, or novel and physiologically arousing.[51] It's hard to come up with an exciting activity that you and your spouse could pull off in seven minutes in a strange room, but these researchers devised a sort of wacky exercise that might ring familiar to anyone who's ever been on company team-building retreats. The activity involved traversing obstacles on a nine-meter gymnasium mat while attached to your partner with Velcro straps at one wrist and one ankle, crawling on your hands and knees the whole time, and carrying a cylindrical pillow that had to be held between your bodies or heads. The neutral activity also involved crawling across a gymnasium mat, but the primary goal entailed rolling a ball to each other. Whether the couples were only dating or long-married, the ones who did the shared novel activity were more likely than the ones who did the shared neutral activity to agree to statements like "I feel happy when I am doing something to make my partner happy" and "I feel 'tingling' and 'an increased heartbeat' when I think of my partner" after the activity than before. Even more impressive was the fact that observers who viewed the couples having a conversation about their future plans judged those who had partaken of the exciting activity to show increased positive behaviors toward each other (e.g., greater acceptance and less hostility) after the activity than those who had partaken of the mundane task.

It's not difficult to imagine that for many couples, completing the crazy crawling assignment might provoke hysterical laughter. As corny as I sometimes find such exercises, I can't ignore the fact that they lead people to feel closer, warmer, and even more attracted toward each other. Surprisingly, the effects of even such brief activities can last for as long as seven hours.[52] However, there's no need for anybody to go out and purchase Velcro straps and cylindrical pillows; the effects on relationship quality are comparable when we simply sit down with our spouses to create a list of things that we would both like to do that we find exciting. Researchers surmise that shared participation in exciting and novel activities triggers positive feelings (e.g., we might misinterpret the apprehension we feel while rock climbing as bolstered attraction),[53] boosts couples' sense of interdependence and closeness (due to the collaborative aspect of many such activities, like the gymnasium mat crawling), leads us to learn new things about each other (as in a study that instructed couples to pick up cards with intimate questions on them and take turns answering them[54]), and generates positive emotions in general (e.g., amusement, pride, curiosity, joy), which tends to color everything in our lives, including our marriages, in more positive, optimistic strokes.

I'VE LOST THE PASSION, OR,
GETTING USED TO SEX WITH YOUR SPOUSE

Even in the happiest of marriages, after a while we no longer obtain the same happiness boost from spending time with our spouse—or with any of the accoutrements of marriage—as we once did. One of the unfortunate corollaries of this naturally unfolding process is that we also ultimately obtain less pleasure from marital sex.[55] None of us should be surprised or perturbed by this, but many clearly are. When we are in the throes of newfound heart-pounding passion, we are so much governed by our in-the-moment emotions, thoughts, and fantasies that we can't possibly imagine the day the intensity of those feelings will ebb.

The unwelcome fact is that sexual passion and arousal, in particular, are uniquely prone to habituation. Laboratory experiments that track changes in sexual arousal in response to repeated presentation of erotic pictures or instructions to engage in sexual fantasies have found that both men and women show reduced arousal (assessed both by simply asking them and also by measuring actual genital engorgement) over time.[56] It turns out that familiarity may not always breed contempt, but it surely breeds indifference. In Raymond Chandler's words, "The first kiss is magic. The second is intimate. The third is routine."[57]

By contrast, novelty can serve as a powerful aphrodisiac, as illustrated by the "Coolidge effect." According to legend, one morning

former president Calvin Coolidge and first lady Grace Anna Goodhue were visiting a Kentucky poultry farm. During the tour, Mrs.
Coolidge asked the farmer why so few roosters yielded such a large
number of eggs. The farmer proudly explained that his roosters performed their duty dozens of times each day. Mrs. Coolidge was very
impressed by that and pointedly replied, "Tell that to the president."
Mr. Coolidge, overhearing the remark about the roosters' performance, asked the farmer, "Is this always with the same hen each
time?" "Oh, no, Mr. President," replied the farmer, "a different hen
each time." The President nodded slowly, smiled, and said, "Tell *that*
to Mrs. Coolidge!"[58]

Whether or not this story is apocryphal, it has given the name to
the phenomenon that most members of social mammalian species
will demonstrate renewed sexual desire and performance when new
receptive partners are introduced. Humans appear to be just as
susceptible to the Coolidge effect as are roosters and hens. Indeed,
evolutionary biologists posit that sexual variety is evolutionarily
adaptive; it evolved to prevent incest and inbreeding in ancestral
environments. The idea is that when our spouse becomes as familiar
to us as a sibling—when we've become *family*—we cease to be sexually attracted to each other.[59]

It doesn't take a rocket scientist to deduce that because the sex in
a long-term committed monogamous relationship involves the same
partner day after day after day, no one who is truly human (or mammalian) can maintain the same level of lust and ardor that they experienced when their spouse was uncharted and new.[60] We may love
our partners deeply, we may idolize them, we may even be willing to
die for them, but these feelings don't translate into sustained passion
over many years.

In support of this notion, numerous surveys have demonstrated
that sexual desire, sexual satisfaction, and sexual frequency drop off

in accordance with the length of a relationship.[61] Amazingly, this pattern has even been found in college students (especially women), who have been dating for as little as a year. Indeed, when it comes to sex, age is not as important a factor as people think. For example, if you want to predict how often a couple engages in sex, you'd be much more accurate if you considered how long they'd been together than their age.

More than one problem marks this state of affairs, beginning with the fact that it patently stinks that passionate love can't last. Furthermore, our general obliviousness to how all-too-human, natural, and commonplace this hedonic adaptation is drives us to blame ourselves (or our partners) for diminished frequency or desire—for raining on our fantasy of what marriage should be like. The consequence can be a vicious cycle: Reduced sexual passion is perceived as a symptom of something being wrong with our relationship (when it's just a symptom of the normal process of adaptation), which prompts even further erosion in our satisfaction with the relationship, which undermines sexual desire even more, and so on.[62] Books with titles like *The Sex-Starved Marriage: A Couple's Guide to Boosting Their Marriage Libido* and *Rekindling Desire: A Step-by-Step Program to Help Low-Sex and No-Sex Marriages* become bestsellers because so many of us—alas, just about all of us—confront this problem at one time or another.

Another fundamental problem concerns gender differences. No one is shocked to hear that differences between men and women come into play in a discussion of sexual behavior. However, the gender differences in question may surprise you. To begin with the unsurprising news, scores of surveys have confirmed the obvious by showing that, relative to women, men have more frequent sexual fantasies, report stronger sexual desire, think about sex more, and wish to have it more often.[63] In line with these results, observational, anecdotal, clinical, and survey evidence (not to mention high-profile examples involving prominent men in politics, sports, and film) point to one seemingly incontrovertible fact—that men are much more likely than women to stray from marriage.[64] Furthermore, men's infidelities—when they do occur—involve a greater number of sexual partners.[65] (For an admittedly extreme example, the alleged count for Tiger Woods was a hundred twenty-one.[66])

Hence, it would stand to reason that men adapt to sex with the same partner more rapidly than do women. But what researchers are beginning to suspect is actually the reverse—it's the women who adapt faster. First, studies show that, in a long-term relationship, women are more likely than men to lose interest in sex, and to lose it sooner.[67] Second, women appear to be physiologically aroused by a much broader range of stimuli than men are[68] and to be most turned on by fantasies of sex with strangers[69]—findings that suggest that a familiar partner might rapidly become less and less physiologically arousing for them. Third, female lust has been described as being dominated by a craving to be the object of powerful, urgent desire—to be ravished, coveted, and needed.[70] Given that his wedding vows have committed the husband to have sex with his wife—and only his wife—forever, the wife would be hard-pressed to persuade herself that his decision to make love to her this Friday night is a genuine signal of his desperate must-have-you-now desire. Partly for this reason, sex researcher Marta Meana argues that women require a more powerful stimulus to activate their sex drive than do men. "If I don't love cake as much as you," she explains, "my cake better be kick-butt to get me excited to eat it."[71] All these observations lead to the conclusion that women's criteria for passionate sex involve a higher threshold for excitement and novelty than do men's. Maybe my male friends are right after all when they claim that, for them, sex is like pizza—there's no such thing as bad pizza or bad sex. It goes without saying that women don't agree.

CAN PASSION LAST?

Two types of relationships have been found to sustain passion— relationships that begin with low expectations and in which love and lust build very slowly (for example, arranged marriages) and relationships characterized by relentless uncertainty (like volatile, abusive, or on-again-off-again romances). However, such relationships carry costs that are too high or are unacceptable for most of us. So, what about loving, stable, committed unions? On the one hand, as described above, many reasons collude to make the pursuit of sustained passion in most marriages a futile endeavor. On the other hand, some recent research offers clues about how intensity and sexual interest can be rekindled and preserved.[72]

Notably, a small but significant fraction of married individuals profess that their sex lives with their spouses are still fantastic, even after decades of marriage. For example, a study of 156 couples together for an average of nine years, determined that 13 percent showed signs of continued high levels of passion, though without the pernicious obsessive component observed in the early stages of love. Hence, it behooves us to get wise to their secrets. Consider one lesson offered by the laboratory of professor Shelly Gable.

Most of us have goals for our relationships, and Gable and her students were interested in studying differences between people who had "approach" versus "avoidance" goals. An approach relationship goal involves striving for positive experiences in our relationship, such as fun, growth, and intimacy, whereas an avoidance goal involves avoiding conflict or rejection.[73] For example, I have approach goals if I take it upon myself to make my relationship with my partner deeper and warmer and if I devise ways for the two of us to grow. I have avoidance goals if I focus my energies on avoiding disagreements and quarrels and strive to make sure that nothing bad happens between us. Although both types of goals have their uses, it turns out that those of us who have approach relationship goals (whether the relationship is with our spouse, friend, child, or boss) are more likely to be satisfied with that relationship, to have a positive attitude, and to be less lonely and insecure.[74]

What do these different kinds of goals have to do with unabated passion? Gable argues that those of us whose primary drive is to pursue positive experiences with our partners may regard sexual activity as an ideal way to introduce positivity and intimacy into our marriages. Consequently, we may think about sex more, and we may resolve to have sex more often to please our partner or to help build intimacy. We may become more sensitive to our partner's sexual cues, act more readily on them, and seek out situations conducive to intimate moments. Having approach goals may also simply put us in a better mood and a more optimistic frame of mind, which in itself can heighten desire.

To test this idea, Gable and her associates conducted a series of studies, in which they tracked their participants' sexual desire on a daily or biweekly basis, as well as their approach and avoidance goals, including sexual goals (e.g., I had sex "to pursue my own sexual pleasure" or "to express love for my partner" versus "to prevent my partner from becoming upset" or "to prevent my partner from losing interest in me").[75] Those participants who had avoidance goals regarding their relationship reported that their sexual desire declined over the course of the six-month study, but those who had approach goals witnessed absolutely no decline. Furthermore, when both sexual desire and various relationship events (a fight over vacation plans, a surprise visit from a mutual friend) were tracked from one day to the next, the researchers found that people with approach goals felt even greater passion on the good days and experienced less of the expected decline in passion on the bad days than people with avoidance goals.

These findings are promising, suggesting that all of us would do well to place our efforts into increasing positive experiences in our relationships rather than avoiding negative ones. Undoubtedly, marriage and sex therapists can offer additional strategies and tools to help many couples, including the importance of periodic infusions of novelty, variety, and surprise, as discussed above. The bottom line, however, is that science has uncovered precious little about how to sustain passionate love, or whether it is feasible within even a minority of marriages. Whether this is good news or bad news depends on how we think about it. My view is that the decline of passionate love—like growing up or growing old—is simply part of being human.

HOW TO NURTURE YOUR RELATIONSHIP

This chapter is about the sinking feeling that, at best, we have a so-so marriage. There's no major crisis, betrayal, or incompatibility—only a gradual awareness of boredom or dissatisfaction. Furthermore, the lack of major trauma can have an insidious effect, leaving us feeling guilty over our own seemingly "trivial" discontent. The discontent isn't trivial, however, and may even represent a watershed moment in our relationship. This is why it's critical to recognize that much of our dissatisfaction stems from the process of hedonic adaptation, that such adaptation is natural and foreseeable, and that empirically validated steps to slow, prevent, or counteract it (as described above) must ideally be taken long before our marriage is in trouble. If we can understand that difficulty is as much a part of committed relationships as is joy—that nearly all of us encounter waning passions and satisfactions—working to mend the relationship will seem less daunting and more worthwhile. In learning that there's no magic formula for happiness in a marriage, more choices about the future will open up for us.

I would be remiss not to mention the many other strategies to strengthen our intimate relationships that have been put forth by numerous theorists, clinical psychologists, and marriage manual authors. Recommended practices include making time to just be together and talk, expertly communicating (that is, truly listening, being "in tune" with each other, and conveying admiration, appreciation, and affection), managing conflict, being supportive, kind, and loyal, and sharing each other's dreams, rituals, and responsibilities.[76] Although not aimed directly at combating hedonic adaptation, these techniques have been shown to improve the quality and satisfaction of our partnerships and, hence, to assuage relationship ennui. I offer here three additional evidence-based strategies.

MAKING THE MOST OF YOUR PARTNER'S GOOD NEWS

One of my favorite lines of research is on how couples share positive experiences with one another. Many would agree that one of the greatest benefits of marriage is having a person you can turn to in the face of stressful, negative, or traumatic events. However, it appears that although we often turn to our partners to help us cope with the worst things that have happened to us—and implicitly judge our relationship by the level of their support, compassion, and sensitivity—we also often turn to them to share the best things.

(Indeed, studies show that people do the latter on a daily basis from 70 percent to 80 percent of the time.)[77] The surprising finding is that the closest, most intimate, and most trusting relationships appear to be distinguished not by how the partners respond to each other's disappointments, losses, and reversals but how they react to *good* news. Flourishing relationships have been revealed to be those in which the couple responds "actively and constructively"—that is, with interest and delight—to each other's windfalls and successes.[78] When your husband tells you he's being promoted, a response marked by joy and enthusiastic questions tells him that you grasp the meaningfulness of his accomplishment (both to him and to you), renders it more memorable, validates its importance, and signals that you care. Both men and women who say that their partners respond in this "active-constructive" way report the highest levels of satisfaction, trust, and intimacy in their relationships.

Unfortunately, we don't always react to our partner's good news (or they to ours) in the most optimal ways and, instead, end up delivering responses that damage our relationships. Researchers have found, for example, that when we learn about our spouse's promotion, if we are silently supportive (expressing little if no enthusiasm), point out its complications or downsides ("You'll have to work on weekends" or "Does this mean we'll have to move?"), or don't say anything at all, we are undermining the happiness, warmth, and trust of our relationship.

In sum, appreciating, validating, and "capitalizing" on our partner's good news is an effective strategy to bolster our relationship and thereby to intensify the pleasure and satisfaction we obtain from it—in short, to preclude hedonic adaptation. One study showed that people who strove to show genuine enthusiasm, support, and understanding of their partner's good news, however small—and did so three times a day over a week—became happier and less depressed.[79] It's not too late to start.

HELPING YOUR PARTNER ACHIEVE
HIS OR HER IDEAL SELF

Much has been said and written about the importance of "positive behaviors" in relationships, similar to the ones I just described (appreciating, validating, respecting, comforting, understanding). Yet, as I will address later, being too positive or being always positive may not serve our marriages well and may even harm them. One particular positive behavior, however, has special properties with respect to enhancing flourishing in both our relationships and in our partners. Researchers call it *partner affirmation*—the act of believing in, supporting, and validating our partner's values, goals, and dreams.

When we are thinking about how to realize our own ambitions and aspirations, chances are high that we are focusing on all the steps that we must take and the efforts we must muster along the way. What we likely undervalue is the role that the people closest to us can play in helping us tremendously—and sometimes unsuspectingly— to achieve our goals. The extent to which we are successful at building our characters, learning new skills, and acquiring new resources is often shaped by other people, and especially by our intimate partners or spouses. Researchers argue that "people come to reflect what their partners see in them and elicit from them"[80]—a finding with the lovely name, the Michelangelo phenomenon, after the Italian Renaissance artist who sculpted Florence's *David*, reportedly saying "I saw an angel in the block of marble and I just chiseled 'til I set him free."[81] Like sculptors, we have the capacity to influence and mold our partners such that they are able to realize their ideal selves—their highest and deepest ambitions for themselves. This process can unfold in gradual and subtle ways. For example, if my husband were very shy, I could help him become more outgoing and convivial by inconspicuously guiding dinner party conversation to create the perfect opportunity for him to regale the guests with one of his most charming stories.[82] Furthermore, my expectation that he'll be sociable may boost his own confidence and give rise to a self-fulfilling (or rather partner-fulfilling) prophecy. I can also bring out the best in him by—consciously or subconsciously—discouraging or holding him back from any goal-thwarting situations or behavior (like steering him away from always sitting next to the one person he knows at a party).

When this sculpting process—the Michelangelo phenomenon—is successful, our partners will have come to resemble the person that they (and we) want them to be, our relationship will have been strengthened, and we both ultimately will have become happier, as individuals and as a couple.[83] When our spouse affirms us and helps us move closer to our ideal selves, we feel not only happier and more vital because we are accomplishing our goals, but because we feel truly understood, gratified, and grateful. Our love grows when we recognize how much our spouse cares for us and is striving to support and encourage us. And, when it is we who are affirming our spouse, we feel a stronger love that derives from the support we're giving ("I must truly adore her if I am doing so much for her") and the increasingly positive view of our spouse that such support entails ("I'm discovering that she is an incredibly creative person"). Finally, we are personally happier because doing good for others has been shown in numerous studies to boost positive mood and overall well-being, likely as a result of strengthened social bonds and enhanced feelings of self-efficacy and optimism.[84]

THE POWER OF TOUCH

When considering the importance of touch in a romantic relationship we are thinking, in all likelihood, of sex. This automatic link between touch and sexual activity is unfortunate, because the import and impact of touch is so much broader and stronger.

A pat on the back, a squeeze of the hand, a hug, an arm around the shoulder. Such gestures are often lightning quick and sometimes nearly undetectable. But just because a slight touch is often inconspicuous doesn't mean it's inconsequential. Indeed, the science of touch suggests that it can save a so-so marriage.

The centrality of physical contact to human life—not to mention animal life—is unquestioned. Researchers in fields ranging from psychology to anthropology to ethology have observed the uses of touch in a wide range of behaviors, including the communication of power or status, flirting, playing, reconciling, comforting, cooperating, and conveying particular emotions.[85] Notably, newborn infants' sense of touch is the most developed of all their senses.[86] Physical contact for infants is tied to better physical and mental health,[87] as evidenced, for example, by the benefits of skin-to-skin "kangaroo care" for premature babies and by the great harm suffered by orphans deprived of touch. Last but not least, as a couple of famous developmental psychologists have powerfully shown, physical contact is critical if a child is to develop a healthy sense of attachment and security in her relationships with caregivers.[88] A parent's touching, holding, and cuddling, for example, makes the child feel safe and protected, and it is this sense of security that gives her license to explore on her own and to take risks, even in unfamiliar situations.[89] Amazingly, even spiderlings (baby spiders) are more likely to explore a novel environment if their mom spider has touched them relatively more.[90] By contrast, both human and animal infants who are deprived of touch show fearfulness, mistrust, and a reluctance to explore.

The importance of touch is undeniable, yet it is remarkably undervalued. Of course, there are striking cultural (and subcultural) differences in the acceptability and pervasiveness of physical contact in everyday life. For example, Greek and Italian couples use touch more when interacting together than English, French, and Dutch couples.[91] One such cultural difference hit home for me personally during my first few weeks in college, which was the first time I had lived away from home. Coming from a Russian family, I grew up with tons of physical contact, kisses, and cuddles, and I didn't realize until college that not everyone behaved the same way. Indeed, I still remember being confounded by a scene from *The Brady Bunch* in which the oldest daughter, Marcia, comes over to her mom to give her a kiss, and her mom responds (not unkindly), "Why did you do that?" Marcia needs a reason to kiss her mother? I have also been astounded to hear from friends that they had almost never witnessed any form of touching or physical affection between their parents (and experienced little for themselves, particularly in the teen years and beyond). In sum, many families and couples in the United States and in scores of other Western and Eastern cultures engage in minimal nonsexual touch behavior.

If you feel bored or lukewarm about your relationship, introducing more (nonsexual) touching and affection on a daily basis will go a long way in rekindling the warmth and tenderness, if not full-fledged passion, that has been lost to time. Studies show that a simple touch can activate the reward regions of our brains, reduce the amount of stress hormones coursing through our bloodstreams, and diminish physical pain by reducing activation in the parts of the brain associated with stress.[92] These findings imply that physical contact is almost like a drug; when our spouse touches us, we experience a mild high, we feel less frazzled, and we observe a diminution of discomfort and distress.

Our spouse can also communicate his feelings to us via touch. Although this observation may seem obvious, people's abilities to decode distinct emotions from a mere pat on the arm have actually been tested. In a series of studies, for example, pairs of unacquainted participants from Spain and the United States were invited to a laboratory, where they were positioned on two sides of a barrier, such that they could not see each other.[93] One member of the pair was then instructed to touch the other on the forearm through a hole in the barrier in a way that expressed a particular emotion. The touched participants (as well as observers who simply watched the touching) were able to identify six distinct emotions conveyed by the touch—love, gratitude, sympathy, anger, fear, and disgust. Furthermore, when their partners were allowed to touch any (appropriate) part of the body, not just the forearm, the participants were able to read two more emotions—happiness and sadness.[94]

This ability to recognize discrete emotions from a single touch can be invaluable in myriad relationship situations in which we find ourselves. A small stroking motion communicating love can de-escalate a fight. A pat communicating gratitude can bolster intimacy. A hug communicating happiness at our spouse's latest success can foster satisfaction. Scientists have also shown that certain forms of touch remind us of the feelings of security we might have felt long ago in our mother's or father's embrace. A pat on the back or the shoulder can thus trigger feelings of security and comfort, which leads us to be more adventurous and risk taking (ideally in fruitful ways).[95] Furthermore, scientists can better predict which couples will stay together or get divorced based on their nonverbal communication (such as touching and gesture) than verbal communication.[96]

Try increasing the level of physical contact in your relationship by a set amount each week. For example, during the first week, brush his or her back or arm every time you pass each other in the kitchen; in the second week, always sit together close enough to touch; in the third week, never let a parting or greeting elapse without a kiss, and so on. Of course, depending on your and your partner's personality, background, and family history, your liking or openness to nonsexual touch may vary greatly. If the comfort level is low for either of you, you would do well to proceed slowly and delicately, and, if it would help in your particular situation, discuss your goals regarding physical contact.

THE PREPARED MIND

Perhaps you thought that you had it all figured out. You found "the one," you married, you were happy. With time, however, the returns stopped being so high. You began having qualms and discontents, then whispers of apathy and dullness, and yearnings for something more. The realization that your marriage is no longer making you happy is not the end of the road, and neither is it the beginning. This chapter accounts for your experiences, legitimizes them, offers direction for ways to reinvest in your relationship, and charges you with a prepared mind.

For many of you, the first reaction to the feeling that you're bored and unhappy is to conclude that there must be something wrong with you or your relationship and to assign blame. Your "first thought" is that if your marriage doesn't fulfill all your needs for intimacy, passion, and companionship, then you (or you partner) have failed. Before you can understand what type of change is possible and what is not, you need to push forward past those first thoughts and heed your second thoughts. This more reason-based perspective involves learning about hedonic adaptation. Gaining an awareness of the ubiquity of this phenomenon may lead you to acknowledge that your marital grievances are natural and commonplace, thereby exonerating both your spouse and yourself, and to take steps to slow down the adaptation process. At that point, you may come to a more positive outlook for your relationship. The optimal course of action is to begin practicing adaptation-thwarting and relationship-building strategies as soon as possible. Which strategy to begin with will depend on your preferences, resources, and needs. Some may initiate mobilizing efforts to inject excitement, novelty, variety, and/or surprise into their marriage. Others may choose to convey appreciation for their relationship, help bring out the best person their partner can be, or respond more enthusiastically when that partner succeeds. Inside and outside the bedroom, you may opt to shift your goals to a more positively oriented "approach" mode or to touch more frequently and regularly.

However, if your efforts fail to bear fruit, it may be time to conclude that your loss of interest and passion either isn't possible to save or isn't worth saving. Hence, this alternative trajectory involves leaving your partner and searching for a new love. This path can bring about great happiness, especially if you are fortunate to find a terrific match. Beware, however, because it can also produce great disappointment, as you may reasonably find your passions waxing and waning in the new relationship much like they did in the old one. You now are all too aware that the natural course of adaptation will undoubtedly replay itself. How to act in the face of that knowledge is up to you.

CHAPTER 2

I Can't Be Happy When . . .
My Relationship Has Fallen Apart

There's a well-known story in academic circles about an eminent professor whose wife had stopped talking to him about anything more meaningful than the day's shopping. One night, at the theater, he had an epiphany. He was watching a play in which the main character acts out his life at age twenty, thirty, forty, and so on, and, with each decade, the man edges closer and closer to living a life of quiet desperation. After the play was over, the professor thought, "This could be me." He decided that night to leave his wife, quit his job in Michigan, and move back to his hometown of New York. Today, both he and his ex-wife are happily remarried, living a thousand miles apart, each with a new family.

Admittedly, this story is a bit extreme; few of us decide in a single moment that we married the wrong person and act on that first thought. Much more often, the thought rises to the surface on and off for weeks or months and even years. Indeed, divorce fantasies are very common, and, not unexpectedly, they are much more common among people who eventually get divorced. Furthermore, the divorce fantasy doesn't materialize out of nowhere. The realization that our relationship is in crisis is usually precipitated by one or more pivotal events—perhaps a feeling of loneliness, being on completely different wavelengths, no longer caring about the other's well-being, or the discovery of an infidelity.

This chapter is about facing a seemingly insurmountable problem in your long-term relationship or marriage. Perhaps the two of you are bedeviled by irreconcilable differences regarding your finances or where to settle down or whether to have a baby. Alternatively, one of you may have irrevocably changed, had an affair, fallen out of love, or refused to stop drinking. It is undoubtedly an extremely punishing and painful time. You fantasize about divorce and yet you are acutely anxious about actually going through with it, convinced your family life will be forever ruined. However, that anxiety and pain can be markedly compounded by an unspoken belief in one particular happiness myth—that you can't possibly be happy after your relationship falls apart or you divorce. As almost everybody knows, the experience of a dying love or broken marriage can be harrowingly difficult at its nadir, yet human beings are masters of surviving and even thriving in the worst of situations. We are exceptionally resourceful at devising solutions and finding positive directions. By describing numerous such solutions and directions, I aim both to refute this myth of happiness and to detail specific ways to rise to the occasion and push forward. A good marriage grants you wings and brings out the best person you can be. A troubled marriage imprisons you and brings out your worst nature. However, a troubled marriage doesn't mean your life is over or your chance for happiness is gone. Research suggests a number of roads to take. One course of action is to remain in the relationship and adjust to it (more on that below). Another is to leave it (also see below). But the most optimistic course is to improve and strengthen it—that is, to try to save your marriage. This is the path with which I begin.

ONWARD AND UPWARD:
STRENGTHENING YOUR RELATIONSHIP

POSITIVE EMOTIONS ARE ANTIDOTES TO
NEGATIVE EMOTIONS

If our relationship is worth nurturing or improving, most of us are likely all too familiar with the many ways to do it. As described in the last chapter, marriage and family therapists advise that we attempt a number of approaches, including resolving not to take our partners for granted, expressing our admiration for them, sharing our dreams with them, and showing them the sort of kindness that we show others. Easier said than done. When plagued by daunting problems and forebodings of a bleaker future, this kind of marital to-do list seems not only overwhelming but patently unrealistic. It's more manageable perhaps to "satisfice" (an amalgam of "satisfy" and "suffice") in our marriages—namely, to strive to be a *good-enough* spouse, with a good-enough husband or wife, in a good-enough marriage.

There are times in life when our paramount goal should be to address directly the negatives in a troubled marriage, and I offer relevant recommendations for this situation in the sections below on coping and forgiveness. However, positive psychologists have learned that sometimes the best path to happiness and flourishing is not head-on but from the side. In other words, instead of focusing on how to fix marital negatives and problems, we can use positive emotions, positive thoughts, and positive behaviors to *neutralize* those negatives. So, for example, instead of striving directly to minimize the negative emotions (such as disenchantment or anger) that churn inside when we're with our spouse, we aim to accomplish the same goal by maximizing our positive emotions (such as tranquility or affection). Instead of striving directly to cut back on our negative thoughts (such as ruminations about being unworthy of a partner), we should aim to build up positive ones (e.g., thoughts about the future being better than the past), with the idea that the positive thoughts negate the negative ones. Instead of striving directly to reduce negative behaviors in our relationship (such as quarrels or contemptuous eye rolls), we should aim to multiply positive behaviors (such as laughter or kind words), such that they countervail the negative ones. When we are at a low point in our relationship—or have hit rock bottom—cultivating more positive thoughts, positive emotions, and positive behaviors may seem like a futile uphill battle. It may be the last thing you want to or have the wherewithal to do. Yet research indicates that at this very moment, this strategy is never more necessary or worthwhile.

Consider an airline's route map—the kind you find at the back of a glossy flight magazine. Because scheduled flights depart and arrive from hundreds of cities, each major and minor city is connected to other cities. Some cities are hubs, so many flights connect to them, and some cities have only a few connections, making it necessary for you to change planes several times to get to your point of destination. Cognitive psychologists, who study internal mental states, contend that all of us have extensive "semantic networks" that look a bit like those airline route maps. Instead of cities connecting to one another in myriad ways, semantic networks are made up of all of our interlinked memories and thoughts. So, Los Angeles is connected to San Francisco with a thick line (representing many flights), but it's connected to Fresno with a very thin line (representing only one or two flights). Similarly, your memory of being bedridden with pneumonia may be strongly connected to a memory of the business trip you were forced to cancel, and weakly connected to a memory of having chicken pox as a child.

If you are disillusioned with your marriage, you are likely to have built up dozens—or even hundreds—of negative memories, pessimistic assumptions, rageful images, and cynical predictions. These are all linked together in your brain's semantic network in such a way that one bad memory leads you to remember another, and one anxious thought activates half a dozen more. This is one reason that, in a troubled marriage, a fight about a petty incident can so easily and quickly escalate into accusations of misdeeds from years ago ("You've never cared about my career; remember that time I got a promotion in 'eighty-eight?") or catastrophizing forecasts ("I just can't see having a child with you"). Not surprisingly, this kind of overwhelmingly negative semantic network can be toxic, leading to vicious cycles by which our problems just get worse and worse. For this reason, cognitive therapists commonly treat depression and anxiety (as well as distressed marriages) by attempting to break up the negative associations in their clients' semantic networks. For example, the belief that you are unattractive may be linked to the memory of the time your wife commented on your weight gain and to the worry that she doesn't love you anymore. The job of the therapist is to dispute these usually distorted thoughts by literally challenging their logic or offering a more charitable interpretation.

Cognitive therapy is remarkably effective,[97] in part because it is often brilliantly successful in divorcing our pessimistic thoughts and memories one from another. However, because not everyone has the time, resources, or wherewithal to see a therapist, I offer an alternative strategy in tackling our negative semantic networks. This one involves not snapping the connection between particular thoughts and specific memories (which often has to be laboriously done one by one by one), but infusing the entire semantic network with posi-

tive emotions, which essentially act to *dissolve or melt* the links between all our negative, resentful, angry, hurtful images, memories,
and thoughts.

How would this work? Positive emotions have remarkable properties, which empower them to serve as foils to negative states. Feelings of joy, satisfaction, interest, serenity, or pride can help us view
our marriages with a broader perspective and provide a "psychological time-out" in the midst of marital strain or trials, thus lessening
the sting of any particular unpleasant experience. Furthermore, such
positive states can directly undo the effects of sporadic negative emotions. For example, an argument with our spouse typically induces
us to become totally wired—we instantaneously experience surges
in our blood pressure, heart rate, and skin temperature. Remarkably,
a mere transient positive feeling (the pleasure of the sun on our cheek,
the anticipation of our lunch out) can speed our recovery from this
unhealthy state. Thus, even brief or trifling positive emotions mar-
shaled in the face of troubles can build our resilience and help us
bounce back.[98]

Studies have also shown that when we experience joy or contentment or curiosity or pride, we feel ready to take on the world, are
more mindful, creative, and open to new experiences, feel more trust
and oneness with intimate others, believe that life is more meaningful, and have the sense of being captains of our own ships.[99] What's
more, the more positive emotions we feel, the more positive thoughts
and experiences we will accrue, to the point where our positive emotions end up developing a life all of their own, triggering healthful
upward spirals. As the world's foremost expert on positive emotions,
Barbara Fredrickson has said that "positive emotions . . . unlock
paths of growth that lead people to become better versions of themselves."[100]

Aim for a three-to-one ratio. We all know—indeed, have always known—that positive emotions, gratifications, and small delights *feel* really good. Now we know that the pleasures of positive emotions belie their true value for us and our relationships. The next step is to puzzle out exactly what it is that we need to do—when, how, and how much—to bring more positive emotions into our lives. Based on more than a decade of research from her own lab and those of other scientists, Fredrickson advises that we aim to experience at least three times as many positive as negative emotions in our lives— that is, a ratio of positive to negative emotions that is at least three to one.[101] She has found that the most flourishing individuals, the most flourishing marriages, and the most flourishing work groups—those that manifest growth, generativity, and resilience—all show ratios greater than three to one. When we are below that ratio, the positive emotions (or positive thoughts or positive social interactions) we experience are too few to buttress optimal functioning. This means that if we experience roughly the same amount of positive as negative emotions—and even if we experience *twice* as many positive emotions as negative ones—we are likely to be languishing, lonely, and distressed.

For example, happily married couples are characterized by ratios of approximately five to one in their verbal and emotional expressions to one another, while very unhappy couples display ratios of less than one to one. Tellingly, the exact same optimal good-to-bad ratios (five-to-one) characterize productive versus less productive business teams. Scientists who keep tabs on people's daily lives also find that those who are most healthy and thriving report that close to three good events happen to them each day for every bad one.[102] Of course, this doesn't mean that negative experiences are three times as bad as positive experiences, but what the science suggests is that the "punch" of one bad emotion, stinging verbal remark, or unpleasant life event can match or outdo that of three or more good ones. Hence, we would do well to strive for three times as many good experiences as bad ones, and ideally close to five times as many. John Gottman, a marriage researcher and couples therapist, contends that he can predict which couples will divorce by simply considering the magnitude of the good-to-bad ratio of their interactions with each other.[103]

My recommendation is to keep a diary of positive to negative events that take place between you and your partner—for example, how many times per week do you fight, show affection, express gratitude, criticize, ignore, and so on. Calculate your good-to-bad ratio and resolve to increase the numerator (or the positive events in your marriage—in other words, make love, not war) and decrease the denominator (or the negative events—for example, anticipate and nip a conflict in the bud). In other words, just as with your bank account, your goal should be to make a lot more (positive) deposits to your marriage than (negative) withdrawals. I suggest asking yourself each morning, "What can I do for five minutes today to make my partner's life better?" Studies have shown that very simple behaviors— for example, sharing a humdrum amusing event that happened to us, disclosing something private, smiling, listening closely to a partner's words, looking enthusiastic, and being playful or humorous— can affect our marital happiness, intimacy, the outcomes of fights, and even our health.[104] One can predict the outcome of a couple's fifteen-minute conversation from the first three minutes.[105] So make those first three minutes count! And, whatever it takes, try to cut short the drip, drip, drip of unpleasant emotions and invidious interactions in your marriage.

Can there be too much positivity? Positive psychologists don't often broach the idea that too many positive interactions or positive emotions might be harmful. However, when it comes to marriage—specifically, when it comes to a severely distressed marriage—even a little too much positivity could be a real risk.

Marriage counselors typically teach couples to think and behave in positive ways toward each other. So, for example, you might be encouraged to practice making charitable attributions about your partner's misdeeds (e.g., "He only yelled at me in front of the teller because he'd had a stressful day"), and you might be discouraged to track how many times this week he accused or rebuffed you. In other words, as Benjamin Franklin advised in *Poor Richard's Almanack,* "Keep your eyes wide open before marriage, and half shut afterwards." Half of all couples, however, don't benefit from this kind of therapy at all,[106] and some scientists conjecture that this is because, instead of keeping their eyes half shut, the most troubled couples *need to* observe how much they have been blaming and rejecting each other. They need to keep their eyes wide open. They need to notice when they are being neglectful or mean. In short, distressed couples need to monitor and acknowledge their problems (even when doing so makes them feel bad or dissatisfied temporarily) so that they can address them.

We may be advised not to sweat the small stuff in our relationships, but the truth is that this stuff may not be small. So when we sugarcoat a fight, overlook a hurt, or bury the hatchet too quickly, we may fail to notice and resolve a major problem surfacing in our marriage and allow the problem to get worse and worse. Researchers have found that couples who are very happy or who have only minor or infrequent problems benefit when they make positive attributions about each other, hold high expectations, and don't monitor hurts or slights. But couples who have major troubles show the opposite pattern. It may seem counterintuitive, but the ones who benefit the most are those who draw fewer sanguine inferences from each other's bad behavior, who express fewer positive expectations, and who keep track of times that they have hurt each other.[107] In short, those of us in very unhappy marriages should still strive to increase our positive emotions and positive interactions, but not at the cost of blinding ourselves to our problems.

THE DANCE OF (SYNCHRONOUS) CONVERSATION

Two of my favorite recent studies measured the extent to which speed-daters and college-age dating couples showed "linguistic synchrony" (otherwise known as language style matching) in their conversations.[108] You and your partner display linguistic synchrony when the words and expressions you use match each other's. For example, you both might use clichés a lot ("those were the good old days"), or you both might speak in flowery language or relatively formal language, or you both might like to invoke emotion words (*sad, eager, dreading*), or use a lot of pauses and *hmm*s, or you both might engage in Valley-speak ("Like, I got some totally grody milk today"). People who show similar styles of speaking and gesturing (gaze, posture, etc.) have previously been found to be more likely to be attracted to each other.[109] In the recent studies, however, couples and potential couples were assessed on whether they subtly (and presumably unknowingly) reciprocated each other's use of function words such as articles (*a, the*) and pronouns (*I, you, we, he*). This might seem fairly esoteric, but it turns out that the coordinated use of function words can reflect the extent to which two conversation partners are trying to engage each other, as well as the extent to which they succeed at communicating and understanding each other.

The intriguing findings were that pairs of first-time daters who matched each other's language styles were more likely to want to date again, and college-age couples who matched each other's language styles were more likely to still be together three months later (considered a long time for a college fling). Those who didn't match were less likely to express romantic interest in each other (in the dating study) and more likely to break up (in the couples study). Researchers have also analyzed the linguistic synchrony in the letters and poetry of famous romantic and platonic couples—for example, Sylvia Plath and Ted Hughes, Elizabeth Barrett Browning and Robert Browning, and Sigmund Freud and Carl Jung. When tracked across the ups and downs of their relationships, analyses showed that their happiest times (e.g., the first four years of Plath's and Hughes's marriage) were marked by the highest linguistic synchrony and their least happy times (the two years before Plath's suicide at age thirty) were marked by the lowest synchrony.[110]

An argument could be made that there's nothing we can do about the extent to which our language matches that of our partners—that the process is uncontrollable and automatic—but I believe that we can deliberately try to match one another's speech patterns, and reap relationship benefits as a result. Women appear to be naturally better at this kind of verbal (as well as nonverbal) mimicry than men,[111] but this may mean that men just have to try harder. Have you ever interrupted a conversation with someone to answer the phone, and instantly found yourself switching your speaking style to match that of the person on the other end of the line? Sometimes this happens effortlessly, but at other times you may be conscious of having to exert mental and verbal control (and hence feel exhausted and relieved after the conversation is over). Your body also acts to match that of your conversation partner. Studies show that two people conversing typically mirror their respective behaviors (e.g., you sit back, she sits back; you rub your chin, she rubs her chin; you laugh, she laughs), often without even noticing.

If you can consciously switch your speaking style, then you can consciously develop linguistic synchrony with your spouse or partner and enhance your relationship accordingly, even if just a little. The primary reason that such synchrony benefits relationships is that it's a signal that we are listening to and truly trying to know and understand each other. Attentiveness is critical. A distracted listener, for example, appears to do more damage to a shared experience than even a hostile listener.[112] Although this may initially seem counterintuitive, when we are sharing an important memory, incident, or life dream with a friend or partner, we tend to prefer a negative reaction to no reaction at all. Hence, linguistic synchrony is especially valuable in troubled relationships, which have a relatively greater share of difficult conversations. If you can mirror your partner's speaking style and gestures during a tense exchange, you are more likely to hear each other, and more likely to sort out the issue of the day.

MEND YOUR LIFE: COPING WITH A TROUBLED MARRIAGE

There are elements of a relationship that are very difficult to nurture or improve. Our partner may have a trait we have difficulty living with (a temper, narcissism, an addiction). He may have cheated on us. His work may take him away from us five days each week. We have tried to change him or the situation with little or no success. When we are facing major struggles in our marriage, we may want to consider a course of action that involves learning to live with our current difficulties and making the best of the situation. Although this path may seem a Herculean effort, at least at first, it will get us through the rocky patch and bring us to the point where we are either ready to make a bigger change or walk away, or else we have surmounted the roadblock and reached more satisfying times.

For those of us who choose this path, the findings from three separate areas of research may be invaluable. The first is seeking solace and joy outside our marriages—in our family members and friends. The second is learning new, balanced ways to obtain closure and to observe and make sense of our daily life. The third is forgiveness.

SOCIAL SUPPORT

The need to belong, to feel cared for, and to depend on other individuals and groups to thrive and survive is an essential part of our human (and primate) nature.[113] Social support is especially critical in helping us manage stressful and painful life experiences. When we have marital woes, turning to a friend, relative, spiritual adviser, or even a pet[114] can instantly bolster our spirits and diffuse our worries. Our companions can make us feel loved and valued, can help us understand our situation better and give us specific advice about how to address it, and can provide us with tangible or financial assistance. In a sense, an ear that listens and a shoulder to cry on can blunt the misery we might feel in our marriage and supply us with the resources we need (such as confidence, information, an escape route) to cope with it or to take action.

When I was younger, I seriously underestimated the value of social and emotional support. I remember once spending hours crying and crying—and ruminating and obsessing—and crying some more over a doomed relationship. And then, after talking about my feelings for about an hour to a close friend, my anguish came down from a ten to maybe a three. How much would I have paid for a pill that had a salutary effect of equivalent magnitude?

When we are confronted with a major problem in our marriage—our partner is unfaithful, we're fighting every day, we fundamentally disagree over whether to have kids—that problem appears so formidable and daunting that it's difficult to fathom that mere warmth and comfort from a friend or family member can make it go away. Of course, most of the time, social support won't make a problem disappear, but it can go a long way in helping us address the problem, mitigate it, and lighten our emotional reactions to it. In a clever study that supports this claim, researchers recruited volunteers who happened to be passing the base of a hill and were either alone or with a friend.[115] Incredibly, those who were accompanied by a friend—especially a friend they were close to and knew a long time—judged the hill to be *less steep* than those who were alone. Serving as a metaphor for the challenges of life—and the challenges of marriage in particular—companions and confidants can make us feel that our problems and stresses are less steep as well.

Sometimes when you feel that you want to leave your spouse, the person you really want to leave is yourself. To be sure, the Michelangelo phenomenon can work in both positive and pernicious ways. Instead of helping you achieve your ideal self, your partner may have instead helped mold you into an individual whom you despise. This is another state of affairs for which friends and family members can provide invaluable support—by helping you keep your eye on the big picture, by renewing your confidence, by recognizing how you may have changed in adverse ways, and by helping you undo those changes.

In sum, if you are struck one day with the sinking feeling that you're married to the wrong person, one of the most invaluable actions you can take is to talk to trusted others. In addition to the psychological and concrete benefits I've just described, you may realize a neurological and physiological bonus. The brains, hearts, neuroendocrine systems, and immune systems of people who have a close confidant show less reactivity to situations in which they are experiencing some hurt or stress, such as feeling rejected or ignored.[116] Furthermore, the mere perception of having social support—for example, the thought that your mom will always be there for you—can reduce stress and boost your happiness level, especially in the face of challenges. And you don't have to be the life of the party, surrounded by a dozen people ready to make sacrifices for you. The benefits of social support extend to those of us who simply participate in groups in our communities (PTA, reading group, running club, church or synagogue group), and/or who can identify at least one mutually close friend.[117] Having many close friends outside your marriage appears to be unnecessary.[118]

THE "FLY ON THE WALL" TECHNIQUE

A troubled marriage wouldn't be called troubled if it weren't marked by a succession of arguments and slights: *She was cold to me today. He humiliated me in front of our friends. She rebuffed my attempt at affection. He made a major purchase without consulting me. She was out late and shut herself in the den after walking in. He gave the kids junk food and completely ignored my objections. She lost her temper over the smallest thing. He made me feel like an idiot. She didn't seem to care about my news.* It makes me feel exhausted and a little sad just to contemplate the emotional sting of such incidents. If one of the above happens to us, a common a response is to chew it over—passively and repetitively—until our heads are spinning with recriminations, worries, rejections, annoyances, misgivings, doubts, and vulnerabilities. In other words, the more we ruminate about a hurt or trouble, the worse we feel, the more negatively biased the conclusions we reach become, and the further we stand from a solution or way out.[119] However, although my own and others' research suggests that we are better off not thinking about such things and should instead redirect our attention to something more positive or just not sweat the small stuff,[120] often this advice is impossible or unrealistic to follow. When our partners are neglectful or contemptuous, their behavior is likely evidence of a problem that will not go away on its own—a problem, for better or for worse, that requires action.

A very new line of research suggests a healthier way to consider painful experiences, namely, that we should analyze our negative feelings and troubles from a "self-distanced" perspective.[121] In other words, we should try to observe and think about ourselves through the eyes of another person, like a fly on the wall. Furthermore, we should *avoid* thinking about and visualizing our past experiences (e.g., replaying that argument or humiliation) through our *own* eyes, as such a "self-immersed" perspective routinely precipitates toxic rumination.

The reasoning behind this is that when we reflect on a bad experience as though we are an observer—as though we are watching ourselves from afar—we are able to reframe the experience in a way that helps us gain insight and obtain closure. By contrast, when we recall the negative event through our own eyes—as though we were right there—we end up rehashing in heartbreaking detail exactly what happened, who said what, and how we felt. Studies show that people who naturally take a self-distancing or "fly on the wall" perspective about a recent episode that made them feel rejected or enraged, or are encouraged to take such a perspective by an experimenter, are more likely to try to solve their problems in a constructive manner and less likely to reciprocate hostile behavior from their partner.[122] Furthermore, self-distancing buffers us against anger, sadness, and pessimism[123] and makes us less physiologically reactive to stress (with, for example, smaller spikes in blood pressure), which is not only good for our emotions but also for our physical health.[124]

So, the next time you experience a minor or major crisis in your marriage, let a bit of time pass, then deliberate on it by assuming the viewpoint of an objective observer, say, your therapist, a fair-minded friend, or even a stranger, thus scrutinizing yourself and your spouse from a distance. Scientists have shown that this exercise will inhibit you from engaging in circular rumination or avoidance[125] and instead will lead you to a clearer and more coherent understanding of the crisis, and even a realization that will allow you to achieve some resolution or sense of closure.

SEALING NEGATIVE EXPERIENCES IN A BOX

There are many troubles in a marriage that we need to acknowledge and work to resolve, but there are some troubles that should be accepted and left behind. These are the ones that we should "seal in a box" and put away. You might wonder what kinds of experiments provide empirical support for this recommendation, or how this idea might be translated to the laboratory. Remarkably, it turns out that no such translation is needed. Researchers have instructed participants to write about very painful memories and then quite literally asked them to *seal* these recollections (though in an envelope, not box).[126]

If you were to emulate this experiment, you would first think about something that makes you feel truly bad—for example, contemplate an event or decision in your marriage that you thoroughly regretted (for example, concerning an infidelity by either partner) or think of a strong personal desire that was thwarted (to have a baby or change jobs).[127] Then you would write about the experience on some loose-leaf paper, which would make you feel even worse, at least initially. Finally, you would fold up the papers, put them in a manila envelope, seal or glue it shut, and give it to the experimenter or discard it. This procedure has been found to weaken the emotional impact of the distressing event and make people feel less sad, less regretful, less anxious, less disappointed, and less angry.

When we talk about managing or checking our emotions, we often use terms related to physical enclosure—for example, burying our grief, bottling up our worries, putting a lid on our rage, or sweeping our feelings under the rug. It turns out that the physical act of sealing, enclosing, or locking up helps us attain psychological closure over our problems and heartaches. Depositing our worries into a package that we then seal gives us a sense of relief and a sense that our emotions are under our control. This technique may seem simple at best and silly at worst, but I would encourage you to give it a try. Sealing an object related to your troubles—whether a diary entry, letter, or photograph—in a container may relieve a great deal of distress, and help you to move on.

IS FORGIVENESS ALWAYS A GOOD THING?

A few minutes ago, at work, you received a phone call from your significant other telling you that she or he had just arrived home after spending the night with a lover. The two of you have been going through a rocky period, but you had been under the impression that the relationship was basically sound. Your significant other apologized and wants to meet with you tonight.[128]

This emotionally charged hypothetical scenario is being used by a team of researchers who are studying how to measure and cultivate forgiveness. Imagine as vividly as you can that this event just happened to you. How would you respond this instant? How would you manage your feelings and your relationship from this day forward? Would you find it in your heart to forgive?

I've always been a bit in awe of genuinely forgiving people. Parents who forgive the murderers of their children. The unjustly imprisoned who forgive the system that betrayed them. Probably the most famous such prisoner was former South African president and Nobel Peace Prize winner Nelson Mandela. At his 1994 presidential inauguration, Mandela is said to have told the audience gathered in front of him, many of whom were dignitaries, royalty, presidents, and prime ministers from around the world, that he was most honored to have as his guests that day three jailers from Robben Island, the prison where he was held for eighteen years, living on meager rations and doing hard labor in a lime quarry. Mandela later explained that if he did not forgive, he would spend the rest of his days living with bitterness and hatred.[129] His view is not only deeply inspiring but is persuasively supported by empirical evidence. Whether the act is extraordinary, as in the dramatic examples above, or involves letting go of everyday transgressions in our lives, forgiving others can liberate us in more ways than one.

WHAT THE SCIENCE SAYS

"To err is human; to forgive, divine."[130] Whether a version of this adage came to us from magazine articles or our mothers, most of us have heard somewhere that forgiveness is good for us. Forgiveness involves a shift in how we view and behave toward people who have hurt us—a shift from bitter and vengeful feelings in the direction of goodwill (or positive thoughts, emotions, and acts).[131] It is said to release our anger and our hatred, improve our relationships, and ultimately make us happier and healthier. Indeed, true forgiveness has been found to reduce grievances, minimize intrusive negative, angry, or depressive thoughts, bolster optimistic thinking, foster contentment with life, promote commitment and satisfaction in a marriage, improve physical health, and even boost productivity at work.[132] If you're pained by your spouse's actions, take time to consider the implications of these findings.

Intervention studies that teach strategies to promote forgiveness have been successfully conducted with many diverse groups, including married couples, incest survivors, parents who have experienced a child's suicide, men whose partners had abortions against their wishes, children hurt in relationships, and divorced couples involved in parenting conflicts.[133] Scientists have established that when our spouse, for example, mistreats us and we don't forgive her, her transgression will spill over into our future marital interactions and conflicts, and ultimately stand as an albatross between us, blocking us from solving our problems. Forgiveness can not only avert this vicious downward spiral in our relationship but trigger warm thoughts and interactions. Indeed, one study even found that forgiving one person (such us our partner or our neighbor) spills over to our other relationships. Simply remembering someone we forgave strengthens our connections with family, friends, and co-workers and makes us more likely to donate to charity or to volunteer for a worthy cause.[134]

BUT . . . THE DOORMAT CAVEAT

If forgiveness is so rewarding, and its illustrious practitioners so virtuous, why are many of us reluctant to embrace it as a regular practice, especially in our relationships? Why do we have mixed feelings when observing long-suffering husbands and wives who forgive their spouse for one sin after another? Evolutionary and social psychologists offer a tenable answer. Our likelihood of survival and reproduction sometimes depends on being forgiving and sometimes depends on being vengeful, and it's critical to differentiate situations that warrant one response over the other.[135] For example, when forgiveness is granted too quickly and uncritically, we may end up wounding our self-possession and self-respect, regretting our inability to stand up for ourselves, and damaging our relationships by preventing our partners from learning a lesson and improving themselves.[136] If we forgive our spouse too hastily and too often, we risk losing sight of our values, ignoring real problems in our relationship, and becoming his or her doormat.

When to forgive and when not to forgive? Scientists have recently established criteria for when forgiveness is beneficial versus harmful. Essentially if, after your husband has committed some wrong, you believe that (1) you and he will stay married and you treasure preserving the marriage, (2) he is not likely to repeat the transgression or hurt you again, and (3) he rarely misbehaves, then forgiveness will have positive consequences. For example, in one study of married couples, spouses who forgave partners who frequently behaved badly experienced growing relationship problems over time (and vice versa), but spouses who forgave partners who rarely behaved badly reported sustained satisfaction with their marriages.[137]

Other studies have shown that people who forgive spouses who are agreeable or have made strong amends experience a strong sense of identity and a boost to their self-respect, whereas those who forgive spouses who are not agreeable or have not make adequate amends feel significantly worse about themselves.[138] In sum, if your wife—who may have been unfaithful or deceitful or mean—signals to you that you are safe and valued in your marriage, then forgiving her will bolster your sense of certainty and worthiness about yourself, preserve your marriage, and improve the inevitable conflicts and problems. However, we need to examine whether our propensity to forgive arises out of a legitimate and well-considered motive to heal our marriage, or whether we are so terrified that our conviction we'd never be happy if our marriage ended will come true that we'd do anything we can to avoid a major confrontation. Forgiveness is a choice that requires a conscious effort, and that effort may pay off in immense dividends—both for you and your relationship. But if all the signs indicate that your partner feels no remorse and will misbehave again, then forgiving will not be the "divine" thing to do.

LEAVING BEFORE IT'S TOO LATE

You've tried everything, but the ratio of positive to negative experiences in your marriage is at best one to one. You're deeply and constantly unhappy and you don't want to waste any more good years. Separation and divorce are such personal decisions that no one—not even an accomplished marriage counselor—can tell a couple whether to go through with it or not. I will not either, but I mean to offer you some vital hot-off-the-presses findings and conclusions from social science, which may (or may not) influence your decision.

THE VALUE OF WAITING

The adage that "time will heal all wounds" is one of those sayings that is probably true, at least in certain circumstances, but is harsh to hear. If your marriage is subject to naturally occurring waves, or ups and downs, and you have been in a trough for a bit too long, it's very possible that you should simply ride it out. I once heard a lovely story concerning a bowl of murky water. The water was cloudy from the dirt inside it and its owner didn't know what to do to make it clear again. Should he boil it? Freeze it? Shake it? Strain it? Does some chemical exist that will absorb or neutralize the dirt? He tried those methods but they didn't really work. What did work was to let the bowl of muddy water sit for a while and settle. So, he discontinued all his efforts, relaxed, and simply let the water stand. After a time, he noticed that the muck started to separate out all by itself, and soon enough the water was crystal clear again.[139]

If you let the marriage settle, you might find that the muck will separate out all by itself.

AFTER DIVORCE, YOU WILL COPE AND GROW

And what if the gunk doesn't break up all by itself? Then, perhaps, you will resolve to separate or divorce, as more than 40 percent of couples do, and the decision will be terrifying.[140] After all, something as momentous as divorce will not only change your life and your family in a million small and large ways, but it can challenge the very story that you tell about yourself—past, present, and future— that imparts coherence and purpose to your life. After all, this isn't the way your story was supposed to end.

People typically experience a range of emotions during and after a divorce, from betrayal and rejection to sadness and relief, from anger and fear to guilty and self-pity. Moreover, sometimes the emotions come and go within a span of minutes, lending new meaning to the term "emotional roller coaster." You may feel like your life is a mess and you're becoming unhinged. You may start questioning your self-worth and value as a mate. You may be facing mountains of paperwork, endless calls with your lawyer, stressful negotiations with your ex about property and custody, and children who are acting out or withdrawing. On top of this, you are likely encountering new financial, employment, and social stresses. You may be feeling considerable pressure to find a job, or a better-paying job. And, just when you need social support the most, you may be feeling isolated and lonely, because friendships change after a marriage ends and some of your "couple" friends may drift away.

Despite the enormous challenges and strains, somehow most people manage to survive divorce and even thrive. Indeed, an analysis of eight different studies that followed people before and after they legally divorced showed that the typical response was one of increasing happiness over time.[141] One of the themes of this book is that human beings are remarkably resilient, with the capacity to turn traumas into assets and bad experiences into growth experiences— for example, to bounce back from a divorce and even emerge from it stronger than before. My favorite take on resilience recasts it as "ordinary magic" and not something possessed only by extraordinary people with special strengths whom we can never hope to emulate.[142] Rather, it is a common characteristic that involves the ability to rally after adversity and to experience positive emotions. However, because most of us aren't aware of the ordinary but remarkable dominance of this ability, we typically underestimate our capacity to weather almost any unhappiness. Because we worry we'll never be happy after an adversity or trauma, such as our family breaking apart, we underestimate the ordinary magic we all possess.

Much has been written—both by researchers and self-help authors—about the particular resources that help us grow and even "benefit" from the kind of loss, pain, and trauma characteristic of divorce.[143] These strengths will help us cope and grow throughout our darkest days. Beginning today, undertake one of the following activities, perhaps the ones that you find most natural or rewarding, or at least the ones you feel least anxious about starting:

- Ask yourself how you have become stronger as a result of your separation and divorce.

- Write a story of what happened during and after the end of your marriage, how you have grown and changed because of it, and what new priorities and purpose you can think of for your future.

- Consider the funniest thing someone has said to you since your divorce.

- Ask yourself what precisely you are feeling, and why, during this period of your life, and give yourself the task of sharing your feelings with others.

- Do something every day—however trivial—that makes you happy at least briefly.

- Try to recollect what has helped you bounce back from previous traumas, and muster those same resources again.

- Reflect on what spirituality means to you and how you can use it to connect to others.

- Connect to another person by helping them or teaching something to them.

These steps will help build and reinforce your capacity to maintain a positive attitude, even when in pain; to make sense of the breakup; to reprioritize what is important to you; and to value more those goals that are newly meaningful and attainable.[144] These activities also aim to "lighten" the burden of the hardship by encouraging you not to take things too seriously, to hone your awareness and sensitivity to your own and others' emotions, and to develop your ability to communicate your feelings and connect with other people.[145] Finally, taking these steps will help you engage more with something bigger than yourself and to rely on other significant relationships in your life outside your marriage.

Last but not least is a resource that nearly everyone needs to reinforce. Because of its momentous influence in many areas of life, self-esteem is one of the most studied of all human traits. Thus, assessing your current level of self-esteem should be a top priority. To do so, rate the extent to which you agree with each of the following statements (1 = strongly disagree, 2 = disagree, 3 = agree, 4 = strongly agree):[146]

_____ 1. I feel I am a person of worth, at least on an equal plane with others.

_____ 2. I feel I have a number of good qualities.

_____ 3. All in all, I am inclined to feel I am a failure.

_____ 4. I am able to do things as well as most other people.

_____ 5. I feel I do not have much to be proud of, compared to most others.

_____ 6. I take a positive attitude toward myself.

_____ 7. On the whole, I am satisfied with myself.

_____ 8. I wish I could have more respect for myself.

_____ 9. I certainly feel useless at times.

_____ 10. At times I think I am no good at all.

To determine your self-esteem score, first "reverse-score" your ratings of items 3, 5, 8, 9, and 10—that is, if you gave yourself a 1, cross it out and change it to a 4; if you gave yourself a 2, change that to a 3; change a 3 to a 2; and change a 4 to a 1. Now add up your 10 ratings to calculate the sum.

The highest self-esteem score that you can get is 40 (if you strongly agreed with all the positively valenced self-esteem items and strongly disagreed with all the negative items) and the lowest is 10 (if you did the opposite). People around the world score an average of 31 on this scale, and people in the United States score an average of 32. So, if you scored lower than 31 or 32, then more than 50 percent of your peers have higher self-esteem than you; if you scored lower than 20, then your self-esteem score is in the bottom third of the population.

If your score is below the average level, then boosting your self-esteem, however challenging, may need to be one of your primary objectives. Start by taking "baby steps" toward goals that help you accomplish something, nurture friendships, act compassionately towards others, and feel better about yourself.[147] Several sections in this book offer guidelines for how to accomplish that.

AFTER DIVORCE, LIFE WILL GO ON

Research on hedonic adaptation shows that we swiftly grow accustomed to most negative events. For example, in one study, during the first two years after a divorce, people experienced a great deal of psychological distress, but then they seemed to rebound.[148] Life carried on, and a multitude of unrelated daily uplifts and upsets captivated their attention much of the time.

One of the reasons that we embrace the myth that divorce (or any other adversity) will make us more unhappy (and for far longer) than it actually does is that we assume we'll be as much preoccupied with our divorce and all its consequences one year or five years from now as we are today. Hence, we fail to consider the myriad other events that will unfold and compete for our attention during the next year and five years.[149] After all, we may need dental surgery or our air-conditioning fixed. We may see our son graduate with honors and we may reconnect with a long-lost cousin. We may learn how to cook sumptuous paella for our friends, and we may take a delightful (or disastrous) trip with our kids to the Florida Keys. In short, our judgment and our participation will be required by many situations completely unconnected to our divorce. Divorce doesn't happen in a vacuum.[150] Life goes on, and other events push and pull and control our emotions as much as, or more than, the original trauma. To truly grasp this notion, emulate what participants in several clever studies were instructed to do: Those who sat down and actually wrote out the many other events and commitments that will demand their time and attention in the future (e.g., the doctor's appointments, dinner parties, car repairs, and salary raises they anticipated next year) were less likely to inflate the heartbreak of the divorce trauma.[151]

In *House Lights,* a book about family life, a father is faced with never living together again with his wife. When he asks his daughter what he's going to do now, she says something that applies to all of us:

> You're going to be sad . . . You're going to miss her. You're going to keep on seeing patients, and meeting with your birders, and recording books for the blind. You're going to see friends, and eat food, and . . . get oil changes . . . buy groceries . . . go to those concerts at the church. Clean your binoculars with your little binocular-cleaning kit. You'll shovel snow, and mow the lawn, and rake the leaves. You'll read, and cook.[152]

The truth is that every month, the fact of your divorce—and its repercussions—will have a smaller impact on your daily life than the month before.

WHAT ABOUT THE KIDS?

You will get over it, perhaps you will forgive if not forget, and maybe your life will be infinitely better, but what about the kids? Surveys show that children are by far the top reason that unhappy couples choose to stay together.[153] This reality is neither unreasonable nor surprising, but it's important to establish whether people's assumptions about the effects of divorce on children, as well as on other important life outcomes, are accurate. The literature on this subject encompasses two extreme perspectives. The first is that divorce has no long-term costs for children, and the second is that it causes permanent harm. As with most debates, the answer is somewhere in the middle, though my reading of the research is that it's closer to the no-long-term-effects view. In sum, divorce definitely has some harmful effects on children, but these effects are often small and don't apply to every family.[154]

On the one hand, not unexpectedly, after a divorce, the ex-couple has a more difficult time being good parents. They have trouble, for example, monitoring, supervising, and disciplining their children effectively and consistently, providing love and affection, and diffusing parent-child conflict. This toll occurs because of new custody arrangements, the fragmenting of family cohesion, and increased depression, anxiety, and stress in the parents. However, the damaging effects are often short-lived or not universal. For example, one researcher tested whether children of divorce were less happy and less self-confident, got lower grades, had less healthy relationships, and showed more behavior problems than children of intact families.

Out of 177 comparisons between these two groups of children, more than half (103) revealed no differences whatsoever.[155] Other studies have found that 75 percent of children whose parents divorce suffer no long-term impediments, and that the effects of divorce on conduct problems, academics, and well-being are smaller than the effects of gender.[156] Of course, this means that fully a quarter of children do suffer from divorce, even over the long term, and this truth should be taken very seriously. For example, our own marriage is twice as likely to end in divorce if our parents divorced, and our health is jeopardized.[157]

Attempts to answer the question of whether divorce injures children have a very important limitation, however. All the studies are necessarily correlational, as it would be impossible (and unethical) to randomly assign some couples to divorce and others to stay married. This means that we cannot rule out the role of genes in any of the findings. Divorce is highly heritable—meaning that the genes that underlie who gets divorced and who does not (which appear to be linked to particular personalities, like being generally negative and unhappy) are passed down from parents to children.[158] So when we learn that children of divorced parents don't do as well in certain domains, the effect may be due to the genes that the children share with their parents and not to the effects of divorce per se.

Another critical piece of the puzzle concerns the question of whether we should stay in a conflicted marriage for the sake of our kids. In other words, is it worse for children to continue to reside with parents who are quarreling and miserable or to undergo the consequences of their parents' divorce? The short answer is that children do better when able (via divorce) to escape their parents' fighting, screaming, and the pressure to take sides. In a home full of pain, quarreling, or coldness, children are essentially exposed to chronic stress, which leads them to develop the habit of staying constantly vigilant and alert.[159] My friend Josie remembers hiding in her room when her parents were fighting and hurling objects at each other. She frequently intervened in their conflicts, joining the shouting and trying to protect her mom, and dreaded hearing her dad's key in the door. Today, she is ultrasensitive to any kind of conflict; when her husband so much as raises his voice, her heart races. Josie has been in therapy and has managed to have healthy and successful adult relationships, but at a price.

When we compare how well children do in homes with a great deal of parental conflict to how well they do after divorce, the answer is pretty clear: The former fare significantly worse. For example, in one study, children exposed to lots of fighting in the home were relatively more likely to act out, to be anxious or depressed, and to have troubled relationships with friends and classmates, but whether their parents were married or divorced had no impact on their problems. So, it's the conflict that matters, not the divorce. Of course, this evidence also means that studies that discover harmful effects of divorce on children may simply be discovering the effects of the inevitable conflict associated with that divorce. Notably, research on health mirrors these findings very closely. Although people who divorce report more health problems—weaker immune system, more heart disease and diabetes, lower cancer survival, and problems with physical functioning in old age[160]—the health of unhappily married couples suffers just as much or more.[161] Indeed, although we may not be aware of it, in the middle of a hostile argument, the functioning of our immune system begins to decline, our physical injuries heal more slowly, and our coronary calcium levels (signaling risk for heart disease) rise.[162] As one health psychologist concluded, a troubled marriage presents as big a risk factor for heart disease as a regular smoking habit.[163]

If you are considering divorce and worried about how it will impact your children's psychological adjustment, academic achievement, behavior issues, and even their future grown-up relationships, you need to consider that a warm, loving, and peaceful single-parent home (or two of them) is more pivotal than a distressed two-parent home. The one caveat is whether you suspect that your grave problems with your spouse are invisible to your child. Although this may seem implausible, we all know of couples who are able to hide their unhappiness so successfully that their separation is a bombshell to everyone, including their closest friends and family members (and sometimes even one of the spouses). It turns out that children who have had no clue that their parents were having problems suffer the most negative and long-term consequences when those parents stun (and devastate) them by divorcing.[164] This state of affairs presents a difficult and perhaps irresolvable dilemma: It's surely unwise to fight in front of your kids just so they are not surprised by an eventual split-up. Perhaps the best way forward in this situation is for the couple who is so practiced at putting up a happy front to continue to forge a warm and nurturing environment for their children, as well as maintaining amicable interactions with each other, throughout the separation, divorce, and beyond.

THE PREPARED MIND

The moment of truth that involves the possibility of leaving or staying in a relationship is one of the most difficult to confront and grapple with. You have the choice to leave. You have the choice to stay and make the best of the lot you're dealt. You have the choice to stay and resolve to improve your partnership. One of the lessons of this chapter is that when you recognize the misconceptions that are likely compounding your crisis point, you will realize that you may have more choices than you think. Accordingly, I present several marriage-coping and marriage-nurturing strategies here. The sooner you begin practicing these strategies—after the first divorce fantasy rather than after the first separation—the more effective they will be. Of course, sometimes a divorce fantasy is just that—a daydream that allows you to discharge your anger and distress before you return to the work of caring for your marriage. But other times divorce fantasies are harbingers of what's to come. In that case, the sooner you consider the research (e.g., that divorce does *not* irreparably harm most children), the sooner you will be prepared to make a decision based on reason rather than intuition (the notion that you can't leave no matter how unhappy you are).

Above all, before making any pivotal decision, you need to consider how much of your marital unhappiness is due to you, how much of it is due to your spouse, how much of it is due to dynamics within your marriage, and how much of it is due to circumstances beyond your control. Such understanding may not change your ultimate decision, but it will influence what element of your marriage or your life you should seek to change. Knowing that this happiness myth is wrong—that your life won't end when your relationship does—opens up new roads and new positive possibilities for how to enact that change.

CHAPTER 3

I'll Be Happy When . . . I Have Kids

was walking with a friend when she confessed something to me that I had never heard anyone say out loud: "I don't like being a parent." She adores her son, probably more than anything. She had tried to have a baby for a decade before she finally succeeded, with the help of multiple fertility treatments. She is grateful for that. But perhaps because the desire for a child had been so strong and so enduring, and the effort so difficult and stressful, it took her several years to acknowledge the reality that parenting just doesn't suit her. She doesn't feel comfortable around a gang of kids, and feels she has to fake "mommy" behavior in front of other parents. She doesn't want to give everything of herself in the service of unconditional concern and care for another. She finds the relentless worries and schedules and disappointments not a challenge or an adventure, as some of her friends and colleagues seem to, but a heavy burden. I should add that an objective observer would have no clue of her true feelings. She is a fine parent, and she knows it; she just doesn't like it.

Many questions may spring to mind when we hear this story. Is parenting something we are supposed to like? After all, how many of us *really* anticipated what it would be like to have a child, even after reading a dozen books and talking to every parent we met? And isn't my friend being premature in her conclusion, given that perhaps no job in the world changes as drastically over time as does parenting? In a few years, when her son is in elementary school, her parenting today will be hardly recognizable, and a few years after that, everything will change again, and so on. Indeed, sometimes huge developments in the child and in the parent-child relationship occur in the course of months. Finally, is this simply an extreme example that does not bear relevance for most of us?

Children are the fount of our greatest joy and the source of our greatest sorrow. It's not surprising, then, that some of our most impactful watershed moments are situated in our family lives. Before we decide whether to resign ourselves to our feelings about parenting, despair over them, or strive to fight them, we need to establish whether our predicament is so very unique. The expectation that having kids will make us immensely happy is not only rooted in our culture but likely evolutionarily wired as well. Although this myth of happiness may keep human beings from giving up on reproducing, it also serves to create a crisis point out of an archetypal human chapter in our lives. When parenting doesn't make us as happy as we expected it to, we feel not only strung out, miserable, and disheartened, but ashamed as well.

PARENTING ISN'T WHAT I EXPECTED: THE SURPRISING FINDINGS ABOUT WHETHER CHILDREN MAKE YOU HAPPY

You may find little joy in being a parent and loathe the myriad chores and worries that the role entails. You may have gotten weary and disenchanted with the eighteen-plus-year grind—the years of parenting behind you and especially those ahead of you. That's bad enough, but to top off these unwelcome feelings, you feel like an aberration and misfit in a culture of fierce family nuclearity, afraid to voice your true feelings about parenting and risk being rebuffed by others. Amazingly, in part because these feelings are so taboo, few people seem to recognize how widely shared they are. An analysis of more than a hundred studies revealed that couples who were followed before and after the birth of a child suffered seemingly permanent declines in their relationship satisfaction.[165] Surveys also demonstrate that, despite many parents' professions of joy and elation at their role, if you are female, young, not married, and unemployed—and if your children are very young or adolescent, step, or troubled—then being a parent likely makes you less happy, and less satisfied with your life and partner (if you have one), rather than more.[166]

Having children is costly, exhausting, stressful, and emotionally draining—so much so that it's a wonder we somehow seem unable to accurately envision parenting's difficulties up until the day we bring the infant home. After that day, however, no parent of an infant will be surprised to hear that when people are asked how happy they are before and after they bring home their first baby, the second report is significantly lower than the first.[167] Furthermore, marital satisfaction soars after the last child leaves the home.[168] And, although the evidence is mixed, a number of studies that simply compare the happiness or satisfaction levels of parents and nonparents drawn from all ages and life circumstances find that parents are less happy.[169] For example, in one oft-cited study, working mothers in Texas reported experiencing fewer positive emotions on a daily basis and more negative emotions. When asked to rate how they felt during every hour of the previous day, they judged taking care of their children as only slightly more enjoyable than commuting and housework.[170]

Clearly, if raising children frequently makes you cranky, irritable, enraged, weary, or worried sick, you are not alone. You are not the only one whose world shrinks after kids come, and you must say goodbye to risky adventures, spontaneous intimacies, and spur-of-the moment opportunities. You are not the only one whose marriage may suffer tremendously—at least when the children are under six or over twelve[171]—to the extent that trifling troubles or irritations are magnified into divorce-consideration-worthy fault lines. Studies show that the two most significant sources of married couples' clashes occur over finances and kids. However, stress and sleep deprivation alone are likely to boost the likelihood of any kind of conflict.[172] As one new father expressed it in indelicate terms, "[Children] are a huge source of joy, but they turn every other source of joy to shit."[173]

I hope that knowing that many other parents share our pain from time to time will make us feel less like outcasts and alleviate some of our guilt. Loving our children is not the same as loving parenting. Nonetheless, we may benefit by focusing on what our children impart to us that may not be captured by the question, "Are you happy?" Even parents who hate parenting have meaningful, joyous, and even euphoric moments that contribute to a life well lived—when our child is born, when he runs into our arms after a separation, when he reads his very first word, when he stars in his first school play, when the thought of him softens the sting of a failed project at work, or when he graduates with honors. In a recent study, my colleagues and I found that parents reported more meaning in life when spending time with their children than during the rest of their days.[174] Part of being alive and a citizen of the world means using our capabilities to the fullest, encountering different dimensions of human experience, growing and learning about ourselves, connecting with others, fulfilling culturally prescribed goals, experiencing a wide range of emotions (from the highest highs to the lowest lows), carving out a unique identity, writing the story of our lives, and leaving behind a legacy that will persist beyond our own lifetimes.[175] Children allow us to do all that and more.

Of course, most of the time, we are not thinking about those transcendent benefits; we are not whiling away our time savoring the memorable and profound moments which our kids grant us. Instead, we focus on the daily tasks and chores, and especially the small crises and big emergencies, that confront us. There is a saying about Jewish mothers, which really applies to all mothers and fathers: "A Jewish mother can never be happier than her least happy child." Psychologists have shown convincingly that the bad is always stronger than the good, such that the heartache from one child easily overwhelms the delight from another.[176] As a result, the obstacles to a parent's happiness—especially that experienced on a moment-by-moment level—are great, and those who respond by admitting that they frequently don't enjoy being parents are being perfectly rational.

Notwithstanding all the evidence that those of us who dislike parenting are not simply irresponsible or mad, when people are asked confidentially about their biggest regrets in life, scarcely anyone ever says that they regret having been a parent. Indeed, 94 percent agree that, despite the heavy costs, the rewards of being a parent are worth it.[177] After years pass, those dreaded middle-of-the-night feedings, heartbreaking moments clasping an inconsolable child, and standoffs over curfews metamorphose into treasured, nostalgic memories that offer satisfaction and delight. However, the regret of not having had children, or not having had more children, is a prevalent one.[178] We must bear both of these facts in mind when we are called into the assistant principal's office once again and feel that we cannot endure another day of being a parent.

DAILY HASSLES WILL MAKE YOU
UNHAPPIER THAN MAJOR TRAUMAS

Parenting is indeed a multi-decade grind, but there are many actions we can take to make the bad moments more bearable and more affirmative. A somewhat counterintuitive strategy is to take time to distinguish the major difficulties you are experiencing in the course of parenting from the minor ones; you might perhaps even list them in two columns—the "big things" and the "little bad things"—side by side.

One family recently described to me their issues in agonizing detail. Sarah and James's younger son has a mild form of Asperger's syndrome (which involves social deficits), as well as attention deficit disorder. He does extremely well in some subjects at school and struggles in others. He has one close friend, but hardly interacts with other peers. In short, the problems from his diagnoses rear their head almost every day. "It's not terrible," his parents said. "There are many good—even great—days and weeks." But there are evenings when they are pulling their hair out and quarreling about how to handle his latest "issue" and what their next steps should be. Their older son seems psychologically well-adjusted, but would much rather be with his friends than study, which means they battle over homework nightly. Not surprisingly, this family's list of big worries comprises their youngest son's mental health, while the small worries include their older son's "homework wars." On the small-issues list, they also include the various trials, stresses, and hurts experienced on a daily basis. In a recent week, for example, Sarah's offer of a play date for her younger son was met with a feeble excuse, and she is convinced that the other mom just didn't want her kid interacting with Sarah's kid. Then their dryer broke, which led to an amount of hassle and inconvenience seemingly disproportionate with the minor malfunction. Finally, their older son couldn't find the new cell phone he had just gotten for his birthday and they spent many frustrating hours searching for it.

Which of these two lists should make this family—and ours— more distressed and unhappy? Although most of us believe that the items in the big-things column deliver the bigger and longer-lasting sting, research reveals this to be a myth. To the contrary, the opposite is true—the hassles and uplifts that we experience apropos of our children on a daily basis impact our well-being more than do the major life events.[179] The counterintuitive idea that annoyances are worse than calamities makes little sense . . . until we consider why.

A number of years ago, when I was single and living alone, I had two bad experiences on the same day—being told by an airline that my long-reserved window seat (the last one) on a cross-country flight was erroneously sold to another passenger, and, later in the day, my car getting totaled ("accordioned") in a freeway accident. The accident wasn't my fault and I walked away, but I was incredibly serene and coolheaded in my response—calling for help, speaking with the insurance company, making plans for a rental the next day, etc. I seemed to have instinctively known that this was an emergency and that I needed to stay calm, think rationally, and muster all the resources and skills I had to manage it. My reaction to the airline's news, however, was the reverse. I felt their error was unforgivable, and I was still seething about it days later, while driving in my stopgap rental car.

Researchers argue that when we experience a significant negative event—a car accident, a layoff from our job, a child's suspension from school—we are acutely motivated to cope with and weather the crisis as best and as quickly as we can. We seek emotional comfort from friends, advice and job training from employers, second opinions from counselors and doctors, and information from books and Web sites. Furthermore, we do a lot of so-called cognitive work to come to terms with what occurred. We might take pains to rationalize, make sense of, or look at the bright side of the accident or layoff. Within minutes of my car accident, I had commiserated with my best friend and persuaded myself that "this is a good thing," because now I could use the insurance money to buy the convertible I had always wanted. By contrast, no such coping efforts take place after small disappointments and irritations. For example, I did not try to persuade myself that the airline worker, undoubtedly a poorly paid employee in a foreign land, made an understandable human error because he was having a trying day. Nor did I seek advice or information from others on how to handle the situation. I would have deemed that overkill.

We tend not to seek social support for the little bad things, in part because we expect that others will not care half as much as we do. (The eyes of even our closest loved ones will glaze over if we go on too long about our ruminations over spilled milk.) Furthermore, studies have shown that disclosing minor traumas leads well-meaning others to express their support by minimizing or downplaying them ("Too bad Charlie had a temper tantrum on the flight, but the trip could have been so much worse") and implying that we shouldn't feel as bad as we do, which has the consequence of making us feel even worse.[180]

In sum, because severe problems trigger efforts to cope and to positively reevaluate our situation, as well as eliciting strong emotional support from others—and not-so-major problems do not—we often paradoxically suffer pain and distress from the little things longer than from the big things.[181] Indeed, "it may be that the little things hurt precisely *because* we call them little."[182] However, most of us are painfully unaware of this. For example, a series of studies showed that people expect to dislike someone who hurt them a lot for a longer time than someone who hurt them a little, but the reality was the reverse.[183] As a consequence, we fail to muster appropriate energies to handle the everyday upsets we confront in life, and especially in our parenting life.

Consider that left-hand little bad things column regarding your kids. Perhaps it includes building irritation over your daughter's computer use, last night's yelling about clothes thrown all over the floor, this morning's worry about your baby's earache, or your dwelling on who will watch your son the morning both you and your partner have super-early meetings at work. It's important to muster efforts to address these seemingly small issues, whether by seeking help, negotiating with family members, reframing the events in more positive ways, or taking time out to relax, recharge, or meditate. If we resolve to focus our attention on the little bad things with respect to parenting, we will recover from them more quickly, be happier, and have the vitality and stamina to face another day.

FINDING BALANCE AND EMOTIONAL MEANING THROUGH WRITING

You will instinctively know not to neglect the "big bad things" column regarding your kids, but this doesn't mean it will be easy. Your teen may have gotten in with the wrong crowd or developed an unhealthy addiction. Your middle-schooler may be being bullied. Your preschooler may have been diagnosed with a chronic illness. Your toddler may not be reaching her developmental milestones. Some parents don't mind the day-to-day slog of parenting, yet come unhinged when a serious problem arises.

Furthermore, your ordeals as a parent may be rooted not in a particular child but in how you are managing parenting as a whole. The constant struggle to keep balance—between you and your spouse, and between parenting and work—has become almost a cliché. Although many parents handle it with aplomb, some feel the strain of juggling as a crushing burden.

From the first day home with a new baby, you realize the dozens, if not hundreds, of negotiations that must take place between you and your partner about how the work of caregiving and maintaining a household must be shared. Who will change the next diaper, wash the next set of dishes, get up next in the middle of the night, make the next decision about naptime, take the baby to the doctor next week, and file the tax returns in April? Moreover, just when you and your partner have supposedly ironed out your conflicts about the division of labor, the child (inevitably) grows or another is born and everything changes. The cycle of negotiation—or worse, feuding—begins again. Who will drive the kids to school, activities, friends, and doctors; make decisions about camps, schools, and medical treatments; complete dozens of registration, health, and school forms; do the disciplining; arrange the child care; help with homework; discuss college applications, or research athletic programs? The list of chores and obligations is endless, and someone always has to be there to pick up the ball.

The home versus work balance is arguably even more difficult to juggle than the chore wars, as there's no panacea for this nearly universal problem. Most parents—even those who have help and whose work is flexible—agree that there are not enough hours in the day to be a great parent *and* a great worker (not to mention, great wife, daughter, friend, etc.). In a 2008 survey, more than half of working parents reported having a hard time managing the responsibilities of work and family.[184]

Balancing the multiple obligations of career and parenting can be extremely stressful and exhausting, as the demands of your different roles compete for your attention, time, and energy and spill over from one area into the other. For example, on a stressful workday, fathers tend to physically withdraw from the family, while mothers behave less warmly and are less responsive toward their children.[185] In turn, problems with children lead to work disruptions, fatigue, and difficulty concentrating at the office. Furthermore, the sheer mental energy required to remain mindful of both the household and office to-do lists and to exert emotional control on both home and work fronts (e.g., to act happy when picking up your child from day care or focus intensely on your supervisor's feedback, even when it's the last thing you feel like doing) can lead to overload and stress and, ultimately, to depression.

Before the stress of juggling turns into hopelessness and depression, it's important to learn strategies that can help you find the right balance, come to terms with your current situation, or make the best of it. One of the most effective such strategies is to use writing or journaling to find emotional meaning in your parenting struggles. Jamie Pennebaker, a professor of psychology at the University of Texas in Austin, discovered that writing out our deepest feelings about our hardships and torments (what he calls emotional disclosure or expressive writing) can bolster our physical and mental health.[186] To date, he and other scientists have completed over a hundred studies supporting this discovery. Emulating the procedures they have used is very simple: Obtain a blank notebook or journal and start writing—at least for three to five consecutive days and ideally longer—your deepest thoughts and feelings about your most difficult and most upsetting experiences as a parent.

When scientists have compared participants who regularly write about their miseries to control participants who write about a neutral or superficial nonemotional topic (like the layout of their bedrooms or a detailed description of their shoes), they have consistently found that the "expressive writers" are happier, more satisfied with their lives, and less depressed. Furthermore, when tracked days or weeks later, the expressive writers end up visiting their doctors less often in subsequent months, show stronger immune function, perform better at school or work, are less likely to miss work, and more likely to find a job after a layoff.[187]

In sum, emotionally expressive writing has clear hedonic, physical, and cognitive benefits—benefits that are likely to mitigate the unrelenting stress of parenting, the anguish of family traumas, and of balancing our own needs and obligations with those of our partners, children, and career. Keeping a journal about our parenting experiences is one of the most valuable strategies that we can avail ourselves of when trying to get a handle on painful or conflicting thoughts and feelings.

Initially, Pennebaker believed that the secret of this strategy's success was the catharsis or "letting go" that it allows people who have been holding in their feelings. For example, we may have been feeling chronically guilty about coming home late from work, angry at our wife for never appreciating our labors, or overwrought about how to handle the travel required of our jobs. But it appears that the secret is not necessarily in airing these feelings but rather in the actual writing about them—the words themselves. Writing about our family worries and troubles helps us reconcile ourselves to them and understand them. Putting our emotional upheavals into words helps us make sense of them, accommodate to them, and begin to move past them; it ultimately prepares us to share these upheavals with close others. So language turns out to be critical. The act of converting intense emotions and images into a coherent narrative changes the way we structure our distress or pain, think about it, and integrate it into our life story. An acquaintance told me once that writing about upsetting experiences *reduces* them—compresses them, makes them smaller. When our traumas and difficulties shrink, they can be stored and diluted more quickly and more efficiently. If we develop the habit of keeping an expressive journal—and putting it to use even after minor traumas and bothers—the practice will pay dividends when major parenting upheavals inevitably come our way. An added bonus is the newfound appreciation, humor, and insight that we will inevitably gain when rereading the journal years or decades later.

SEEING THE BIG PICTURE

Life with children—whether they're infants, preschoolers, tweens, or teens—can mean life in a house full of disorder and chaos, constant demands on our time, attention, and pocketbook, and not-infrequent waves of irritation, embarrassment, regret, and rage, not to mention panic about paying for it all. Some of us are so plagued by the sense that we are shackled to our present life as far into the future as we can imagine that we become miserable and disillusioned or, worse, apathetic and depressed. At these moments, it's helpful to contemplate the "big picture" perspective—why we chose to have children in the first place, how our parenting experience will shift and improve with time, and what we wish to contribute to society and to future generations. Such a broad perspective prompts us to ask the big questions—what is the purpose of our lives, and what are we doing here?

We can also consider a more personal perspective—about our priorities and prime concerns during different stages of our lives. Perhaps waking up every day before sunrise to be with your kid is something you need to do right now, pushing him to raise his grades is something you will need to do in ten years, and calling him to offer emotional support is something you will need to (and want to) do in twenty years. Older people, especially, benefit greatly if they have positive relationships with their adult children, and report that having grandchildren is one of the best experiences of their lives.[188] Despite the fact that people are bearing children later than ever before, and that those children are living at home longer, monumental increases in the human life span mean that parents have an unprecedented number of post-empty-nest years to spend together with their adult offspring—a remarkable 30.5 years on average for mothers and 22 years for fathers.[189] In interviews about the wisdom they have accumulated during their lifetimes, older adults underscore the importance of taking a lifelong view of their relationships with their children. Summing up their advice, "What are you doing when your child is age five, ten, or fifteen that will create a lasting, loving relationship over the much longer time of his or her adulthood and your middle and old age? Because, believe me, as your life goes on *you will want your children there* . . . When you are in your seventies and beyond, your children provide you with continuity, meaning, attachment, and ultimately an overarching sense of a greater purpose in life."[190] In sum, the payoff for your trials today will be hard-earned, long in coming, but much treasured.

But what about now? Knowing that I'll be delighted when my children help me in my old age doesn't really soften the blow of a preschooler's temper tantrum or a teen's casual brutality. Taking the big-picture view about parenting is difficult and requires real effort, just as it's challenging to be forgiving after a snub or to think positive thoughts after a disappointment. We humans are so seduced by the narrowness of the here and now; we find it so easy to say yes to immediate gratifications rather than delay gratification in order to labor on meaningful pursuits. The capacity to do the latter involves what psychologists call self-regulation (or self-control), and, not surprisingly, self-regulation failure is the root of many of society's ills. But if you can manage to get yourself to work even on days that you detest it or floss your teeth without any evidence of a reward, you can manage to sustain the relentless parenting duties with a longer view.

During a visit to a business school in North Carolina, I was told a revealing story by one of the professors there, John Lynch, about a middle-school science teacher's lesson to his students. The teacher begins the lesson by taking out a big empty clear glass vase, with a wide neck, and filling it with big rocks. "Is the vase full?" He asks the kids. They say yes, it is. So he leaves the classroom for a moment and returns with a handful of smaller rocks, which he dumps into the vase. The small rocks fill in the gaps between the larger ones. He again asks the kids again, "Is the vase full?" Now they get it and they say no, it's not completely full. "How do you fill it up even more?" They suggest using even smaller rocks. So the science teacher leaves the room again to fetch some sand, and he packs the vase with sand, such that all remaining visible holes and gaps are filled. He now asks, "What is the lesson of this demonstration?" That we shouldn't jump to conclusions, some say. There are many ways of solving a puzzle, others offer. "No," he says. "The lesson is to put in the big rocks first."

The science teacher's lesson is, commit first to the "big" meaningful projects and goals in your life—contributing to your community or working on your marriage or raising your kids—even if it takes times away from the "small" immediately gratifying plans. Starting today, decide what the big rocks are in your life, what are the small rocks, and what are the handfuls of sand, and precommit yourself to the big ones.

TAKING TIME OFF

The blur of the intensive parenting years makes it very difficult to ever step back and reconsider our priorities and possibilities. When we don't have time to think, we may become blind to viable alternatives to our routines. One such possibility is taking breaks from parenting.

In the last two decades, the family has undergone seismic cultural shifts, and one such shift is the push to spend more time, and more quality time, with our children.[191] Even full-time working mothers, for example, spend only ten fewer hours per week with their kids than full-time stay-at-home moms,[192] and both are pressured to engage in labor-intensive hyper-parenting that involves a seemingly endless stream of child-enriching activities.[193] The result is chronic levels of anxiety, winner-take-all parenting, and a perfectionism that leads many to feel that they are falling short no matter how much of a child-rearing martyr they strive to be.

This pressure to lead a child-centered life renders the idea of taking time off from parenting nearly unthinkable. If we felt guilty about bringing store-bought cupcakes to the preschool fund-raiser, how will we feel skipping whole afternoons, days, or even weeks of our child's life? Yet raising children has historically been a collective obligation.[194] Our ancestors brought up young children in the context of a larger village, clan, or tribe, which allowed child-care responsibilities to be shared across many family members and neighbors. In some cultures and subcultures, this approach endures until today. Even my own parents, not so very long ago, back in the old country, used to send me and my baby brother to our grandparents for entire summers, starting at age two. Moreover, the grandparents lived 1,500 kilometers away in Kyshtym, Russia, the site of the world's third-worst nuclear disaster, which had taken place a decade earlier and led to thousands of radiation poisoning deaths.[195] I would never dream of doing such a thing with my own kids (though my parents, now grandparents themselves, still futilely implore us to send them their grandchildren every summer), but surely there are middle-ground alternatives.

If we are burned-out and unhappy—or worse, depressed—we simply cannot be outstanding parents. Taking a break from the daily grind can revitalize us, restore us, fortify us, and remind us which are the big rocks in our lives. Taking time off from parenting could mean asking a family member to take over child care while we (alone, with partner, or best friend) go away for a period of time. My husband and I used to escape for one weekend a year to a nice hotel in an interesting neighborhood that we'd never explored. It was no more than a half-hour's drive from home but felt like an ocean away. Taking time off could mean trading babysitting with a friend or hiring someone for a few hours each week just so we could relax and do absolutely nothing. It could mean sending the kids to sleepaway camp or on a getaway with their best friends' families. The possibilities are plentiful. We may miss the kids much less than we expected, or else, we'll ache for them so much that our attitude toward being a parent, and toward our priorities about family versus work, will be transformed forever.

THE PREPARED MIND

If you subscribe to the myth that you can't be truly happy without children, then learning that you don't love parenting—or that it's much more punishing and unpleasant than you expected—can precipitate a crisis moment in your life. In this case, I would wager that the very first thought that came to mind when you realized that you didn't enjoy being a parent was a version of "I must be a bad person." The problem is that this first thought is not only toxic to your happiness and to the quality of your parenting, it is plainly wrong. Learning what the research has to say about the ordinariness of this feeling and, hence, the falsity of your beliefs about how much joy your children will bring, will go a long way toward making you feel that you are not alone. Considering a big-picture view of parenting, reflecting on which situations impact your happiness the most, maintaining your balance through journaling, and taking time off from parenting will fortify you with the resolve to weather the low points of child rearing and empower you to revel in the high points. For, when all is said and done, "To the world you may be just one person, but to one person you may be the world."[196]

CHAPTER 4

I Can't Be Happy When . . .
I Don't Have a Partner

received the following letter from a woman who had been trying a variety of happiness-increasing exercises:

> [The exercises] have helped tremendously in almost every aspect of my life. Being happy has become easier for me, but the thought of not having a companion really gets me down. I can spend the day in gratitude, expressing kindness and love but when I see happy couples my heart drops and my attitude changes. On the inside I feel so down and alone even though I'm faking my smile when a couple sees me gazing at their blessing of love and companionship. Even though I'm grateful for what I have, I become so sad that I have no one to share my love with. How can I find a way to get myself over the hump of sadness and unworthiness I feel towards relationships?[197]

As demonstrated by this woman's experience, the pain of being alone can be acute. If the thought that you'll always be alone haunts you every day, you are faced with several diverging paths of action or inaction. Before you can determine which path will make you happiest and most fulfilled, you need to understand the meaning and implications of being single, and the sources of why you feel the way you do about it.

THE MYTH OF THE SAD SINGLE

Most people in the United States eventually marry or enter into a long-term relationship,[198] and if you are one of the few who hasn't, you may have borne a variety of emotions over the years, from disappointment and loneliness to rejection and anger. You may even have been discriminated against by employers, the IRS and the political system, stigmatized by society, ignored by researchers, and snubbed by newly coupled friends.[199] If you've always wished for a fairy-tale wedding or cooking dinner every night with your partner, remaining single is undeniably very painful. It's wise, however, to examine the extent to which your romantic fantasy has been kindled by societal norms (which stipulate what all of us are expected to accomplish at each life stage) and fueled by your parents, in-laws, and married friends. It's a fantasy that carries the assumption that you'll find true happiness only when you find a partner or a spouse. Before you decide how to feel or how to act, it's important to examine the truth value of this myth of happiness.

A great deal of media and scholarly attention has focused on the idea that the happiest individuals are those who are married. Although this is technically true, researchers have shown that being married only leads people to report that they are happier with their lives as a whole (in part because the question "Are you happy overall" probably compels them to weigh the fact of being married as signifying greater happiness), but being married does not necessarily lead people to experience more happiness moment to moment.[200] For example, a study that tracked how married women occupy their time during every hour of the day found that marriage confers both benefits and costs to women, and that these benefits and costs appear to cancel themselves out. Married women spend less time alone than their unmarried peers and more time having sex, but they also spend less time with friends, less time reading or watching TV, and more time doing chores, preparing food, and tending to children. (Notably, nearly all the findings regarding marriage apply to long-term committed romantic relationships as well.)

Furthermore, although married people do report being more satisfied with their lives overall than their unmarried peers, it turns out that this difference is strongest or only evident when the comparison is between the married and the divorced, the married and the separated, or the married and the widowed.[201] Always-single individuals fare extremely well. These data are also consistent with a study I had described earlier—an investigation that tracked 1,761 single individuals who got married and stayed married over the course of fifteen years. This study found that newlyweds derive a happiness boost from getting married that lasts an average of about two years; after the second year of marriage, they are back to where they started, at least in terms of happiness.[202] Single people don't get to experience the boost, but neither do they suffer the decline.

A parallel story can be told about singles and health. For example, although married people who have never divorced are healthier and live longer than those who divorce, people who have always been single are just as healthy as those who have always been married and live just as long.[203] This might seem surprising, as marriage, love, and intimate relationships appear to be the source of happiness, identity, and meaning for so many of us. Some even argue that our culture is one of "intensive nuclearity," so much so that single people are perceived to have missed out on life's most transcendent experiences and thus, like the anonymous woman who wrote me, must be more lonely, more sad, more deprived, and even less mature.[204] They're not.

People who remain single all their lives are assuredly not deprived, because they draw value and purpose from other sources in their lives—from their friends, siblings, extended family members, communities, jobs, or dedication to a great cause. In a word, they seem to heed the well-worn advice not to place all their eggs in a single basket. Instead of banking on the benefits of marriage, a single woman who has separate identities as stockbroker, sister, friend, cyclist, and gardener is unlikely to lose her self-assurance, sense of competence, and joie de vivre when something goes awry. No matter her choices, or lack thereof in life, she will always have something to excel at and enjoy, whether it's an intense triathlon, a fancy lunch with her best friend, a successful presentation at work, or a prank on her siblings.

The most notable fact, however, is that single people do have rewarding, lasting, and meaningful relationships. Relative to their married (or once-married) peers, they tend to be closer with their siblings, cousins, and nieces and nephews; they continue to develop new friendships as they age; and they stay in better touch with friends. Indeed, researchers point out that the close companions of singles are people they have chosen, whereas the close companions of marrieds are frequently chosen for them (e.g., their kids' friends' parents, their in-laws, their spouse's friends, etc.). Notably, older women who have always been single typically have up to a dozen important, meaningful friendships, which they have maintained for decades.[205] Married readers—and parents in particular—can you say the same for yourself?

No one individual—not even the love of our lives—can be all things to us at all times and in all situations. Sometimes we long for emotional support over a personal crisis. Sometimes we want intellectual stimulation or insight about the latest political development. Sometimes we require technical or financial advice. Sometimes we need an enthusiastic pat on the back. Other times we are desperate for someone to give us a push out of a rut. Those of us who rely much of the time on our partners—who can't possibly fill all these needs—are at a disadvantage. Single people who have several circles of friends—the kinds of friends they can call for help in the middle of the night—whom they have cultivated and nurtured for decades are at least as well, or even better, positioned to benefit during emergencies, troubles, stresses, and triumphs.

In short, an abundance of research demonstrates that strong, warm, fulfilling interpersonal relationships make us happy.[206] However, the key relationship doesn't have to be a sexual or romantic one.

BECOMING YOUR BEST POSSIBLE SINGLE SELF

When we have an acute sense that we will never be happy without a romantic partner, we can pursue one of several routes. One is to strive our best to put ourselves out there and meet and date as many people as we can. It's likely that in due course one of them will turn out to be "the one." Although I do not discuss this option, copious words of wisdom, articles, and books can help us realize this goal. Another route—addressed in the section to follow—involves deciding that we can indeed be happy without a romantic partner, releasing ourselves from that goal, and building for ourselves a full and rich life as a single person. Of course, we are free to leave the door open for a future relationship, while precluding it from being our overriding dream in life. Finally, we can do our utmost to become the most happy, optimistic, well-rounded, and successful person we can be, and be confident that this new person we will have become is likely to attract the best possible mate for us.

I begin by considering this third option—that a positive, happy, optimistic person will not only enjoy his present solitary life to the fullest, but will make a coupled life a great deal more possible. Indeed, more positive individuals are perceived as more physically attractive, intelligent, warm, moral, and socially skilled than less positive individuals; not surprisingly, they have been found to be more likely to find marriage partners and to erect enduring and fulfilling partnerships.[207] In one of my favorite studies, for example, women who signaled positivity in their college yearbook photos, taken at ages twenty or twenty-one, were relatively more likely to be married by age twenty-seven and less likely to still be single at forty-three.[208]

How can we become that authentically optimistic person? Several recommendations can be found in the scientific literature. First, we must consider how such a trait as optimism is defined, as some of us may have the wrong idea about it. Many people characterize optimism in a way that harks back to the definition offered by Voltaire in 1759—that it's "a mania for maintaining that all is well when things are going badly."[209] In truth, many researchers like myself opt for a far narrower definition—one in which we hope "that everything would somehow sort of maybe turn out not too bad."[210] When we feel lonely and alone, creating our best possible self calls for this kind of "small optimism," at least to begin with—the expectation that we will get through the day; that we may not accomplish everything we want, but we'll accomplish some of the things we want; that while we won't always get what we want, we'll get what we need; that it's okay to put our trust in life; that we shall not be overcome; that even if things don't turn out well, they will get better.

Whether our optimism is big or little, many of us waver in our expectations for the future. Fortunately, numerous research-tested activities have been shown to boost positive thinking. The most robust strategy involves keeping a journal regularly for ten to twenty minutes per day, in which we write down our hopes and dreams for the future (e.g., "In ten years, I will be married and a home owner"), visualize them coming true, and describe how we might get there and what that would feel like. This exercise—even when engaged in as briefly as two minutes—makes people happier and even healthier.[211] Furthermore, it's a good idea to practice our optimistic muscles when we're confronted with the small confidence-testing questions (Should I sit next to the guy reading my favorite novel?), so that we'll be better prepared when the big ones come (Am I cut out for love?).

But what if our goals and dreams about finding a mate are highly difficult or challenging or even impractical? What if our expectations are inordinately high? Even the most successful die-hard optimists will face barriers to their positive expectations. Research shows that optimistic thinking helps us forge ahead, in spite of barriers and adversities.[212] When we practice optimism, we become more confident, more motivated, and more energetically engaged with our goals, we take more proactive steps toward achieving them, and we are more committed, persistent, and task focused. In other words, we behave in ways that boost the probability of attracting the right partner.

However, undoubtedly, there will be times when our optimistic thoughts will fail to stand up to harsh realities and we will allow ourselves to be swayed by negative inferences and conclusions. In such situations, we can try a valuable exercise that helps combat negative thinking by deliberately finding ways to reinterpret our circumstances more positively. For example, we might write down (1) our present problem or stumbling block (e.g., intrusive thoughts such as "I'll never fulfill my dream of finding true love"), (2) our initial interpretation of it ("Because I've screwed up every relationship I've had"), and, finally, (3) our positive *re*interpretation ("I have matured a lot during the last five years and I am much better at judging people").

Of course, at times our fatalistic verdict about a particular goal being beyond our reach is simply true. When my anonymous correspondent wrote that she has "no one to share [her] love with," her conclusion may have been pessimistic, but it was not baseless or irrational. In that situation, optimists have actually been found to be more likely than pessimists to give up an impractical goal (e.g., a thirty-nine-year-old who is determined to be married and pregnant by forty) and, at the same time, to paint the situation in the best possible light.[213] In essence, practicing optimism grants us the flexibility and big-picture perspective to judge our goals and dreams realistically, let go of unattainable ones, recognize how much we have grown or learned about ourselves from the challenges we've faced, and move on by finding new, meaningful goals to pursue.

Learning to be more positive and optimistic means learning to see opportunities in difficulties,[214] to construe the world as full of possibilities and wonder. If we feel that we'll always be alone, we may be right or we may be wrong, but we won't know unless we remain engaged, keep a positive perspective, and keep trying.

REDIRECTING YOUR GOALS

While some of us will continue searching for Mr. or Ms. Right, others may choose to liberate ourselves from this pursuit entirely. The reasons we will do so may be complicated, and to unravel them, we may need to explore why we are currently alone. If we have a habit of sabotaging relationships because we've had poor role models, little relationship experience, or we're fearful of the next steps (intimacy, commitment, compromise) or of potential pitfalls (infidelity, rejection, being hurt), we may consider seeking professional therapy or guidance from friends and self-help books. Alternatively, perhaps we actually prefer to be alone but do not recognize this about ourselves (or do not wish to). Or, we have run the cost-benefit analysis and, in view of our present circumstances, decided that we are either better off without a partner or that the probability of finding a partner who will fit our personality and lifestyle is very low.

If we choose to disengage from the goal of spending the rest of our lives with an intimate soul mate, how do we go about doing it? Scientists have learned a great deal about the benefits of equanimity in the face of unfulfilled dreams, as well as about the fortitude and flexibility necessary to relinquish unlikely goals in favor of better-suited ones. Indeed, research shows that people facing unrealistic goals are significantly better off if they are able to relinquish those goals and to take up new and meaningful activities.[215]

Studies show that three steps are necessary to move forward responsibly.[216] First, we begin to reduce our efforts at finding a mate—for example, by telling our friends to stop setting us up and by regarding new people we meet not as possible dates, but as potential friends and confidants. Second, we begin to feel that the mate-finding goal is not as meaningful or important or critical to our happiness as we had previously believed,[217] perhaps by drawing on research about the myth of the sad single. Third, we identify and start pursuing alternative activities (such as strengthening our relationships with old friends, adopting a child, or going back to school), and gradually learn to think about ourselves and our identities differently (e.g., as a great friend versus a potentially great spouse). Half of all adults in the United States today are single, and recent surveys show that more and more people are embracing singlehood as a lifestyle choice.[218] Connecting with a positive singles community can be both comforting and empowering. In short, our time, energies, and efforts invested in the goal to find a lifetime partner become rechanneled to the goal to become an exemplary friend, leader, or uncle.

The importance of these three steps have been investigated in people confronting a variety of situations—from those newly separated to couples in which one partner is dying from AIDS to parents of disabled children. In all the studies, the individuals who were able to move forward and sustain their happiness were the ones who were successful at (1) downplaying the importance of the original (but now unattainable) goals to their well-being (e.g., the goal of curing their partner's illness or having a brilliant career while caring for their special-needs child) and (2) upgrading the importance of alternative, more realistic goals.[219] For example, if our partner is chronically ill, we may put our career on hold and instead focus on being the best possible caregiver and companion.

More relevant to the issue of being alone, researchers have also looked at people's pursuit of new intimate relationships in the wake of a recent separation.[220] They found that those who faced limited opportunities in finding a new romantic partner (in this case, older versus younger people) were more likely to give up the mate-finding goal, which ultimately led to greater happiness over time. Younger people, by contrast, were less likely to give up such goals, and those who did became less, rather than more, happy over time.

Although this research might seem rather depressing, the implications are worth pondering. At what point do we continue to brood over our single status, or hope to chance on that ideal person who may not exist? When do we accept and embrace our present life and move forward with other plans? In the 1950s, eminent psychoanalyst Donald Winnicott introduced the concept of the "good-enough

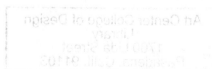

mother"—a woman who does not perfectly strive to immediately meet all her child's needs, yet allows the child to grow into a well-adjusted adult.[221] Perhaps those of us confronting the reckoning point at the heart of this chapter should consider whether we are leading a "good-enough single life." For many of us, the answer will be no, and we will persist at becoming our best possible self—a person who will be more likely to attract a fitting mate. Some of us, however, may be surprised to learn that the answer is yes, at least for the time being.

THE PREPARED MIND

The "I'm alone and feel that I always will be" crisis point is undeniably painful for many individuals. If you find yourself at this crossroads, you have the choice to continue to brood about your situation and to remain miserable in it. Alternatively, you can do something proactive about it—strive to flourish as an individual and stay open to the possibility for connection. Or you may discover that you don't need a man (or woman) to make you happy. If your first thought is, "I'll never be happy alone" or "I'm a loser," consider whether your desire to get married is authentically yours or whether it's dictated by your family or the larger culture. Research shows convincingly that married people are no happier than single ones, and that singles have been found to enjoy great happiness and meaning in other relationships and pursuits. If you don't like your single life, change it. If you can't or won't change your life, change the way you think about it. If truth be told, the happiness myth that you can only be happy with a partner is as powerful as it is wrong. Knowing this should give you pause—and hope—and open up new avenues and prospects.

PART II

WORK AND MONEY

IF we work part-time in college and then forty hours per week through age sixty-seven, we will have worked almost 100,000 hours over our lifetimes, with a quarter of our waking time devoted to our jobs. The average workday in the United States is nine and a half hours long, with 35 percent of us working on weekends, and 31 percent working more than fifty hours per week.[222] Of course, "average" means that half of us work more—and often a lot more—than that. Most of us with jobs or careers accept them as a vital part of our identities, replete with triumphs and disappointments. Furthermore, our jobs arm us with the money to support ourselves, to enjoy ourselves, or to suffer by making far too little or by spending what we make unwisely. Indeed, when people are asked if they could have anything in the world right now, most report wanting "more money."[223] It's not surprising, then, that myths about what brings us the greatest happiness (finding the ideal job, being successful and rich) and the greatest unhappiness (making too little money) would permeate our working life and our income-generating life, stretched over four or five decades, and create troubling crisis points for us. In the next three chapters, I dismantle the evidence for these myths of happiness and offer numerous ideas for ways you can surmount these crisis points and prosper.

CHAPTER 5

I'll Be Happy When . . .
I Find the Right Job

D o you find your work no longer satisfying—or worse, unbearable? If so, recent surveys show that more Americans than ever before share your experience.[224] You may be burned-out, bored, or weary of your job, or you may feel that professional success has decisively and irrevocably eluded you. What's more, the feeling that your work is no longer what it used to be can instigate a painful crisis point that pushes you to question your judgment, your skills, your industriousness, and your motivation. The heart of this chapter is about the happiness myth that stokes this crisis point—namely, that whatever happiness may have eluded you thus far will materialize after you acquire the "right" or perfect job. Grappling with this myth requires an understanding of the true sources and ubiquity of malaise about your job or your level of success. Only then will you be prepared to make the healthiest choices and to take next steps. A number of these steps are detailed here.

GETTING USED TO YOUR JOB

In chapter 1, I focused on the turning moment when you decide you are bored with your marriage. Might there be a parallel point when you acknowledge that you are bored with your job? Although love and work may seem to have little in common with each other—why else would there be a need to "balance" them?—they are both, as Freud aptly recognized, mainsprings of our mental health.[225] Furthermore, like interpersonal relationships, work is an aspect of your life to which you are prone to hedonically adapt and take for granted—a situation that gives rise to the apathy and ennui that fuel that painful feeling that your work has lost its pleasure and you'd be so much happier doing something else. One course of action, of course, is to find a new career path. Alternatively, you could try to identify how much of your ennui is due to your unique (and problematic) work situation and how much to the widespread and foreseeable process of hedonic adaptation, which is likely to repeat itself at your next job. If the latter, a number of empirically supported approaches exist that can ward off the feeling that your work is no longer satisfying and stop hedonic adaptation in its tracks. Before you make a drastic decision, give these strategies a trial run to determine whether they would succeed for you, or whether your job situation is beyond repair. Above all, know that when your work isn't fulfilling any longer, there is hope.

I have colleagues who change jobs often, moving their families from coast to coast every two to three years. They seem sincerely thrilled with every fresh opportunity and throw themselves anew into redesigning their work commitments and lifestyles. Then, inevitably, after a year or so, like second-year college students experiencing a "sophomore slump," they begin to feel a bit bored or antsy or develop justifiable complaints about their new supervisor, colleagues, obligations, or daily commute. Little by little, they begin to fantasize about something out there that's even better—a job with a more reasonable boss, perhaps, or a lighter commute, more helpful colleagues, and less burdensome obligations.

Of course, not everyone has the option of routinely relocating and shifting jobs, which suggests that many more only dream of doing what some people are fortunate enough to be able to do. Yet are these professional roamers truly lucky? Are they genuinely happier with each new position and, if so, does this benefit outweigh the costs of severed friendships, dislocation from roots and neighborhoods, and transfers to unfamiliar school districts? Although each of us must balance the personal pros and cons ourselves, we would benefit from considering the research illuminating why all of us are prone to become spoiled by perfectly decent jobs and whether there is anything that can be done about it.

A seminal study on this topic followed high-level managers for five years to track their job satisfaction before and after a voluntary job change, such as a promotion or a relocation within the same company to a more attractive city.[226] The managers were mostly male, mostly white, and averaged forty-five years of age and a $135,000 annual salary. They were doing well. What the researchers found, however, was that these managers experienced a burst of satisfaction—a honeymoon period, in essence—immediately after the job change, but their satisfaction plummeted within a year, returning to their original pre-move level. In other words, they experienced a sort of hangover effect. By contrast, managers who chose not to change jobs during the same five-year time period experienced negligible changes in how much satisfaction they felt about their jobs. So, while I (for example) remain at the same position and am no more or less happy with it year after year, my itinerant colleagues experience repeated slumps and surges.

The so-called hangover effect is persuasive evidence of hedonic adaptation to our jobs. Human beings are capable of adapting to almost everything about their work life, and especially anything that stays the same. One of my former students wrote me recently to confess that when she first arrived at her new job in San Francisco

. . . I was so enamored by the view across the bay I snapped photos of it. Now I am amused every time the double-decker red bus comes by my [office] window and everyone on board scrambles to snap a picture. I know the view is amazing because people come by and tell me so, but I have already experienced 100 percent adaptation—actually, I would say I've fully adapted to the entire lifestyle here, and I'm back to baseline.

We get used to the cities where we live, to our favorite ice cream, our favorite artwork, and our favorite songs; to new houses and new cars, to pay raises (more on that later), and, as I detailed in chapter 1, to relationships and even to sex.[227] When we have reached one goal, we are content for only a short while before we begin to feel that we won't be satisfied until we reach even higher. In this way, we continually escalate our expectations and desires. Generally, this is not a bad thing. A ceaseless striving for more is surely evolutionarily adaptive; if realizing our goals left us all feeling entirely complacent and content, our society wouldn't witness much progress. If we were always content with the status quo, we'd never strive to accomplish more, like building better cabinets, publishing more books, learning more languages, finding new sources of nourishment, and making more scientific discoveries. If we remained in a self-satisfied euphoria about our latest triumph, we would not be able to compete effectively with others and we might fail to recognize dangers and opportunities in our environments.

Before we survey possible ways to combat, prevent, or slow down the process of becoming satiated with our jobs, it's important to learn exactly what happens to us during the process of adaptation, and why. There are really two chief explanations at work—we experience less and less pleasure over time and our aspirations rise.

When we commence working in an enviable new position, we get a big boost of well-being, even euphoria. We think about the new job (and what we love about it) often, and we experience lots of positive emotions as a result of the chain of positive events set into motion by the job—by the newfound opportunities for new connections, challenges, learning, and adventures. However, in the words of one of my graduate students, those puddles of pleasure slowly dry up and eventually evaporate completely. The thrill of our new work responsibilities continues to decay after the tenth and twentieth time we experience them, and so on. The excitement, happiness, and pride we used to feel happens less and less, as we focus less and less on the novelty of the job and turn our minds toward the countless daily hassles, uplifts, and distractions of life.[228] After a while in the office or at the job site, we don't even notice the things that used to make us smile.

At the same time, as we obtain less and less pleasure from our new position, another critical thing occurs—our expectations rise. Indeed, this is something that can undermine our happiness *even* if we are blessed to have a job that brings us the same quantity of joy today as it did in 2011 or in 2001. So, the job that used to be special now becomes our right and privilege. Whether it's the boost in our compensation, authority, flexibility, or control over our time, we begin to feel that we deserve no less. We begin to feel that our novel and stimulating work experiences have simply become part of our new life—our "new normal"—and we come to expect the happiness that we now have. This new (and extremely common) development has the unfortunate consequence not just of dampening our happiness—causing us to go back to whatever we felt before we even moved—but pushes us to up the ante, to want more and more, so that we are almost never content with what we have, even when we are fortunate to have plenty. In an extreme example, after *Thriller* became the best-selling album of all time, Michael Jackson declared that he would not be satisfied unless his next album sold twice as many copies. In fact, it sold 70 percent fewer. Most musicians would have killed for sales of thirty million, but for Jackson the contrast with his earlier success was stinging.

So, for much the same reasons that we adapt to our relationships, we adapt readily and rapidly to our jobs. Knowing this should give us pause and, perhaps, force us to hesitate a bit before we resolve to jump ship. But just because hedonic adaptation is natural and evolutionarily adaptive—the way hunger for sweets, sexual jealousy, and a fear of angry beasts all are natural and evolutionarily adaptive—doesn't mean that we can't tamper with it.

REINING IN YOUR ASPIRATIONS

Immoderate aspirations are toxic to happiness. On the one hand, the more we attain, the happier we become. But, at the same time, the more we attain, the more we want, which negates the increased happiness. A nice example comes from the finding that people who are more highly educated are (surprisingly) less satisfied with their lives.[229] In other words, the enhanced life satisfaction that I might derive from my Michigan MBA (e.g., from the accompanying friendships, business connections, and prestige) is outweighed by my increased aspirations and their attendant risk of disappointment and regret ("I got an MBA at a highly ranked school—why can't I land a lucrative position on Wall Street?"). A new job that is more highly compensated, more stimulating, and more gratifying than our old one will make us happy, but, before we know it, we begin to *require* high compensation, stimulation, and gratification to declare ourselves happy.

How do we prevent ourselves from taking our jobs for granted? One of the most effective—and the most difficult—strategies is to ratchet down our desires and curb the inflation of our expectations.[230] I don't mean that we should expect less from our jobs. We should simply not allow our desires to continue escalating to the point where we end up feeling entitled and convinced that we would *only* be happy if we got more and more of this or that. Given the inherent challenges involved in reining in our aspirations, we will need a full arsenal of psychological tools at our disposal to accomplish it. I suggest trying, then fine-tuning multiple approaches (often at the same time) and not easily giving up. Five such psychological tools are described below.

CONCRETELY REEXPERIENCE

Remind yourself on a regular basis and in a tangible way what your former (less satisfying) work life was like.[231] If you were paid less, set certain time periods (say, one week per month) to limit your spending to match your earlier consumption habits. If you used to have unfriendly colleagues, have lunch by yourself once in a while. If you regularly worked nights, periodically force yourself to stay late again. Such reexperiencing will encourage you to appreciate your current job and to obtain more pleasure from it by simply remembering or mentally transporting yourself to (less fortunate) times past.

CONCRETELY OBSERVE

I visited one of Google's offices once to give a talk about happiness, and we ended up discussing how easily people adapt to the good things in life. A group of employees gave me a tour and told me how they love their jobs but that they are totally spoiled by working at Google and feel that they can never work anywhere else. They have free hot lunch and dinner every day, an abundance of snacks, guest authors visiting, and plenty of games and toys (including a drum and guitar room). They can even bring their pets to work. They said that these perks seemed awesome when they first began their jobs but that they lost no time becoming accustomed to them and even found things to complain about (e.g., "Not the crab cakes again!"). My recommendation was that they should make an effort to observe other workplaces—maybe even their own former offices, if they could.

Make occasional visits to your friends', acquaintances', or former colleagues' places of business and unobtrusively compare them to yours. Such observations will leave a more lasting impression on you and help you feel a sense of privilege in your own work life.

BE GENUINELY GRATEFUL

Keep a gratitude journal—a list in your head, on paper, or in your smartphone[232]—that regularly helps you contemplate the positive aspects of your job. Nothing undermines gratitude like too-high expectations, and the higher your expectations, the less gratitude you will feel. If you expect to go home at five p.m. tomorrow, and then you do, it's highly unlikely that you'll be grateful for it. The problem with the practice of gratitude, however, is that it's extremely challenging to maintain and carry out in a sincere, genuine way. But so is maintaining a rigorous fitness program or a healthy diet or self-imposed daily practice on a musical instrument. The key is to muster effort and commitment—two attributes that are available to all of us.[233]

SHIFT YOUR REFERENCE POINT

When you think about your dream job, what is your reference point? For many of us, it's a higher-paying, less stressful, more engaging, more cushy, and more fulfilling one. Perhaps it's the job that our high school friend now has or the job featured in the article we read or in the movie we saw. More likely, our reference point is a fantasy job that may not really exist. Do you dream about being a pro football player, film director, senator, homicide detective, investigative journalist, neurosurgeon, best-selling author, or marine biologist? If you do, you are likely overlooking the fact that even such fabulous-sounding jobs have periods of high stress, monotony, possibly unpleasant colleagues, thankless tasks, exasperating outcomes, and long commutes. For example, the job of video game tester, ranked in the top twenty of "incredible dream jobs,"[234] requires long stretches of concentration, which can be stressful and exhausting. As one such tester described her first full day of video game testing: "The last two hours, I feel nauseous. Severely so."[235] Former international spies tell a similar story. According to Lindsay Moran, the author of *Blowing My Cover:* "You know, certainly I didn't expect it to be James Bond to a T, but at the end of the day, the CIA is a lot of people in sensible shoes sitting in cubicles, and that's kind of a reality that's probably a shock to a lot of people like me who come into the agency expecting something more glamorous."[236]

My point is that the dream job is a poor reference point. Change it to a more appropriate or gratitude-inducing one—like the similar but somewhat less rewarding position you once applied for, or the job you had before your promotion, or the completely dissimilar job in the nearby school, hospital, mall, farm, factory, or office park. Also important is to shift your reference point from time to time, to exercise your ability to visualize alternative types of jobs and situations.

MAKE THIS DAY AT WORK YOUR "LAST"

I'm currently conducting a one-month-long "happiness intervention" in which participants are instructed to live the month as if it's their last month. Their instructions are not to pretend that they have a terminal disease but rather to imagine as fully and faithfully as possible that they are about to move a very long way from their jobs, schools, friends, and families for an indefinite period of time. Previous research hints that this exercise should prompt us to appreciate in a profound way what we are preparing to give up. When we believe that we are seeing (or hearing, doing, or experiencing) things for the last time, we will see (or hear, do, or experience) them as though it's the first time.[237] Thus, the Google employees might appreciate afresh their crab cakes, the intellectual stimulation, and their pets under their desks; and we might appreciate our fair-minded manager, flexible schedule, and opportunities to travel.

FINAL THOUGHTS

You may have noticed that many of the foregoing techniques have the consequence of heightening our appreciation for our current jobs. This is no coincidence, as appreciation may be one of the most effective ways to rein in expectations. An authentic sense of gratitude for our career is simply incompatible with an addiction to ever-increasing levels of satisfaction.

An Indian student approached me at a conference once to tell me that her parents had had an arranged marriage and that she had always wondered how they made it work. When she asked, they told her that their secret—at least in their first years together—was having *no expectations at all*! "That way," her father said, "when my wife did anything wonderful—or nice or even ordinary—I was happy." It's truly remarkable to me how this couple managed to rein in their expectations. It must require talent, or at least very hard work. The lesson to the rest of us, however, is that if this couple can hold zero expectations, then we can at least succeed in restraining ours.

Nonetheless, a minor stumbling block remains. A great deal of research has shown that high goals and high expectations are critical in the domain of human performance.[238] If we aim and expect to do well on a job interview, the medical boards, or a first date, we are more likely to succeed. Ambitious goals can foster self-confidence, fuel greater effort, combat anxiety, and create self-fulfilling prophecies. So, how do we reconcile these findings with the recommendation to *lower* our aspirations? The answer lies in considering, first, our history, and second, the domain in question.

First, do we have a history of flitting from job to job (or relationship to relationship and home to home)? If our position is truly unsatisfying or stagnant, then it's worth our efforts to aim in a different direction or to aim higher. But if, by most people's standards, we have a perfectly good job, then our expectations are overbalancing our reality and robbing us of all but the most fleeting pleasures.

Second, when I advise ratcheting down our aspirations about our jobs, I am referring to aspirations regarding our career, position, and work life in general ("Is this job good enough for me or do I deserve something better"), not to our specific work performance ("Am I confident about my PowerPoint presentation tomorrow?"). When it comes to our performance and specific accomplishments at work, we should always aim high.

BEATING THE ULTRADIAN DIP

On August 9, 2010, a JetBlue Airways jet arrived at John F. Kennedy International airport in New York from Pittsburgh, Pennsylvania. As it was taxiing down the runway, an altercation occurred between a passenger and a flight attendant. The flight attendant, Steven Slater, apparently decided that he couldn't take it anymore, directed several profanities at the passengers through the intercom ("Go f*** yourselves!"), grabbed two Blue Moon beers from the beverage cart ("I'm outta here!"), and deployed the emergency evacuation chute, sliding down and disappearing into popular history. Although the reckless deployment of the slide endangered individuals on the tarmac and cost the airline $10,000, Slater became an instant working-class hero, striking a nerve with disgruntled employees everywhere who wished that they, too, could tell their bosses to take their job and shove it.

Yet we don't feel disaffected by our jobs all of the time. More likely, we experience the malaise or exasperation on a periodic basis. Would you be surprised to learn that these low points—the moments when you yearn to walk out or slide down the chute in brilliant fashion—occur every ninety minutes? If we understood this fact, we could anticipate those moments and head them off. The fed-up flight attendants and wage-earners of this world would think twice.

Most of us have heard of circadian rhythms—daily cycles that regulate when we feel sleepy (close to bedtime and throughout the night) and when we feel alert and awake (upon waking and throughout the day). The word *circadian* means "about a day," so a circadian rhythm occurs once in a twenty-four-hour period. The circadian rhythm is essentially our internal biological clock, which is sensitive to light and dark.

Few of us, however, have heard of another type of bodily cycle, called the ultradian rhythm. We cycle through ultradian stages every 90 minutes or so (but no longer than 120 minutes) during sleep. What's more, we continue to experience these 90- to 120-minute cycles while we are awake as well. Practically, this means that for about an hour and a half to two hours after rising in the morning, we feel particularly vigorous and focused—able to sustain concentration and energy throughout our activities. At the end of that interval, however, we experience a twenty-minute period of fatigue, lethargy, and difficulty concentrating. This is the "ultradian dip."

Business gurus have shrewdly commandeered these ideas to serve as the foundation for practical advice when they coach executives and leaders. Their message is that all employees should be aware of their ultradian rhythms and when they feel the twenty-minute period of flagging focus coming on, instead of pushing through it (thus risking inefficiency and errors), eating a candy bar, or smoking a cigarette, they should take a break that brings about revitalization and renewal. At these times we need to relax or switch our activity to something completely different—for example, take a twenty-minute power nap (the length shown to give us the most "bang for the buck"[239]), take a walk outdoors, meditate, listen to music, read a chapter of a novel, or gossip with colleagues (but not about work).[240] In a study conducted with employees of twelve Wachovia banks in New Jersey, those who were prompted to renew their energies in these ways reported being more engaged and satisfied with their work, showed improved relationships with customers, and produced 13 percent more revenue from loans and 20 percent more revenue from deposits than did a control group.[241]

Think back to the last time you felt particularly dissatisfied or stressed at work. It's highly probable that you were weathering one of those twenty-minute ultradian dips. This doesn't mean, of course, that those feelings of disaffection or vexation aren't symptomatic of a real problem, but it means that we should be cautious about over-interpreting them. Many of us have moments when we feel power-fully that we've "had it"—with our careers, spouses, children, and even our lives. With hindsight, we recognize that these thoughts are typically ill-considered and short-lived. A sound tip is to be mind-ful that the ultradian rhythm recurs throughout the day and that the times when our bodies move from a high-energy peak to a low, lethargic trough are opportunities for our most pessimistic thoughts to occur. Before acting on any hasty decisions, neutralize your ultra-dian dips by taking relaxing, channel-switching breaks. If the thoughts persist and persist, then it's time to take them seriously.

EDITING THE MOVIE REEL OF YOUR LIFE AND VISUALIZING A BRIGHTER FUTURE

The feeling that our work is just not satisfying anymore may wash over us one day, and when it does, it may be so powerful that we won't be able to see past it. Any of the job's virtues from the past or possibilities for growth in the future will pale next to the force and vividness of that day's emotions. Before we allow the feeling to dic-tate our actions and decisions, we must step back and impartially review our past experiences and our future possibilities.

YOUR PAST

In the memoir Christopher Reeve published five years before he died, the actor who was, to many people, Superman before a riding accident left him a quadriplegic, wrote the following: "It took me quite a while to learn that the movie reel and real life were two different things. This continues to be helpful to me today when I remember that the stories of my life, my interpretations of events, are like a movie reel and that I can change those reels."[242] This is a profound insight, suggesting that our past is neither a completely blank slate nor a fixed set of circumstances, experiences, and events. Rather, we have a degree of control over our story, because we have control over which experiences we emphasize and which we minimize, which events we selectively remember and which we forget, which circumstances are vivid in our minds and which are faint or distorted. Do we truly believe that the last eight years of our careers have been a misspent, unproductive, and unrewarding slog? If yes, how biased and invested are we in culling the evidence from our work history to support this view? Might an objective observer reach an entirely different conclusion? To choose the best course of action for yourself, these questions—and their implications—should be considered honestly. Writing out the evidence for both the pessimistic and optimistic view of our work experiences may help illuminate the facts and clear our vision.

YOUR FUTURE

Although we have a great deal of control over how we view and experience our past, we possess many times that amount of control over how we view our future. The reason is obvious: The future has not yet come to pass and thus is rife with possibilities, opportunities, and unexplored vistas. Unfortunately, instead of envisioning an attractive future landscape for our current work life, many of us fixate on the mountains of obstacles along the way. Instead, it's far easier (and more enjoyable) for us to indulge in "escape fantasies," which allow us to imagine an alternate dream job that has all the positives we currently lack and, of course, none of the negatives.

Before we pack it in to track down that dream job, I think it's critical to reexamine our predictions about what may happen in our current one. For example, in the same way that cognitive therapists teach their depressed patients to combat their negative thoughts ("My manager has it in for me") by finding evidence that disconfirms them ("She complimented my work last week in front of the whole department"), we can learn to rethink and dispute our pessimistic predictions. As I previously discussed, I don't propose that we should persuade ourselves to believe that everything will be forever rosy. Positive future-thinking can simply mean saying to ourselves, "Look, this project is going to be hard, but I'll get through it" or "My past few assignments have been mind-numbing, but if history's any guide, there'll be a big challenge coming soon." The bottom line is that we train ourselves to construe the periods of stress or monotony in our work as short-lived and contained, as opposed to long-lasting and with far-reaching implications. This new perspective will provide clarity about how truly miserable—or reasonable—our current job really is.

I'M NOT GETTING POWERFUL OR FAMOUS OR WINNING A NOBEL PRIZE

We had grand ambitions. We worked hard. We did many of the right things. Yet, despite our efforts and accomplishments and some turns of luck, we are struck one day with the idea that our success has stalled and fizzled. We see friends, friends of friends, and former colleagues outdistance us, leaving us in the dust. While our career has flatlined, they are celebrating prosperous businesses, buying second (and third) homes, appearing as talking heads on television, and being lionized at awards ceremonies. What has gone wrong? Why aren't we among the 2.1 million Americans considered top executives?[243] Why haven't our talents been recognized?

When we find ourselves dwelling on such questions, it's time to step back and reexamine our priorities, our goals, and our reference points. Like the feeling that our work is no longer fulfilling, this crossroads is fueled by the happiness myth that "I'll only be happy when . . . I am successful" and thereby has the potential to create false feelings of dissatisfaction. However, the sense that we have failed to achieve our professional dreams calls for new recommendations. Following the suggestions I describe below will help us weigh our accomplishments more realistically and more forgivingly and prevent these nagging questions from arising in the first place.

THROWING OFF PERNICIOUS COMPARISONS WITH OTHERS

Much of the time, it's impossible *not* to compare ourselves with others. Whenever we have dinner at a friend's house or ask our neighbors or spouses how their day is going or turn on the television set, we are inundated with information about other people's victories and tragedies, opinions, lifestyles, personalities, and marriages. We are bombarded by images of Hollywood mansions versus garden apartments, beautiful faces versus overfed bodies, violin virtuosos versus inept has-beens. We are confronted with individuals whose successes seem to magnify the degree of our own squandered potential—people whose careers seems to exist solely as a rebuke to our own.

Social comparisons arise naturally, automatically, and effortlessly. Not surprisingly, studies have shown that comparing ourselves with others—whether it is a child noticing that his classmate has a cooler backpack or an executive finding out that she is making a higher salary than her colleague—has a profound effect not only on our evaluations of ourselves, but on our moods and our emotional well-being.[244] Indeed, it's comparisons to other people that are primarily to blame for our feelings of inadequacy and discontent. For most of us, feelings of deficiency or not living up to some lofty standard stem from observing others' successes, real or imagined. Instead of asking ourselves, "Does my career (or productivity or income) meet my needs?" we ask "How good is my career, my productivity, and my income compared with my neighbor's?" Instead of feeling personally richer and richer, we instead feel that we are attaining new levels of relative poverty.[245]

Yet we cannot simply close our eyes to all comparisons or pay no heed to other people. Mindful of this fact, during my third year of graduate school, I began investigating the question of what can be done about the comparisons we make. This line of research, as we shall see shortly, revealed that the secret to being satisfied with our achievements lies not in ignoring other people's strengths and accomplishments, but in not suffering the negative consequences of those observations. In other words, don't let the social comparisons get to you.

I conducted a series of studies to test whether those of us who have the capacity to shrug off the sting of unfavorable comparisons with our peers are indeed happier about ourselves and our lives in general than those who do not.[246] For example, in one experiment, I brought in two volunteers at the same time and asked each of them to use two hand puppets—Chipmunk and Otter—to teach a lesson about friendship to an imaginary audience of first-graders.[247] The two volunteers took turns doing this in front of a one-way screen while being ostensibly evaluated and videotaped. After they were finished, we created a small deception by leading each volunteer to believe that he or she had performed very poorly on this task (that is, that they received an average rating from judges of 2 out of 7), but also to believe that the second volunteer had performed even worse than they had (receiving a disappointing rating of only 1). By contrast, a second group of volunteers were led to believe that they had performed extremely well (having obtained an average score from judges of 6 out of 7), but that their peer had performed even better (receiving an outstanding score of 7). I also had some participants do the task alone—without a peer—and receive either "excellent" or "poor" feedback without learning anything about how another participant might have performed.

Years later, I'm still somewhat taken aback by the results. To analyze the data, I divided my participants into those who, before performing, reported being very happy and those who reported being relatively unhappy. When I examined the "before" and "after" data of my very happy participants, I found that those who learned that they had performed very poorly reported feeling less positive, less confident, and more sad after the study was over. Their reaction to ostensible failure was perfectly natural and not at all surprising. By contrast, the very happy participants who learned that they had performed extremely well (a 6 out of 7) subsequently felt better on all dimensions, and, notably, learning that someone did *even better* did not dilute the pleasure of their ostensible success.

The results for my unhappiest participants, however, were dramatic. Their reactions, it appears, were governed more by the reviews they heard given to their peer than by their own feedback. Indeed, the study paints a stark and quite unpleasant portrait of an unhappy person. My unhappiest volunteers reported feeling happier and more secure when they had received a poor evaluation (but heard that their peer did even worse) than when they had received an excellent evaluation (but heard that their peer did even better). It appears that unhappy individuals have bought into the sardonic maxim attributed to Gore Vidal: "For true happiness, it is not enough to be successful oneself . . . One's friends must fail."

My conclusion from this study, as well as half a dozen other studies I have conducted on this topic, is that when we ask ourselves the question, "How good (successful, smart, affable, prosperous, ethical) am I?" those of us who typically rely on our own internal, objective standards are happiest. Such habits render us less likely to be buffeted by the winds of external judgments and outside realities (e.g., discovering that our neighbor is directing a television pilot or that our former classmate is on the cover of *California Lawyer*). By contrast, those of us who base our self-evaluations on comparisons with others are the unhappy ones, and the practice turns out to be rather unwise. Think about it: Feeling glum or personally deflated as a result of other people's successes, accomplishments, and triumphs, and feeling relieved rather than disappointed or sympathetic in the face of other people's failures and undoings is a poor prescription for happiness.

The habit of social comparison begins early in life. In childhood, we learn that good performance is most frequently measured in relative terms. We're often being compared with the good manners of our siblings, the talents of our classmates, and even with the As and trophies that our parents earned as children. Consequently, we have been conditioned to want to learn how we stand relative to others, and preferably, learn that we are better off. As a result of this early conditioning, making social comparisons is unavoidable and inevitable. The habit is so deeply ingrained that, like humans, even capuchin monkeys have been found to be sensitive to comparisons with their simian peers.[248] However, because there is always someone better off—wealthier, more talented, more popular, or slimmer—those comparisons will make us feel bad more often than they will make us feel good.[249] The goal, as my studies show, is to rely a little less on others when determining our self-worth and to rely a little more on our personal standards.

If you conclude one day that you haven't "made it," is that conclusion based on your personal goals or on some norm or standard set by others? Are your feelings about your past triumphs (or lack thereof) dictated by what other people think? If your answer is yes, my research suggests that you should strive to ignore such invidious social comparisons whenever possible—for example, by crying "stop" or distracting yourself immediately with a pleasant task when you catch yourself doing it. And when it's not possible to turn a blind eye, you should strive to experience *schlep naches* (Yiddish for "deriving pleasure from the achievement of others") rather than *schadenfreude* (German for "deriving pleasure from the misfortune of others"). When "there is no expense, no feeling of impoverishment, no hints of anxiety connected with discovering that somebody else is much better than you are in a particular field,"[250] you will have achieved greater maturity—and hence, happiness—than the average person. Instead of bemoaning your lack of achievements, you will recognize your efforts up to now and take action to reach the next step.

THE PURSUIT OF HAPPINESS AND
THE HAPPINESS OF PURSUIT

Perhaps your worries about not having attained what you wanted to attain at this point in your life are not entirely unfounded. If so, then your priority would be to remedy the situation—to identify what you are passionate about and to take action to pursue it. A great deal of research—some old and classic, some new and leading-edge—suggests the optimal ways for us to inspirit ourselves, find meaningful goals, and strive toward them. Applying these findings to our own lives will increase the likelihood that we will be happier and more successful. Yet we must always bear in mind that the realization of our dream is not the magic formula for happiness; as I explain below, the striving's the thing,

When scientists study "goal pursuit," they are essentially studying the infinite variety of projects, schemes, plans, tasks, endeavors, ventures, missions, and ambitions (both large and small) that we undertake in our daily lives. When it comes to our vocations and avocations, numerous investigations have shown that those of us who are merely *striving* (and not necessarily achieving) are happier, especially when our goals with respect to work and hobbies are realistic, flexible, valued by our cultures, authentic, not materialistic, and not impinging negatively on other aspects of our lives.[251]

However, the research exposes an irony. The crisis point at the heart of this section concerns our anxiety about not having yet achieved our dreams, yet the empirical evidence reveals that the critical factor in whether goal pursuit makes us happy lies in enjoying the journey and *not* in realizing the end-goal (dream). This finding, of course, contradicts many people's strong beliefs and intuitions that goal achievement is the gold standard. Indeed, it contradicts one of the primary myths of happiness, which tells us to wait for happiness until we realize our dreams. Yet when we finally land that part in a Broadway play or that promotion or that award, we feel an immediate thrill, but that thrill is often followed by satiety, increased expectations, and even letdown.[252] After economist and *New York Times* columnist Paul Krugman learned that he had won the long-coveted Nobel Prize, "His wife Robin's reaction, once the initial thrill wore off, was 'Paul, you don't have time for this.'"[253] In similar fashion, one of my colleagues won his field's highest honor, the American Psychological Association Distinguished Scientist Award. When asked how long the happiness boost lasted, he replied, "One day."

By contrast, if we enjoy the struggle along the way, we will derive pleasure and satisfaction by simply pursuing or working on our goal. We will ideally stretch our skills, discover novel opportunities, grow, strive, learn, and become more capable and expert. Whether in our chosen fields or hobbies, our gradually added knowledge and expertise will afford progressively increased opportunities for appreciation and delight, as well as the satisfaction (according to some scientists) of our innate need for being challenged and using our potentials to the fullest. Whether our valued goal is inventing something special or finishing school, it will give us something to work for and to look forward to.

Furthermore, goal pursuit in and of itself imparts structure and meaning to our daily lives, creating obligations, deadlines, and timetables, as well as opportunities for mastering new skills and for interacting with others. Hence, in the course of our pursuits, we may attain a sense of purpose in our lives, feelings of efficacy over our progress, and mastery over our time. All of these things make people happy. And once we accomplish a step along the way (e.g., completing an internship or an article), we would do well to savor that accomplished step or subgoal (which should deservedly give us a small emotional and ego boost), before moving on from the accomplished goal to a new one.[254] In sum, instead of focusing too much on the finish line in the first place, we should focus on—and enjoy as much as possible—carrying out the multiple steps necessary to make progress.

THE BILLION-DOLLAR QUESTION

Numerous writers and researchers, from Malcolm Gladwell (author of *The Tipping Point* and *Outliers*) to Dean Simonton (creativity scholar at the University of California, Davis), have explored the question of what makes people successful.[255] Is it innate intelligence or hard work? Is it conscientiousness or talent? Many have concluded that the simple answer is diligence—namely, that we need to put in approximately ten thousand hours of a particular kind of effort, or deliberate practice, before we can expect to become a true expert or success in any field, whether it's playing the violin, writing novels, pitching baseballs, or performing brain surgery. I have found these arguments extremely interesting and persuasive,[256] but I have always believed that a critical piece was missing from the discussion. That piece is really the billion-dollar question: How do we compel ourselves to complete those ten thousand hours?[257] Where does one get the spark or motivation to force oneself to practice the violin for five hours a day or, as Benjamin Franklin did, to laboriously copy out and rewrite entire published essays (from prose to verse and back again)? Where does one come by the drive to get up at five a.m. every morning to accomplish these things? If the answer is either inborn temperament (that some are naturally more driven and conscientious than others) or the presence of a draconian parent, spouse, or trainer,[258] then many people's hopes for achieving some semblance of greatness are likely fruitless.

The research doesn't bear out this pessimistic conclusion, however. We now know a great deal about that spark or motivation we need to give our all; we know what undermines it and we have some good ideas about what might stimulate it. Essentially, whether we want to be a small-business owner, filmmaker, policy analyst, insurance broker, or food blogger, we are much more likely to succeed and to be happy trying if we are working toward these goals because they are inherently interesting and enjoyable to us, or if working toward them conveys our most important values—in other words, if our motivation is intrinsic.[259]

Although any goal—even a misguided or malicious one—can potentially be intrinsic, generally speaking, the ideal goals are ones that nourish our basic drives to grow, feel competent and self-sufficient, connect with others, and contribute to our communities. It makes us unhappy—and less likely to succeed—when we are pursuing goals that are not truly our own and when we are doing so simply to obtain approval (say, from our parents or colleagues) or to avoid guilt. Such "extrinsic" goals include striving to become rich, beautiful, popular, powerful, or famous.[260]

When you pursue a career or undertaking for its own sake, you are more likely to experience intense concentration, engagement, flow, curiosity, and persistence. But how do you acquire that kind of spirit and motivation? You have to begin at the beginning. That is, the most important pivot point is the one from which you initially make your choice of what it is you really want. Ask yourself the following questions about your so-far unrealized ambition or dream.

- Is your goal—say, to start your own business—attainable?

- Who is the owner of the goal—you or someone else?

- Does it conflict with a long-held plan (e.g., to spend a lot of time with family or travel around the world)?

- Do you truly feel "yourself" when you are pursuing your ambition or fantasizing about it?

- Do you expect to grow in the process or to develop lasting relationships?

- Would you still do it if the compensation were much more modest?

You don't have to agree with these sentiments *all* the time. I have a passion for my work yet I'm still peeved when it encroaches too much on my family/leisure time or when it is a grind. But if your answer is a broad no to at least two of these questions, it will be extremely challenging, if not impossible, to will an intrinsic motivation that isn't there. In that case, you will want to shift your priorities and goals—for example, from running a bank to running a nonprofit, from wealth to philanthropy, from teaching to writing, or from writing to teaching. Alternatively, it is sometimes possible to reframe your work. Perhaps there is a noble purpose behind it that you have not considered. Perhaps you have a talent—writing, public speaking, networking, organization—that has gone unnoticed and that you can bring to bear in your current position.

Finally, if there are repetitive or dead spells in your work, perhaps you can take advantage of them by growing in some way. Many jobs involve periods of time in which you are waiting for something to happen. A sales associate may be idle waiting for the next sale and a cabbie waiting for the next ride. Other occupations involve manual tasks—typing letters, clicking through online ads, machine work, house painting—that leave the mind to wander. Why not use that time to learn or grow? For example, long-haul truckers, data entry clerks, and halibut fishermen report discovering new ideas and enjoying their days more when they spend their work time listening to podcasted courses from universities all over the world on such diverse topics as existential philosophy, world classics, and theoretical physics.[261]

Once we have chosen or reframed our goals in such a way that they become personally meaningful, need-satisfying, and compelling, we can draw on several other lines of research to sustain our commitment and drive. First, studies show that we are many times more likely to succeed when we make a public resolution to accomplish something, whether it's to apply for that long-delayed certification or to begin a full-time job search.[262] Second, we should make great efforts to win over those who are closest to us about the value of our pursuits and then engage and cultivate their aid and comfort. We will be much more successful at keeping our motivation alive if our partners or best friends not only support our dreams, but if they inspire us by treating us as though we already possess the expertise, authority, accomplishment, or title that we seek.[263]

Finally, we would do well to follow psychologist Abraham Maslow's recommendation to choose growth over security—in other words, to take potentially worthwhile risks instead of choosing to do what is known, comfortable, and familiar. Consider your pursuit of that elusive dream—the one you are distressed over not having accomplished yet—and ask yourself whether taking a risk might bring a potentially large payoff. Writing out two columns—one for a list of the anticipated benefits and one for the likely costs—will help you to reveal the answer. I'm not partial to the expression "moving out of our comfort zone," but that is essentially what I am suggesting we attempt—that is, do something to advance our dreams that we have wanted to reach but have been reluctant to follow. People who have tried this exercise find it extremely challenging, yet also expanding, empowering, and inspiring.[264]

THE PREPARED MIND

If we have lived our life with the belief that winning the perfect job will bring a lifetime of happiness, it can be deeply distressing to learn that once that job is ours, the resulting happiness is not as great, or as enduring, as we imagined it to be. In other words, at the root of this happiness myth is the misconception that, although we're not happy now, we'll surely be happy when we make partner at our firm, when we're managing our own projects, when we land our first gallery exhibition, when we sell our screenplay, when we're running our own store, or when we win the Nobel Prize. We encounter a problem, however, when acquiring that seemingly perfect job doesn't make us as happy as we expected and when that happiness is ever so brief. What explains this unwelcome experience is the inexorable process of hedonic adaptation. Hence, a critical first step is to understand that everyone becomes habituated to the novelty, excitement, and challenges of a new job or venture. This new awareness will suggest to us an alternative explanation for our occupational malaise. To wit, there may be nothing wrong with the job or with our motivation or with our work ethic. The fact may be that we are simply experiencing a naturally occurring, all-too-human process.

The second step is to understand what it is that we can proactively do to slow down or even reverse the process of getting progressively bored with our jobs, and to start practicing the relevant strategies as soon as possible. If such efforts are ultimately futile, if the job is truly substandard, or if the work is a poor fit for our preferences and abilities, then we'll be more confident that moving on is a decision we have made with a prepared mind—that is, one based on reasoned analysis and effort, not on emotion-based gut instinct.

Alternatively, we may find ourselves deeply discontented because we are not at the point in our professional lives today that we thought we would be. Yet the message of this chapter is that if we want success—recognition, authority, rewards—because we think our happiness depends on it, we are limiting our happiness now and jeopardizing it in the future. The reason comes from a storm of research, which fortunately (or unfortunately) can be summarized with a cliché: "Happiness does not come from outside of us; it dwells within." As trite as this statement might seem, sometimes a truth is disguised as a truism. We may genuinely bemoan the fact that we have not yet attained this or that (while our friends have), and this bemoaning genuinely makes us unhappy, but the attainment of this or that is not the answer to our unhappiness. Distracting ourselves from toxic comparisons, concentrating on our own internal standards, and focusing on the journey in pursuit of our dreams, rather than on the end result, will redirect our attention and energies from the "I'll be happy *when* ____" mentality and toward more fruitful horizons.

CHAPTER 6

I Can't Be Happy When . . . I'm Broke

One of the most traumatic turning points in life is learning that we have lost our home, our job, or our retirement savings. *Foreclosure, bankruptcy, pink slip, eviction*—these are words that push our panic buttons, lead to sleepless nights, and precipitate hopelessness and dread. We may initially be plagued with a stream of devastating feelings—we've lost everything, we are defeated, and we have no prospects. We can't imagine ever being happy again.

Some of us may climb out of the financial hole and live to prosper, but many will endure the experience of living paycheck to paycheck, unable to afford anything beyond the bare necessities, barely scraping by, fearful of the next downturn, or miserable about being poor. Recent years have prompted even those who are relatively comfortable to feel financially insecure. Thirty years ago, the chance that one of us would suffer a loss of income was 17 percent, and roughly the same number were worried about being laid off; today that chance is one in four and the majority are worried.[265] Even if or when the world economy improves, the anxiety about being broke will likely still prevail. In light of our personal—and largely uncontrollable—financial downturns, how do we manage this anxiety? How do we live an impecunious life that we call good?

DOES MONEY BUY HAPPINESS?
FINALLY, A CLEAR AND PRESENT ANSWER

It's the rare individual who doesn't believe that she could ever be happy without money. My first aim in this chapter is to examine this happiness myth and challenge the deeply held belief that we need money to be comfortable, secure, and content. My second aim is to offer research-based recommendations for how we can sustain a good quality of life with a small or unstable income—how we can turn lemons into lemonade, make the best of less, and spend the little we have in wise and thrifty ways.

Much has been said and written about whether or not money makes people happy, and the conclusions offered can differ radically, depending on which psychologists, economists, or commentators we listen to. I have read a great deal about the link between well-being and the triumvirate of wealth, income, and material possessions. I have also spoken to (and heard from) numerous experts on the topic. The data are confusing and contradictory, but I believe that I can offer some reasoned and data-based conclusions.

FIRST, INCOME AND HAPPINESS *ARE* INDEED SIGNIFICANTLY CORRELATED, ALTHOUGH THE RELATIONSHIP ISN'T SUPERSTRONG[266]

In other words, it's true that the higher we are on the economic ladder, the happier we report ourselves to be. In many ways, this finding is not at all surprising, given that having money not only gives us opportunities to acquire conveniences and luxuries, but affords us greater status and respect, more leisure time and fulfilling work, access to superior health care and nutrition, and greater security, autonomy, and control. Wealthier people lead healthier lives, have the wherewithal to spend time with people they like, live in safer neighborhoods and in less crowded conditions, and enjoy a critical buffer when faced with adversities like illness, disability, or divorce. Indeed, it's a wonder that the correlation between money and individual happiness isn't stronger than it is.

Two important caveats are in order, however. First, the relationship between happiness and money only holds for a certain *kind* of happiness. When people are asked to consider how happy or satisfied they are in general, those with more money report being happier and more satisfied. But when people are asked how happy they are moment to moment in their daily lives—e.g., "How joyful, stressed, angry, affectionate, and sad were you *yesterday*?"—then those with more money are hardly more likely to have experienced happy feelings.[267] This pattern of results suggests that wealth makes us happy when we are thinking about our lives ("Am I happy overall? Well, I'm making a good living"), but money has a much smaller impact on our feelings as we actually live our lives ("Am I happy today?").[268]

The second caveat, which may be even more important than the first one, is that when psychologists, sociologists, and economists discuss the relationship between money and happiness, they invariably assume that money is the causal factor. But, of course, the causal direction could (and undoubtedly does) go both ways. That is, money buys happiness, but happiness also buys money. Indeed, several studies have suggested that happier people are relatively more proficient or gifted at earning more.[269]

SECOND, THE LINK BETWEEN MONEY AND HAPPINESS IS A GREAT DEAL STRONGER FOR POORER PEOPLE THAN RICHER ONES[270]

That is, when our basic needs for adequate food, safety, health care, and shelter aren't met, an increase in income makes a much larger difference for us than when we are relatively comfortable. Another way to put it is that money makes us happier if it keeps us from being poor. After all, those of us who have very little are more likely to be evicted from our homes, go hungry, live in a crime-ridden community, have a child drop out of school, lack the resources to obtain medical care, or be unable to manage the pain, stress, and practical demands of a disease or disability.[271] Even a modest increase in income can alleviate or prevent some of these adverse situations.

These ideas help explain why money makes poorer people happier, but why does money have a relatively weak effect on richer people's happiness? One answer is that as income rises beyond a certain level, its positive effects (for example, the ability to fly first class or retain top-notch medical specialists) may be offset by some negative effects, like increased time pressure (longer working hours and commutes) and increased stress (from holding powerful positions, feeling anxiety about investments, and problems with overindulged children).[272] Because wealth allows people to experience the best that life has to offer, it can even reduce their capacity to savor life's small pleasures.[273]

THIRD, THE LINK BETWEEN MONEY AND HAPPINESS IS EVEN STRONGER WHEN NATIONS (AS OPPOSED TO INDIVIDUALS) ARE COMPARED

In other words, those of us who live in wealthier nations are a great deal happier than those who live in poorer nations.[274] A huge caveat, however, is that wealthier nations don't just have higher GDPs than poorer nations; they are also more likely to be characterized by democracy, freedom, and equal rights, and they are less likely to experience political instability or rampant corruption and graft. Consequently, it's not clear what really drives the relationship between wealth and happiness at the level of nations.

FOURTH, IN MANY COUNTRIES, AS PEOPLE'S ECONOMIC FORTUNES HAVE IMPROVED, THEIR AVERAGE REPORTED HAPPINESS LEVELS HAVE NOT BUDGED[275]

This last finding seems puzzling in light of the fact that people who have more money are happier. Hence, it's this particular finding that is usually behind any proclamations in the media or elsewhere that money does *not* buy happiness. From my previous descriptions of research, you can probably already speculate about why, for example, Americans have not gotten happier as their incomes have tripled.[276] First, higher incomes foster higher aspirations, such that we now consider necessary—a vacation, a car, or indoor plumbing—what we once considered extravagant or optional. And, second, higher incomes force a shift in our social comparisons, such that we now feel poorer relative to the people in our neighborhoods and offices who have a bit more than we do.[277]

HOW TO BE HAPPY WITH LESS
BY APPLYING THE ANCIENT VIRTUE OF THRIFT

The bottom line from the hundreds of studies on the subject is that having money *can* make us happy, and not having it can definitely make us unhappy, but the power of money is a great deal less than we'd expect. For example, although financial hardship can exert many detrimental effects upon our lives, its influence on our happiness is comparatively small, because, as we've learned in this book, many other factors influence our happiness in even more potent ways. Knowing this, if we have little, whether by circumstance or choice, is it possible to live our lives in such a way that our financial want or insecurity does not bar us from flourishing and prospering? Or, is being happy with less simply a corny fallacy propagated by the wealthy?

Empirical evidence suggests that being happy with less is not a fallacy. For some time now, my graduate student Joe Chancellor and I have been pondering this question—a question that has become even more urgent in light of the world's economic troubles, which have translated into record unemployment, indebtedness, and bankruptcies facing countless U.S. households. The outcome of our work together is the following proposal, which can be summarized thus: If individuals on meager budgets wish to extract the maximum happiness from spending less, they should bring to bear lessons from the ancient virtue of thrift.

Although some of us associate *thrift* with acting cheap, miserly, or stingy, the term actually originates from the word *thrive*. At its essence, thrift is about the optimal, most efficient use of limited resources. Historically, thriftiness has been equated with industry (i.e., the harder we labor for rewards, the less likely we are to squander them), temperance (i.e., we control excess by practicing moderation and self-restraint), and the pursuit of fulfilling and fruitful activities (i.e., so we avoid wasting our resources on frivolous ones). Thrift has an old and honored history, having been promoted and lionized by writers, philosophers, entrepreneurs, and thinkers as diverse as Socrates, King Solomon, Confucius, Benjamin Franklin, Alexis de Tocqueville, Max Weber, and, most recently, Warren Buffett.

We all can apply the principles of thrift in order to spend less while enjoying more, as well as to strive to ensure that limited wages don't wholly undermine our happiness. What's more, thrifty behavior in and of itself can make us feel good (by highlighting our better natures), impart a sense of control (by highlighting our abilities to manage our finances), and even foster success. For example, studies show that children who have the capacity to delay gratification (a critical feature of thrift) grow up to receive superior teacher evaluations, score higher on college entrance exams, get accepted into better colleges, be less likely to become bullies as adolescents, and be less likely to have drug problems as adults.[278] Research from my laboratory and others' reveals a number of strategies and practices to make thrifty behavior possible.

DON'T BE THE BORROWER WHO BECOMES SLAVE TO THE LENDER

Albert Einstein once mischievously defined relativity with the following aphorism: "Put your hand on a hot stove for a minute, and it seems like an hour. Sit with a pretty girl for an hour, and it seems like a minute." Psychologists refer to this truth as "bad is stronger than good"[279] or "pain is more potent than pleasure." As I mentioned in chapter 2, two decades of research has demonstrated that we net a much bigger emotional "hit" from negative experiences (from which we sometimes never bounce back) than we obtain a boost from positive experiences (which we rapidly get used to).[280]

What these findings mean for us is that if a major purchase thrusts us further into debt, the thrill of the acquisition will be powerfully outweighed by the strain of the indebtedness. This example isn't merely hypothetical, as unsecured consumer debt in the United States averages almost $8,000 for every man, woman, and child; and one in every two Americans admits to worrying about the debts they owe.[281] Although it may seem obvious to the thrifty, borrowers who have little or no reserves yet rely on credit to continually spend and consume will suffer constant anxiety about making payments, losing income, and defaulting on loans. Unless we are taking out the loans to pay the electricity bill or save our child's life, the costs of overspending and indebtedness hugely outweigh the benefits of even the most alluring purchase.

Another example involves the tremendous psychic costs of being house-poor. Living in a bigger house with a bigger backyard gives us pleasure, but this pleasure diminishes over time until we barely notice the square-footage or the updated bathrooms. More critical is the fact that our pleasure from the house can't come close to matching the pain and worry of eking out monthly mortgage payments. Shifting from being house-poor to being house-rich means less daily stress and more moment-to-moment happiness.

What does all this have to do with how we can be happy with less? Happiness is not just about feeling good—it's also about not feeling bad. Because diminishing negative experiences (like the worry associated with debt) brings a three- to fivefold greater return on happiness than creating positive experiences (like buying a new television),[282] the wise course of action—and step one to embark on any strategy to enjoy living with less—is to reduce or eliminate debt before committing our money to any nonessential services or goods.

SPEND YOUR MONEY ON EXPERIENCES
RATHER THAN POSSESSIONS

Growing evidence reveals that it is experiences—not things—that make us happy.[283] Many experiences, such as hikes with friends or family game nights, are virtually free. And many others—road trips, boozy dinners, sports tournaments, cooking lessons, and rock concerts—cost money. Of course, sometimes a fine line runs between experiences and things. A Wii game console is both a material object and the channel of experiences, learning, and adventures. Thus, it appears that the happiest people are those who are most skilled at wringing experiences out of everything in which they invest their money, whether it's a guitar, a plane ticket, a picture book, a dress, a camera, cake decorating lessons, or running shoes.

Before we shift our spending and consumption habits in an entirely new direction, it's important to consider the reasons and science behind doing so. Why are experiences superior to things?

First, because most possessions don't tend to change after we've bought them, we adapt to them a great deal faster. Once we open the box and put our new item on the shelf or in the closet, it won't be long before we feel like it's been there forever and we won't even notice it anymore.

Second, experiences are intrinsically more social—more likely to be shared, anticipated, and relived with other people—than are things. Vacationing or bowling with a friend is a lot more likely to cement our friendship than talking about or showing off our new wristwatch or bedroom set.

Third, in light of research underscoring the peril of social comparisons, it's not surprising that one reason experiences make us happier than possessions is that we are less likely to compare them to those of others. The primary rationale is that it simply requires a great deal more effort and imagination to equate our honeymoon spent lying on the beach with our friend's honeymoon spent sightseeing. Even if we could, knowing that our neighbor is having a terrific time is unlikely to diminish our own pleasure. My husband and I loved the Paul McCartney concert and we did not care a whit about whether the people in the eighth row might have loved it even more. But we might delight in a new hatchback just a tiny bit less every time our neighbor drives by in his convertible.

Fourth, relative to things, experiences are also less prone to yet another kind of comparison—the comparison with what might have been.[284] Because store-bought gadgets and handbags (but not ballet lessons or excursions) are so easy to set side by side, we are far more likely to regret purchasing the former, even if it's entirely satisfactory, when we discover an even better value. For similar reasons, it's more difficult to choose among material things than among experiences, and a less-than perfect choice of an item that you can hold or touch is more likely to gnaw at us long after it's made.

Fifth, whereas material objects typically grow old and dull with time, until we are eager to replace them, experiences can actually grow even more positive and more enjoyable as time passes. A wonderful weekend, dinner, or a conversation can become burnished and embellished in our memories, such that we forget or overlook any of the stresses (e.g., getting lost on the way, suffering through traffic) or hassles (spilling hot coffee, bad weather) and only remember the positives.[285] We are more likely to mentally revisit our past experiences than our purchases,[286] and the more we revisit and replay them, the more they blossom and the richer stories they provide.

Sixth, experiences make us happier than things do because we are more likely to identify with them and less likely to want to trade them.[287] After all, we are the sum of our experiences, not the sum of our possessions. When we own something, it is outside us—on our shelf, shoulders, or living room. When we experience something, it is inside us—inside our minds and memories.

Seventh, experiences—like climbing a mountain, visiting a remote location, or learning to dive—may involve challenges and adventures, and it makes us happy to exert effort to endure a difficult lesson or journey and relish the feeling of hard-won accomplishment. Unless our new possession is a snowboard or a hang glider, it is unlikely to deliver the same level of stimulation and challenge.

Finally, things don't make us as happy as experiences because an inappropriate focus on acquiring material possessions begets many costs. As I will describe in more detail in the next chapter, materialists report less satisfaction and meaning in their lives, have emptier social relationships, are more insecure, and are less liked by others than people who are not materialistic.[288]

In sum, the research on the superiority of experiences over possessions is hugely persuasive, and all of us—but especially those of us with meager budgets—would do well to apply its recommendations. However, it's important to remember that material things can also make us happy—as long as we turn them into experiences. We could take along our family and friends in an adventure in our new car; we could throw a party on our new deck; and we could practice a self-improvement program on our new smartphone.

SPEND YOUR MONEY ON MANY SMALL PLEASURES RATHER THAN A FEW BIG ONES

A simple thrift strategy is suggested by research on the emotional benefits of forging positive experiences that are frequent rather than intense (e.g., several modest restaurant dinners rather than a single blowout)[289] and separated rather than combined (rationing out our favorite *Sopranos* episodes week by week rather than splurging on several at a time).[290] Thus, although advertisers might tell us otherwise, we should aim to spend our money on a series of small intermittent pleasures (e.g., bouquets of fresh flowers or long-distance phone calls to close friends) rather than one big costly amenity (like a fancy sound system).

This practice turns out to be both gratifying and relatively cheap. The reason is that when we savor a positive experience—whether it's a gripping movie, half an hour in a massage chair, or a delicious piece of lemon cake—"the banquet is in the first bite."[291] In other words, with each passing minute, hour, or week, our capacity to savor the same experience dwindles. However, our capacity to savor and enjoy can be replenished after a break.[292] Thus, carving up our consumption into smaller doses and separating it out by time can multiply those "first bites" and increase our pleasure. We will obtain more enjoyment from a bittersweet chocolate bar if we cut it into squares and eat one piece per day, instead of devouring the whole thing in a single sitting. We will obtain more pleasure if we divide our spending money, however scant, into several portions, and dole it out to ourselves once or twice a week. One researcher, for example, interviewed people of all income levels in the United Kingdom and found that those who frequently treated themselves to low-cost indulgences— picnics, extravagant cups of coffee, and treasured DVDs—were more satisfied with their lives.[293] Other scientists have found that no-cost or low-cost activities can yield small boosts to happiness in the short term that cumulate, one step at a time, to produce a large impact on happiness in the long term.[294]

RECYCLE HAPPINESS AND RENT IT

Another set of strategies that will help us extract the greatest possible satisfaction from the smallest wage involves the thrifty practices of renting rather than buying, and getting the most out of what we already own. Human beings instinctively seek variety and novelty in their environments,[295] and this innate drive is undoubtedly one of the reasons that many of us feel the need to purchase something new each week. Yet the pursuit of variety need not result in spendthrift and environmentally costly behavior. Instead, we can recycle happiness by being more mindful and appreciative of the material things we already have. As the poet Allen Ginsberg observed, "You own twice as much rug if you're twice as *aware* of the rug."[296]

We can also recycle happiness by using our existing possessions and purchases in novel ways, which can generate for us a stream of positive experiences and positive emotions free of charge. For example, we can reformulate our possessions into activities by sharing our apartment and car with friends or by using our iPod to learn sign language. We can deliberately plan to use our garden in different ways or seek out new opportunities and friendships by taking out our bike or our computer. We can dust off our yoga mat to begin a new fitness program or reread all the classics on our shelves. We can loan our washer and dryer to a needy friend.

Even when a purchased experience (e.g., family trip) or acquisition (e.g., home or car) is long in the past, we can still extract pleasure from it by savoring and reminiscing. Flipping through a photo album or watching old video clips (us at the Grand Canyon, me driving my motorbike) helps us relive the positive experience and the positive feelings we had at the time.[297] As we reminisce, a photo might remind us of a pleasant or funny detail we had forgotten, like the cute waiter who flirted with us or the rainstorm that drenched

us. By paying concentrated attention to our momentary pleasure—
say, as we reminisce about a long-ago vacation or throw on the old
denim jacket that we used to love—we heighten our pleasure even
more. We can savor it by closing our eyes and luxuriating in a memory, scent, or sound, by sharing the experience with others, and by
rolling with the pleasure rather than overthinking it. In these ways,
mentally revisiting and relishing memorable experiences and things
that we had purchased long ago can continue to generate happiness
boosts for us even today. Rather than allowing our paid-for possessions and experiences to gather dust on shelves and in closets and
memories, we can either literally reexperience them in the present
(e.g., by taking out the faded Trivial Pursuit) or metaphorically (e.g.,
by reminiscing about spring break), thus simultaneously saving our
money, reducing our ecological footprint, and feeling happy.

Another thrifty happiness-lifting strategy has an unfortunately
bad rep—renting. Many of us believe that we extract significantly
more happiness from an object that we own rather than rent, yet our
experience merely reflects a well-known cognitive bias that prompts
us to like something (anything!) more after we acquire it.[298] However, like most cases of biased thinking, we can overcome this bias
with a little bit of effort and know-how. The cost difference between
buying a book and borrowing it from a library, between buying a
DVD and renting it, or between buying a mountain cabin and renting it is often immense. Yet we need not enjoy a rented movie, book,
or cabin any less because we don't have title to it. Indeed, rented
items aren't privy to the diminishing marginal utility that character-
izes owned goods, because we obtain less and less pleasure from the
latter over time. Also, rented things enable us to enjoy greater variety
and hence greater pleasure, because we can lease something different
each time or travel to mountain cabins in multiple locations instead
of one. Finally, rentals do not bear the costs, hassles, and stresses

that often characterize purchased acquisitions, such as malfunctions, losses, and repairs. For example, consider two groups of individuals that are fairly similar in their incomes, health, and types of residences. The only difference between them is that one group owns their homes and the other rents. Researchers have found—contrary to popular beliefs about the "American dream"—that home owners are less happy than renters, derive more pain from ownership of their homes, and spend more time on housework and less time interacting with their friends and neighbors.[299] If you can't afford many of the things in life that gratify, amuse, or make daily life easier, rent them.

BENEFITS OF LIVING WITH LESS: HOW LESS COULD BE MORE

The scary new economic era that confronted the world in 2008 prompted much public hand-wringing about the decline of our current way of life amid a handful of hopeful notes. The pessimists opined about the demise of life as we know it. By contrast, the optimists predicted that the shock and toll of looming financial disaster and widespread insecurity would shift our attitudes and better our consumer behavior, ultimately lending our lives greater meaning and greater appreciation for what we have and fostering much-needed disgust with the materialistic culture that pervades our lives and harms our planet. Supporting this perspective, scientists have shown that managing the slings and arrows of life's adversities necessitates expressing gratitude for our relatively good fortune (rather than yearning for more), cultivating a sense of connection with family and friends, building competence and expertise, and looking outside oneself to contribute to others.[300]

Is it simply an unfortunate cliché, or can less truly be more? Many people feel that they don't earn enough to truly enjoy life, and that being told that their hardship has a bright side is offensive. I intend to convince them otherwise, although my arguments apply only to those who have not been impoverished so much by financial circumstances or setbacks that their basic needs fail to be met. Research suggests that a new attitude toward money, time, spending, and possessions can stimulate people to rise to the occasion in ways that they previously had not envisioned, to contribute more positively to society, to thrive via cooperation and interdependence, and to live more authentically and more lightly on the earth. Here are some specific ways that having less can actually improve our lives and challenge the veracity of the myth that no one can be happy without money.

COMING TOGETHER

Having less means we are more likely to pull together, show concern for others, and help one another. We've all heard stories about how families during the Great Depression of the 1930s bonded around the fireplace, the radio, with board games, on walks and museum visits, and other free or low-cost pursuits. This is clearly a sanitized and idealized vision of hardship (as a thought experiment, just think of the "wonderful" experiences you'll have bonding with your parents when you move back in with them, as friends of ours were forced to do last year), but the portrait has kernels of truth. Furthermore, if your job has been eliminated or curtailed, you may choose to spend more time performing community service, and if you're spiritual or religious, you may turn to your faith community. All of these consequences are positive ones.

SHIFTING PERSPECTIVES AND PRIORITIES

Losing our job may open up an ideal opportunity to find something that we are passionate about. The feeling that we've lost everything could fuel immense ambition and drive if only because we have no other choice. *Not* losing our job when those around us have been laid off may foster a sense of gratitude that we are still employed (even if we used to endlessly complain about it), as well as bolstered motivation to show our very best work. Recognizing that money is not the Holy Grail helps us shift our priorities to the things in life that really matter, like our families, our health, world peace, or nature's beauty. When life is hard, counting our blessings and savoring the little things in life becomes even more important. When life is hard, we recognize that we are stronger and more capable of taking care of ourselves and our loved ones than we ever imagined.

GETTING CREATIVE

When we have a lot of money, we can walk into a store and buy the first object we covet. When we have little money, we are forced to learn how to make hard choices—to reconsider what is truly worth buying and what is not. We are also forced to be creative about how to obtain what we need. During the height of the 2008 U.S. recession, garage sales rocketed, with people getting rid of "stuff they don't need" and selling it to others who do. Others started innovative barter systems to accomplish the same goal. It's no wonder that innovation and enterprise flourish during economic downturns.[301] Starting out with little or nothing gives us the freedom to take chances and to rebuild anew.

CONSERVING

Finally, the less money and fewer possessions we have, the less likely we are to damage the environment. We buy less, consume less, and drive less. We slow down and spend our time in a less resource-intensive way. To economize, we are more likely to put on a sweater than turn on the heat, or walk instead of drive. We also waste less. We are more likely to reuse old things—linens, toys, jars—instead of throwing them away, and we are more likely to finish every bite.

A CAVEAT

In sum, both empirical and anecdotal evidence suggests that living with less has some clear benefits. Yet I don't want to downplay or trivialize the hardships and privations faced by people who are deprived not only of luxuries, but basic securities. When my family immigrated to the United States, I was young, but I have indelible memories of the anxiety and powerlessness of living from paycheck to paycheck, the fear of the next unforeseen event (car breakdown, illness) turning our whole life upside down, and the pain of not being able to have the clothes or toys that my peers had. A bit like people who came of age in the 1930s and never lost their frugal habits, I have never forgotten what it's like to be poor. Most of my other indelible memories, however, involve my entire family sitting around the dinner table every night, eating turkey cutlets and fried potatoes, and talking for hours about politics, literature, and movies, and fantasizing about our futures. It wasn't all bleak, but if I knew then what I know now, my family would have been better positioned to make the best of it.

THE PREPARED MIND

Some of us arrive at the point where we must acknowledge to ourselves that, because of one giant misfortune or a string of small reversals or hard luck, we may be broke for a very long time. Others have only ourselves to blame, perhaps making poor choices about how we spend, consume, and overspend, or lacking willpower, industriousness, or drive. For most, the answer is likely a lot more complicated than that. But no matter the cause, if our intuition tells us that we can't be happy without a great deal more money, it's critical to contemplate the data I present in this chapter that suggest otherwise. Exercising one or more of the four thrift principles described above—and doing so sooner rather than later—can both prevent economic disaster and help you extract the greatest amount of happiness from the smallest things. Instead of brooding about our misfortune, we can focus on the ways that we can be happy with less and spend our money right.

CHAPTER 7

I'll Be Happy When . . . I'm Rich

*J**ack Barnes wears a crisp pumpkin plaid shirt to our interview, a navy-striped silk tie, Cartier watch, and a bit too much hair product for a man of fifty. His skin is dark and leathery—a fact I under-stand better after he describes his $2.5 million condominium in Ha-waii. Jack talks in a confident, even self-important tone, but he is friendly and smart. We are at a fancy restaurant, and he tells me to order whatever I want off the menu. I ask for sweet potato fries and he frowns. "You know, those are loaded with bad calories."*

Jack had dreamed of being a doctor since he was four years old, play-ing an MD with a doctor's coat he got for Halloween. "As children, we often want to be a hundred different things. A spy, a cowboy, a clown. I've always wanted to be a doctor." Jack attended Brown University and graduated with a list of academic honors, several athletics trophies, and a near-perfect MCAT. Jack laughs with a cocky grin and confesses he only applied to the top three medical schools, and got into all three. "I had all my ducks in a row. I just knew that's what I wanted to do. By fifteen, I knew my specialty would be plastics. I knew I wanted to make people feel beautiful. There is something powerful about that feeling of being able to say, 'Look, this is where you are at, and in no time, I can bring you here.' It's like playing God—having the potential to literally recreate human life. I get to decide how people look and how they feel."

Jack had a flourishing private practice by the time he was thirty. He was introduced to his future wife by a friend but she was not interested.

"I told her she was beautiful, and I told her to go on a date with me. I was a total nag. I left messages for her every night after our first meeting. Finally, she called back and said no. I told her she was silly, because we were getting married, and two months later, I proposed. We fell in love like blazes."

Jack and his wife enjoyed married life, spent time traveling, and reveled in Jack's professional successes. As his practice grew, Jack capitalized on his specialty by developing a niche practice that catered specifically to high-net-worth socialites in New York, Connecticut, and Massachusetts. The money came in, the money went out, and in the span of four years, Jack bought two vacation homes, two sports cars, and a cruising yacht. *"I had more dough than I knew what to do with. I mean, literally, my wife and I wanted for nothing. First-class everything, rare wine, diamond rings, country club. I was making reams of money."*

For a while, Jack enjoyed his professional successes and prosperity. He loved the power that money brought him. But soon, he noticed that the meaning in his work and in his lifestyle started to seep away. *"I had difficulty feeling motivated, and I had difficulty getting out of bed in the morning. That's what I remember the most. I remember literally feeling like it was a strain. I used to have so much spirit. I'd get up at five-thirty a.m., go to the gym, and see my first patient at eight o'clock. I'd operate till noon, eat at my desk, and then come back and work until eight p.m. Part of my niche was that I'd see patients twenty-four-seven."* Jack began to really struggle—he stopped taking new clients, and starting lying to his wife about the number of patients he was seeing.

At this point, realizing he had everything he wanted but was completely miserable, Jack began seeing a prominent psychiatrist three times a week. *"One day I was lying there and I was going on about feeling empty again, and Dr. G said, "Why don't you do something else? Obviously, what you're doing doesn't bring you happiness like it used to. Do you want to die miserable?" He slammed me over the head. I couldn't die miserable, and it hadn't been in my vocabulary to just change my focus, to change my life. I guess I felt obligated to stay where I was, and just make do the best I could."*

When I ask Jack about the specific moment he realized that his money and success were no longer making him happy, he says it came in waves, but the defining moment was a day when a new patient, after several consultations, asked if she could have her breasts done on Christmas Day, because it was the only day she was available. She wrote a check to Jack for $75,000 as a down payment. "I remember looking at it and staring at it. It was just not where I wanted to be anymore."[302]

Instead of realizing that we've lost everything, what if we realize, like Jack, that we appear to have it all—at least on paper—yet we're still not happy? In some ways, the crisis point I focus on here is the mirror image of the preceding one. To wit, I describe those moments when we have finally reached our goals—especially with regard to making money—and the often unexpected turmoil that follows. Why? Because we fall prey to the assumption that once we attain wealth or success or whatever it is we've dreamed of, we'll *finally* be happy, and when that happiness proves elusive or short-lived, we weather mixed emotions, letdown, and even depression. Such experiences are regrettable, because they are preventable. In this chapter, I demystify this process by explaining that the thread that runs through experiences like making it big and striking it rich is hedonic adaptation to very positive events (rather than the more typical life changes discussed earlier). Understanding the role that adaptation plays in our reactions to this crisis point—to the moment we've finally made it—can not only help prepare us for that moment but boost our chances that we will thrive and move in a positive direction rather than falter and sink into discontent.

MONEY ISN'T ALL IT'S CRACKED UP TO BE

My doctoral adviser was fond of saying that there are very few things in life that are all they're cracked up to be. This bit of wisdom is particularly applicable to wealth. Our fantasies about our first million or the dream beach house are almost never as thrilling in reality as they are in our imaginations, and even when they are, they don't retain their rush of pleasure for very long.[303] Worse yet, our tendency to be satisfied only briefly—to obtain merely "a froth of fleeting joy," in Shakespeare's words,[304] and nothing more—has the pernicious consequence of undermining the happiness of finally achieving a measure of prosperity.

Why is this so? The first part of the answer is that we can never experience something for the first time twice. This is the essential truth about arriving at the top of the mountain or the career ladder. The moments, weeks, or years leading up to the summit can be draining but exciting. There is a headiness, self-possession, and even boldness when we are close to achieving a dream. It is said that before a hurricane is about to strike, people experience a heightened level of focus, connection, and engagement.[305] That's how it feels when we've made it or are about to make it, and it feels wonderful—for a while. In his book, *The Pursuit of Perfect*, Tal Ben-Shahar describes the sense of accomplishment and true happiness he felt after he became his country's youngest national squash tournament champion. That feeling lasted for three hours.[306]

Some of us have had similar experiences—when the satisfaction with finally striking it big or striking it rich seems to have declined in direct proportion to the distance from the starting point of our success. The interesting part is the variation in what comes next. For Ben-Shahar, the moment of triumph was almost immediately followed by a decision that his victory was not all that significant and that what he really yearned to achieve was world-champion status. He began training right away. Jack Barnes, the plastic surgeon, took his psychiatrist's advice not to make any rash decisions. Instead, he went on a three-week silent meditation retreat, where he spent his days reflecting and talked to no one. He returned with a renewed sense of self and the firm decision to turn part of his practice to pro bono work for families without health insurance to repair both congenital and accidental disfigurements in both children and adults. Today, in his fifties, Jack has funded four mobile craniofacial surgery clinics in South America and frequently travels as a medical volunteer to conduct cleft lip and palate repair surgery there. He has never looked back.

In contrast, a well-heeled, powerful developer who once gave me an hour-long ride in his limo from the airport related his experience of "becoming a multimillionaire at age twenty-nine" and ending up with a major drug and alcohol problem "due to the emptiness that came from that." He spiraled downward for years, until a kick in the pants from his parents helped turn his life around. And Anthony, a hedge fund manager I interviewed, told me about how, in the decade after college, he found his earning capacity leapfrogging over all his family members, friends, and former classmates. Instead of feeling ecstatic, he found himself consumed with guilt about his success, and had a distinct sense that others either envied him or belittled what he believed he deserved. Finally, I know an actress who reached the apex of her career in her early forties, at which point her performances commanded earnings that trounced many of her peers'. Again, instead of being happy, she reacted with staggering insecurity. If the magic and "specialness" did not continue, she said, she would want to kill herself.

Some of these examples may seem extreme, but they reflect the sense of being "spoiled by" or "hooked on" money and success, and then doing something—or not—about it. When we finally become our boss's boss, we feel a high, and when that high doesn't endure, as it generally doesn't, we may experience an emptiness, a lack of fulfillment, and a letdown. After all, human beings are programmed to desire, not appreciate, and to strive for more, not be content with what they have.[307] Research suggests that after extremely positive events, mildly positive experiences (like lunch with a friend) become neutral or dull, and mildly negative experiences (like getting stuck in traffic) become intensely negative.[308] Another reason that people can react negatively to success is that even long-desired accomplishments and prosperity can unsettle and disrupt our lives (e.g., necessitating a relocation or new unfamiliar responsibilities), our roles (e.g., shifting from creative to managerial), and our view of ourselves. No matter how positive, these changes are stressful, and, accordingly, are associated with increased incidence of mood disorders, illness, and even hospitalization.[309]

GETTING USED TO MONEY

For many of us, money and success are one and the same. In the latest survey of U.S. college freshmen, when over two hundred thousand students at 279 colleges and universities were asked about their most important life goals, 77 percent checked off "being very well off financially."[310] Being well off can bring numerous conveniences and advantages—besides offering us the ability to afford more stuff, it helps us meet potential mates and provides security and stability—but an unavoidable fact is that we get used to it. For example, economists have found that two-thirds of the benefits of a raise in income are erased after just one year, in part because our spending and new "needs" rise alongside it and because we begin to associate with people in a higher income bracket.[311] Furthermore, as I described in the last chapter, although having more money boosts our satisfaction with life, it has little if any impact on the daily positive and negative emotions and the uplifts and hassles that we experience.[312]

In the beginning, greater wealth brings us a higher standard of living, and the extra comforts and extravagances bring extra pleasure. Then, we get used to—and perhaps even "addicted" to—the higher standard of living, to the extent that we are not satisfied unless we up the dosage by acquiring even more. However, those of us not *au courant* with the latest findings from psychology and economics fail to anticipate this development and end up assuming that increases in wealth should bring more happiness than we actually get.[313] Furthermore, when we don't obtain the expected pleasure, we presume that the fault lies not with human nature but with our failure to purchase the right object, steering us right back to the mall, realtor, or car dealer.

More than two centuries ago, anticipating the research showing that people get used to money and the material things it brings, Adam Smith wrote about how societal norms can create new "necessaries," such that one becomes ashamed to go without.[314] To use an example not available in Smith's era, once we travel business class, and notice that our income coequals always do so as well, we can't go back to coach.

Speaking of income coequals, it appears that what our peers are making determines our happiness even more than what *we* are making, no matter how generous it is. In other words, the average person (though, as we learned earlier, not the happiest one) cares more about social comparison, about status, about rank, and about so-called positional goods than about the absolute value of his bank account or reputation. A famous 1998 study showed that people prefer to live in a world in which they receive an annual salary of $50,000 (when others are pulling in $25,000) than an annual salary of $100,000 (when others are making $200,000). Similarly, researchers in the United Kingdom have demonstrated that people would rather give away some of their own money if it means that others would have less.[315] In sum, the reasons that we get used to having money are many, and the consequences unwelcome.

COSTS OF CONSUMPTION AND MATERIALISM

The more money we have, the more we get used to it, and the more we want. This reality has two potentially harmful outcomes, one less fortunate than the other. First, we fail to enjoy our wealth as much as we ought to. Second, our craving to purchase and possess in ever-greater quantities in order to achieve the same level of pleasure can put us on the path to runaway materialism and acquisitiveness, such that more and more money is spent and less and less happiness is derived from it.

Would all of us recognize materialistic tendencies in ourselves when we saw them? If you're not sure, rate the extent to which you agree with each of the following statements (1 = strongly disagree, 2 = disagree, 3 = neutral, 4 = agree, 5 = strongly agree):[316]

_____ 1. I admire people who own expensive homes, cars, and clothes.

_____ 2. The things I own say a lot about how well I'm doing in life.

_____ 3. I like to own things that impress people.

____ 4. I try to keep my life simple, as far as possessions are concerned.

____ 5. Buying things gives me a lot of pleasure.

____ 6. I like a lot of luxury in my life.

____ 7. My life would be better if I owned certain things I don't have.

____ 8. I'd be happier if I could afford to buy more things.

____ 9. It sometimes bothers me quite a bit that I can't afford to buy all the things I'd like.

To determine your materialism score, first "reverse-score" your rating of the fourth ("keep my life simple") item—that is, if you gave yourself a 1, cross it out and change it to a 5; if you gave yourself a 2, change that to a 4; change a 4 to a 2; and change a 5 to a 1. Now add up your nine ratings to calculate the sum. Researchers have found that, on average, people score a 26.2 on this scale. This means that if most of your responses were inclined to "neutral" and one or two were "disagree," then your materialistic tendencies are average. If you scored closer to 36.0 (i.e., agreed with most of the items), then your materialism score is in the top 20 percent relative to your peers.[317]

Why are materialistic tendencies important to identify? A mountain of research has shown that materialism depletes happiness, threatens satisfaction with our relationships, harms the environment, renders us less friendly, likable, and empathetic, and makes us less likely to help others and contribute to our communities.[318]

A first consideration is the macro-level damage that unbridled materialism inflicts, which includes fueling economic bubbles, booms, and busts, and devastating the planet, as materialists tend to use more of the world's resources and engage in fewer environmentally friendly behaviors.[319] Second, at the individual level, materialistic individuals are less satisfied and grateful for their lives, have less purpose, feel less competent in general, are more antisocial, and have weaker connections with others. Indeed, when it comes to relationships, those with materialistic goals not only rate their own social interactions more negatively, but people in general rate their relationships with materialists as less satisfying as well.[320]

Not everyone who is prosperous is focused on fame, power, and riches; not everyone catches the so-called affluenza virus.[321] But it's a risk that threatens our happiness as we sit surrounded by conveniences and luxuries. As philosophers, religious figures, and humanistic psychologists have long contended, the pursuit of money and reputation redirects our energies and passions away from deeper and more meaningful social connections and growth experiences and prevent us from achieving our full potentials. As we spend more of our time making money, the opportunity "costs" of reading poetry, playing catch with our child, or taking a walk with a friend become so high that it becomes "irrational" to do such things.[322] All the more reason to learn what research has to say about how to avoid the excesses of consumption and materialism and spend money in ways that make us happy.

HOW MONEY CAN MAKE YOU HAPPY

The American dream, rooted in the U.S. Declaration of Independence but first expressed in 1931, has always included the desire for prosperity and material plenty.[323] Over time, however, I believe the dream has changed its shape from simply wanting to get rich—and pronto—to enjoying both wealth *and* happiness. As a famous Lexus ad pronounced, "Whoever said money can't buy happiness isn't spending it right."[324] Psychological science suggests six principles to live by if we want to maximally enjoy our money. Four are described below and two others (concerning spending money on experiences and segregating those experiences) in the previous chapter.[325]

SPEND MONEY ON NEED-SATISFYING ACTIVITIES

If money isn't making us happy, it's likely because we are spending it to keep up with the neighbors, validate our wealth, or flaunt our looks, power, and status. The problem, then, isn't in the money but in how we use it. Perhaps the most direct and most reliable way to maximize the happiness and fulfillment that we can extract from money is through need-satisfying pursuits—for example, by spending our capital on developing ourselves as people, on growing, and on investing in interpersonal connections. In other words, the purchases or expenses that will yield the greatest emotional benefit are those that involve goals that satisfy at least one of the three basic human needs—(1) competence (i.e., feeling capable or expert), (2) relatedness (i.e., belonging and feeling connected to others), and (3) autonomy (i.e., feeling a sense of mastery and control over one's life).[326] Such activities have been shown by researchers to bring happiness and, equally important, *not* to stimulate ever-increasing addiction-like desires for more and more.[327]

Finally, spending money on need-satisfying goals, like mastering a new sport, celebrating a friend's achievement, or taking one's nephew on a safari, can trigger "upward spirals"—that is, streams of happy moods, optimistic thoughts, and kind acts that gain momentum, propagate, spill over, and reinforce one another as they unfold.[328] I acquire beautiful-sounding strings for my violin, which delights me, which prompts my daughter to laugh and give me a hug, which leads me to feel competent and grateful, which galvanizes me to bring my husband his favorite coffee drink, which reinforces our marriage. Sometimes it's amazing how spending money on a single item—in this case, one that supports a gratifying hobby—can precipitate so many happy repercussions.

Which types of activities should we pay for that will satisfy our needs for competence, autonomy, and relatedness? It depends on the person. For one, it may be purchasing software that will improve her French, flying out to visit an old friend, or buying a surprise gift for a teacher. For another, it may be something entirely different, depending on his circumstances, preferences, and talents. Furthermore, many kinds of activities not only bring pleasure in the moment, but satisfy multiple needs simultaneously. Traveling to a distant land in order to aid victims of a natural disaster, for instance (or to repair cleft palates), is a contribution to a community, an opportunity to learn basic nursing or construction skills, and a chance to forge new lifelong bonds. Indeed, spending money on need-satisfying activities may yield more "bang for the buck" than any other strategy.

SPEND MONEY ON OTHERS, NOT YOURSELF

Having money means that we have the ability to contribute substantively to our communities and even change the world. Whether through philanthropy (e.g., donating to the local school district or helping immunize whole nations) or sharing our wealth with family and friends, our money can profoundly influence our own and others' happiness. Perhaps surprisingly to some, the wealthier the individual, the smaller percentage of his or her income goes to charity, with American families making over $300,000 a year donating a mere 4 percent of their incomes and billionaires donating even less.[329]

In a groundbreaking set of studies, University of British Columbia professor Elizabeth Dunn and her collaborators set out to test the notion that money *can* buy happiness, but only if it's spent pro-socially—that is, when we invest in others rather than in ourselves.[330] First, they surveyed a nationally representative sample of over six hundred U.S. residents on their spending habits, and found that the more they spent their money on gifts for others and charitable donations, the happier they were. Notably, the amount they spent on gifts for themselves, bills, and expenses was unrelated to their happiness. Next, the researchers asked similar questions of employees before and after they had received a sizable financial windfall—namely, a bonus from their company averaging $5,000. Surprisingly, the extent to which the bonus boosted the employees' happiness depended neither on its size nor on whether it was spent on buying something for themselves, on bills or expenses, or on mortgage or rent payments. What did matter to happiness was what percentage of the bonus was spent on charities or buying something for others.

Both of these studies are correlational, which means that we cannot definitively conclude that it was the pro-social spending that caused greater happiness as opposed to the reverse. To confirm the direction of the causal link, the same researchers did an experiment in which they approached random people walking about the University of British Columbia campus, handed them an envelope with either $5 or $20 inside, and asked half of them to spend the money in the envelope on an expense, bill, or gift for themselves, but asked the other half to spend the money on a charitable donation or gift for someone else. The instructions and envelopes were handed out in the morning and the spending had to be done by five p.m. When the participants were contacted in the evening, those who had spent the money on others (whether it was $5 or $20) were significantly happier than those who'd consumed it themselves. Indeed, even thinking about spending money on others makes people happier than thinking about spending it on themselves, and this effect has been shown not just with North Americans but East Africans as well.[331]

Why investing our wealth in other people makes us happy seems too obvious a finding to explain.[332] When we give to others, we feel not only more positive about ourselves (that is, as a compassionate, altruistic person) but about the recipients as well (that they are worthy of our kindness and respect). We feel less distressed about the poverty and suffering in the world and in our neighborhoods, and we gain a greater appreciation for our good fortune. We are distracted from our own petty problems and ruminations. Sharing with others, when it's not done anonymously, also, of course, stimulates positive social interactions, generates new friendships and relationships, and improves old ones. Because of all these reasons, as experiments from my own laboratory have shown, extending generosity or kindness is one of the most powerful ways to bolster and sustain well-being.[333]

Even those with modest means are able to contribute a small share of their incomes to others, but those who have an abundance, like Jack Barnes, are truly blessed by the capacity to use their money to change lives. Our money can support hospitals or schools, provide for those who are hungry, offer health care for the ailing, and teach those who are illiterate. On a smaller scale, taking a colleague to lunch, a child to the circus, or a boyfriend to the Lakers game can bring even more joy to the giver than to the receiver.

SPEND MONEY TO GIVE YOU TIME

We live in an age in which time is said to be a more important resource than money. This wasn't always true, of course, and it's still not true for many individuals and cultures. But if you are lucky, you have enough money to afford yourself ample leisure time. The irony is that, in the United States, the more wealth people have, the greater number of hours they work. (This pattern appears to be reversed in Europe.)[334]

If we spend our money to open up more "free" hours in the day—for example, by reducing our work hours (because we already make enough) or paying others to perform time-consuming chores (e.g., fix the plumbing, stand in line at the post office, fill in tedious documents, call airlines)—we can spend our time enjoying those things in life that both empirical and anecdotal evidence suggests make us happy. Essentially, these activities include the kinds of need-satisfying pursuits I discussed earlier—for example, connecting with friends, nurturing intimate relationships, socializing at parties, consuming art, music, and literature, learning new languages and skills, honing talents, and volunteering at our neighborhood hospital, church, or animal shelter. Tellingly, these are precisely the activities that people on the brink of death, like mountaineers caught in a blizzard on Mount Everest,[335] wish they would have spent more time doing in their everyday lives.

Therein lies the rub. The critical issue is how we consume the extra time we buy. If, instead of doing something meaningful, engaging, fruitful, or growth-promoting, we fritter the hours away by mindlessly watching television shows, obsessing over our looks or gadgets, or drifting aimlessly from one undertaking to the next, then happiness will surely not come from riches.

SPEND MONEY NOW, BUT WAIT TO ENJOY IT

A frequently overlooked source of pleasure in purchasing something new—whether a vacation or a telescope—is the anticipation of waiting. Regrettably, many of us equate anticipation with apprehension and waiting with boredom or impatience. I hope to convince you otherwise. Consider the following thought experiment, borrowed from one of my favorite studies. You just learned that you will have the opportunity to kiss your favorite movie star—say, a hot and brilliant actor or actress on whom you have a massive crush. (This is hypothetical, so assume that you are single and available.) Critically, the kiss will take place in either three hours or three days. Which do you prefer? If you are like most people, you will opt to wait three days.[336] Apparently, the pleasure of the anticipation is valued almost as much as the experience being anticipated.

Although researchers have yet to conduct a study in which people's happiness ratings are tracked before, during, and after kissing their favorite celebrity, they have been able to carry off similar investigations with other types of positive experiences. For example, a month before embarking on a guided twelve-day tour of several European cities, eager travelers report expecting to enjoy their trip significantly more than they actually do during the twelve days. Identical results are found when students are surveyed about their expectations three days before their Thanksgiving vacation, and when midwesterners are surveyed three weeks before a bicycle trip across California.[337] Indeed, researchers who studied a thousand Dutch vacationers concluded that by far the greatest amount of happiness extracted from the vacation is derived from the anticipation period, a finding that suggests that we should not only prolong that period but aim to take several small vacations rather than one mega-vacation.[338]

The time period between the day we purchase something (a future trip, fancy Italian dinner, or expensive champagne) and the day we actually collect it appears to possess special qualities, giving us the opportunity to share our anticipation and plans with friends, to relish the future object or experience (e.g., fantasize about cycling through the Tuscany countryside), and to plan and prepare for it (e.g., fast the day before the five-star meal). For my fortieth birth-

day, my husband took me on a surprise trip. He told me vaguely
what to pack, drove us to the airport, and held my boarding pass so
I couldn't make out the destination. Even on the plane, which I
eventually learned was headed to the San Francisco Bay Area, I
couldn't possibly guess all the surprises that the trip promised (and,
remarkably, delivered). My fortieth ended up being by far the best
birthday I'd ever had, with a meal so stunning that we pledged to
name our (unlikely) future child after the chef.[339] But the surprise
trip suffered from one unexpected limitation—I couldn't anticipate
and savor it in advance.

The obvious recommendation from all this research is that we
should pay for our desired object days or weeks before we hold it or
experience it. By this approach, we will always have something wonderful to look forward to in the future. Of course, since the advent
of swift and easy credit, many individuals do the exact reverse, duti-
fully following the principles of economics—instead of paying now
and enjoying later, they enjoy the purchase now and pay for it later.
This opposite approach promotes impulse shopping and, by my
count, encourages at least four of the Seven Deadly Sins (gluttony,
greed, sloth, and lust).[340] Even if we can afford to impulse-buy as
much as we desire, these types of "instant gratification" purchases
are not the types that make us lastingly fulfilled.[341] Instead, defer
the vacation, store the Burgundy, and schedule the gadget delivery
for next month. You'll be happier for it.

DON'T LET SUCCESS MAGNIFY YOUR FAILINGS

In her memoir, Oscar-winning actress Goldie Hawn writes about
how she had initially believed that making it in Hollywood would
make her happy—but it didn't, not at first.

I think I had to become successful to understand . . . that
success only enhances who you are . . . People who are nasty
become nastier. People who are happy become happier. People who are mean hoard their money and live in fear for the
rest of their lives that they will lose it. People who are generous use their gifts to help people and try to make the world a
better place.[342]

We all have friends or partners who bring out or magnify our personalities, preferences, and habits. We grow more liberal when we're
with them or we become more macho, more intellectual or more outgoing, more catty or more coarse. If arriving at the pinnacle of success brings out our greatest strengths and our worst failings, then the
time to prepare for that moment is *now*. Identify the weakness that
you fear might become emphasized and develop a self-improvement
program (based on your grandmother's advice, a self-help video, or
simply common sense) to overcome it. Here are some examples.

Do you have a tendency to be short with the people you employ
or supervise—your office assistant, perhaps, or your gardener or
nanny? If you do, achieving success may lead you to lash out at those
lower on the hierarchy. For the next four weeks, when your are dissatisfied with someone's work, and the urge comes on to be curt or
harsh, resolve to imagine that the person is your therapist, minister,
or boss, and treat them accordingly.

As another case in point, perhaps you have a weakness for impulse purchases on the Web—for buying gadgets, toys for your kids,
and other things that you don't really need. If you do, this quality is
likely to be exacerbated by greater wealth. From now on, make a
decision to wait forty-eight hours whenever you have an itch to shop
and revisit that desire later. Better yet, at the beginning of each
month, write out a list of the items that (1) you really need and

(2) you really desire, and consign yourself to a set spending limit, stipulating that the second list cannot be touched until the first list is exhausted.

Alternatively, do you frequently forget to be appreciative, and are you afraid that success might make it even harder for you to be grateful? Fortunately, you have several empirically supported gratitude exercises to choose from. Resolve to write a letter to yourself each week contemplating a different aspect of your good fortune.

THE PREPARED MIND

When we've achieved—at least on paper—much of what we have always wanted to achieve, life can become dull and even empty. There is little around the corner to look forward to. Many prosperous individuals don't understand why they aren't truly happy and thus may be tempted to conclude that sustained happiness cannot be bought with success, money, or material possessions. As should be obvious from the prime message of this chapter, I believe that this happiness myth is wrong. Don't be a slave to the hedonic treadmill. The practices I describe here will help prevent you from suffering the downside of good fortune. And if you're particularly tenacious or particularly lucky, your efforts will pay considerable hedonic dividends. The key to buying happiness is not in how successful we are, but what we do with it; it's not how high our income is, but how we allocate it.

PART III

LOOKING BACK

THE primes of adulthood, middle age, and beyond beget a number of critical turning points, involving summoning up our pasts, muddling through the present, and managing the adversities that no life, however lucky, can elude. This is a time of life when our unfulfilled potential can seem increasingly salient to us, when we may wonder whether some of the years behind us were just frittered away, when we yearn to be young again, when we weigh our regrets and grapple with the might-have-beens. What's more, these significant yet foreseeable life passages are likely to instigate crisis points for us if we believe that we cannot possibly be happy after an inauspicious diagnosis, after we realize that the time to achieve many of our dreams has run out, or when we're "old and gray." It's time to reconsider these fear-fueled beliefs and discover healthier strategies to respond to life's passages and revelations.

CHAPTER 8

I Can't Be Happy When . . .
the Test Results Were Positive

Some reckonings involve a dawning realization or an epiphany. Others involve events beyond our control that slam us rather than awaken us. Receiving a dire diagnosis or bad news about a health condition represents such an event. In her memoir, *Resilience*, the late Elizabeth Edwards describes learning that her breast cancer had come back—that no longer could she continue believing that she would die of something else. She remembered . . .

. . . what I was wearing, the weather, the words the doctor used, where [husband and daughter] John and Cate sat. From that first tiny hospital room . . . where we first heard the word "cancer" spoken aloud to the basement room with a bed and a sink where John and I sat for hours waiting for the results of the bone scan and the CT, to the latest room . . . where we heard that it was no longer contained and had spread to a couple of new places, the quiet life-changing moments grow to an imposing size. . . . The cancer was back. Well, I suppose the doctors would say that it had never really gone. In that moment, when I found out for certain that I would have cancer in me every single day until the one day it finally took my life, all the reasons to live and the reasons to die, the way to live if I could, all danced before me . . . until I chose a partner from among them. Live. Die. Fight. Curl up. Look for a hug. Give a hug. Cry. Cry. Cry. [343]

When we reluctantly consider such shifts in circumstances happening to *us*—or when our worst fears are realized—we can't imagine getting beyond the crying and despairing stage. We can't imagine experiencing happiness again. I hope to convince you in this chapter that your reactions and forebodings about this worst-case scenario are governed by one of the myths of happiness. Much can be done in the face of positive test results to increase the chances that your time living with illness will not be all misery and purposelessness—indeed, that it can be a time of growth and meaning—with hundreds of studies to substantiate it.

YOU SEE WHAT YOU AGREE TO SEE

When we receive a fateful diagnosis, we are compelled to focus on a particular piece of information or problem, and to call to mind specific details or symptoms, even when we don't wish to. However, even in this situation, when bad things happen *to* us, it turns out that we have a lot more control over our realities than we believe. Edwards understood that her disease would eventually take her life. When it would do so was not under her control, but what *was* under her control is what the disease takes away from the here and now. She wrote:

Part of resisting the disease is captured in simply not letting the fear of tomorrow control the quality of today . . . Powering through the fear may seem like denial, but fear doesn't change the prognosis. It only changes the way I would feel between now and whenever the inevitable occurs.[344]

Appreciating this idea—that we have the power to decide what our experience is and isn't, that we have the power to settle on what our life has been like in the past and will be like in the future—has life-changing potential.[345] Consider that during every minute of your day, you are choosing to pay attention to some things and opting to ignore, overlook, suppress, or withdraw from most other things. What you choose to focus on becomes part of your life and the rest falls out. You may have a chronic illness, for example, and you can spend most of your days dwelling on how it has ruined your life, or you can spend your days focusing on your gym routine, or getting to know your nieces, or connecting to your spiritual side. We can change our lives simply by changing our attitudes of mind.[346]

This approach to illness is captured in one of my favorite quotes of all time, from the 1890 *Principles of Psychology*. "My experience is what I agree to attend to," the philosopher William James wrote. "Only those items which I notice shape my mind."[347] This idea— which is really mind-boggling when we think about it—suggests that our life experience is that on which *we choose to focus*. If we are not seeing, hearing, or otherwise sensing something, it's as though it doesn't even exist—at least not for us. Why is it that sometimes the prospects for our health seem bleak and at other times rife with promise? Why does time race sometimes and at other times stand still? Because a large part of how we experience the world is determined by what we concentrate on. Out of the myriad stimuli in our environments—our current trains of thought, memories, and anticipations; the faces, needs, and conversations of other people in our lives; all the sights and sounds surrounding us; and all the objects in our sightline, natural and human-made—we ultimately choose (or feel compelled to focus on) a few, and disregard all others. This process of homing in is actually adaptive, promoting our survival. Human beings could not possibly attend to everything available to their senses; if they did, they would be overloaded, overwhelmed, and rendered entirely dysfunctional. (For example, the disease of schizophrenia, which leads to complete impairment when untreated, is characterized in part by the brain's failure to filter out irrelevant information; schizophrenics are bombarded by too many stimuli, of which they have great difficulty making sense.[348]) Indeed, the very term "to pay attention" implies a cost—a hedonic stake, perhaps—that we must forfeit. When we pay attention to one thing, we necessarily cannot pay attention to other things. The cost is both in the energy it takes and in the objects of our attention that we must necessarily forsake.

Most of us know at least one person who is prone to zone out from time to time, and when he does so, we have the distinct impression that he is entering his own little world. The "own little world" metaphor is actually more accurate than we think. Try to recall the last time you had a conversation with a group of people—say, while having lunch with colleagues or chatting with fellow parents while waiting to pick up your kids. Would you be surprised to learn that the different members of your group were focusing on entirely different things? One may have been so distraught by recent heartbreaking news that it was all she could think about. Another's heart was racing because his crush had just walked in. A third may have had difficulty focusing on anything but the fact that his shoulder was in tremendous pain. And another person may have been having intrusive thoughts about her next day's appointment. In short, it would not be inaccurate to say that, although the several individuals in the group were essentially in the same situation at that moment, each of them was residing in a separate subjective social world.

This makes the question of what "reality" is rather thorny. Your reality is different from my reality and the difference comes from what each of us spends our time selectively focusing on. The memories that shape the story of your life—and of mine—are subject to the same constraint; I may choose (perhaps subconsciously) to remember particular facts about my earlier years (or even yesterday), and you may choose to remember something quite different. As a result, sometimes two individuals will share a set of experiences (e.g., growing up together or caring for a sick child together), yet when they look back at that shared past, their recollections and perceptions are so divergent that it's as though they didn't share the same set of experiences at all.

One of my favorite studies provides empirical support for this "different realities" idea.[349] Both members of a couple were asked to check off what activities and events had taken place in their lives during the previous week. For example, last week, did you and your spouse have a fight? Watch television together? Have sex? Attend a sporting event? Deal with a problem with the kids? The amazing finding from this study is that husbands and wives completely failed to agree with each other. Indeed, if a stranger instead of your husband had filled out the questionnaire and had merely guessed what events took place in your family life last week, his answers would have matched yours as well as your husband's answers. In short, these findings suggest that your spouse is experiencing a totally different world from you.

Although the reasons for some of our unique "worlds" have to do with the slings and arrows that outrageous fortune dispenses us, researchers have discovered a great deal about how we can go about shaping those worlds consciously and deliberately. Perhaps in no situation are these lessons more important than when we face a health crisis. In this chapter, I touch on a number of healthy ways to respond when the test results are positive or, better yet, habits to develop long before the day those test results come in.

YOUR FOCUS MATTERS

In brief, psychological science is persuasive about the notion that we have power over what we see, focus on, or overlook. But how do we succeed at the often daunting task of deciding to perceive the world in a particular way, especially when events from that world—bad news, harrowing diagnoses, and everyday torments and insults— often impinge on our attention in a rather compelling way?[350] I will respond by beginning with an admittedly extreme example, bor- rowed from the eminent economist and writer Robert Frank:

> A Holocaust survivor once told me that his existence in the camps took place in two separate psychological spaces. In one he was acutely aware of the unspeakable horror of his situa- tion. But in the other, life seemed eerily normal. In this sec- ond space, each day presented challenges, and days in which he coped relatively successfully with them felt much like the good days of the past. To survive, he explained, it was critical to spend as much time as possible in the second space and as little as possible in the first.[351]

The way this individual was able to accomplish what he did in- volved, in William James's words, "taking possession of the mind"— or focused attention. All of us are capable of this feat, although much effort and commitment may be required. One reason it can feel exhausting to resist depressing pessimistic ruminations about our illness (or to focus on the silver lining) is that these efforts can deplete our vital energy and mental resources. Hence, some researchers argue that we should regularly give our attention a breather.[352] We can do this by sleeping (although there are only so many hours that we can or would wish to sleep) or by relying more on our automatic or habitual behaviors and thoughts, although that can be harmful, too, if we have many bad habits.

Nature's peace. One intriguing suggestion for how we can "rest" our attention when we find ourselves mentally taxed, thereby shoring up our capacity to maintain focus on the things that make us happy (or at least less unhappy), is to spend more time in or around nature. Researchers have found that when we experience natural environments—sitting under an oak tree, viewing a sunset, or even browsing through nature photos—our attention is captivated through our senses (smelling the ocean, picking out the colors of a rainbow), which requires little or no mental effort and allows for reflection.[353] By contrast, when we experience unnatural environments—sitting on a metal bench, watching an airplane, or texting on our phones— our attention is captured dramatically, by force (a police siren, a Toyota billboard), requiring us to muster our mental efforts to direct our attention elsewhere, for example, by trying to read despite the car horns or to ignore the pictures in the ads. It's not surprising, then, that unnatural (typically urban) environments, with all their powerful and ubiquitous distractions, are not very peaceful or relaxing.

So, while urban or artificial environments give rise to weary minds, most people find natural environments restorative; nature boosts happiness and relieves stress.[354] But nature is also restorative with respect to our powers of attention.[355] Spending time rowing on a lake, picnicking under a canopy of birch trees, weeding a garden, or lying flat looking at clouds will replenish our mental resources for dealing with the problems in our lives. For example, one series of studies showed that people who spent fifteen minutes strolling in a natural setting not only experienced more pleasure, but were better able to resolve a minor problem—or "loose end"—in their lives, than people who strolled in an urban setting or those who watched videos of natural settings.[356]

Meditation's peace. Another way for us to develop the ability to redirect our attention—say, from intrusive negative thoughts about our health to pleasant thoughts about an imminent trip—is by training our minds through the practice of meditation strategies. There are many different styles of meditation. They may be rooted in different cultural traditions and rely on different techniques, but, at their core, most of the techniques share a great deal in common. Meditation involves relaxing our bodies, practicing our breathing, and being mindful of the here and now. It is usually done in a special place, set aside for that very purpose, and away from quotidian concerns. One of its central goals is to achieve an inner quietness or stillness, free from the seemingly automatic thoughts that trickle constantly through our minds.

Despite the diversity of meditation techniques practiced around the world and throughout history, three methods stand out. The first, used in Hindu meditation, involves repeating a word or phrase (aka mantra or incantation). A second technique (in Buddhist meditation) involves focusing on our breathing, which fortuitously is always with us, or on repetitive activities like sweeping a floor or folding cloth (in Zen meditation). Finally, a frequently used meditation technique, which is somewhat hard to describe, requires that we let our thoughts run through our head without interfering with them. That is, we simply observe our thoughts passively and roll with them, without being judgmental about them or trying to grasp them or push them away. In each of these techniques, when we find ourselves faltering (e.g., we let an intrusive thought upset us or we permit our attention to wander away from our breath), we are taught to monitor and recognize the failure and to bring our focus back.

Thus, the more we practice meditation, the better we get at noticing when our mind is wandering, the better we get at disengaging with an undesired object (e.g., the thought "I can't manage this"), and the better we get at redirecting our attention onto a desired object (the thought "I'm strong").

Why do people meditate? Many do it out of a desire to find a respite from the grinds, stresses, and distractions of daily life, to achieve a sense of peace and tranquility, and to regain energy and concentration. Getting to that place is very difficult, requiring a great deal of effort, practice, discipline, focus, skill, and even struggle. However, the benefits are vast. In experiments in which people are prompted to practice meditation (versus a neutral activity), meditation has been found to enhance empathy (as shown by brain circuits linked to empathy "lighting up" in brain imaging studies during meditative states), foster bursts of positive emotion, alleviate stress and health symptoms, strengthen immune function, and even increase intelligence scores.[357] Of greatest interest are findings of meditation's salutary effect on attention.[358] As we might expect, when we devote time and effort and persistence to practicing meditation, our capacity to focus, direct, and redirect our attention significantly improves.

In sum, the power of attention. What we focus on, what we pay attention to, what we selectively see in our worlds is critical. If we choose to attend to the fact that we are still capable of climbing the stairs and choose to ignore the family member who always makes us feel guilty, we are in effect single-handedly and powerfully weakening the influence of the environment—of the world's slings and arrows—on our well-being. When we are confronting illness or any grave prospect, what we choose to attend to governs, in large part, the quality of our life.

THE MATTHEW EFFECT

- The rush of a sugar high from a dense dark chocolate

- A throaty laugh

- A sip of fine dry wine

- A well-deserved day off

- The glow of a supervisor's praise

- A moment of connection with a child

- A satisfying cry

- A feeling of oneness

- A flash of awe in a museum

These are the big and small moments, indulgences, fulfillments, and hard-won gratifications that add sunshine to your life. They don't seem to belong in a chapter about positive test results, yet you will see that they do. As I described earlier, a growing body of research by Barbara Fredrickson and others has now shown that bursts of positive emotion and pleasure not only *feel* good, they *are* good—good for you, your friends, families, communities, and even the society at large. [359] In other words, positive emotions have tangible and enduring consequences for your intellectual facility, social competence, psychological resources, and even your physical skills. Furthermore, positive emotional experiences generate so-called upward spirals. Pleasure begets pleasure, which enhances your immune system; renders you friendlier and more approachable; leads you to be more productive, more creative, and more persistent at achieving your goals; compels you to see your life as more meaningful; and bolsters your capacity to deal with conflict, stress, and setbacks.[360] So, positive emotions engender success, and success begets yet more success. Sociologists called this the Matthew effect,[361] after the parable found in the Gospel of Matthew: "For to all those who have, more will be given, and they will have an abundance."[362] Fortunately, the richer you are in positive emotions, the richer you will become in all domains of life—your work, your relationships, your leisure, and your health.

In my teaching, research, and interviews with regular people, I have been amazed to learn that most people are surprisingly unaware of which experiences make them happy (or curious, enthusiastic, tranquil, affectionate, absorbed, or proud) and which do not. For this reason, I began teaching people to keep a "daily experience" journal to track their emotions at specific times throughout their day (say, at 9 a.m., 2 p.m., and 7 p.m. every day for a week) and document which events, situations, people, or activities attend these emotions. So, for example, at 9 a.m. on Tuesday, to what extent were you feeling confident, happy, tense, calm, or engaged? Where were you? At home, in your car, in a coffee shop? Were you alone or interacting with someone (and, if so, with whom)? What exactly were you doing? This is a simple and effective way to determine which daily experiences generate positive emotions for you. Once you know that you always laugh with Gary, stay engaged and focused listening to world news, are affectionate with your cat, and feel joyful eating sushi in the park, you should try to partake of those things more often and to savor them more when you do.

Are such positive experiences too run-of-the-mill to truly impact our happiness and help us cope with real hardships? Given what we know about the benefits of positive emotions, should we strive to experience big, intense highs rather than aiming for frequent ordinary bursts of pleasure? In chapter 6, I recommended that we spend our money on many small pleasures rather than a few big ones. This is because the results of research favor the ordinary over the intense. It turns out that the key to happiness and health (and to all of their auspicious by-products) is not how intensely happy we feel, but how *often* we feel positive or happy.[363] For example, in a study that followed people aged eighteen to ninety-four over the course of thirteen years, those with more frequent positive moments (but not more intense positive moments) lived longer.[364] Indeed, seemingly trivial behaviors can offer regular mood boosts that cumulate over time. As researchers from MIT, Harvard, and Duke have written, "One cannot win the lottery every day, but one can exercise or attend religious services regularly, and these repeated behaviors may be enough to increase well-being over time."[365] These researchers tested the idea by surveying a gym, two yoga classes, and thirty-seven places of worship for twelve religions. As expected, they found that working out several days a week and attending religious services each week supplied people with a stream of reliable (albeit small) boosts to their happiness. Furthermore, the more frequently they participated in those activities, the happier they were.

The scientific evidence delivers three kernels of wisdom—first, that short bursts of gladness, tranquility, or delight are not trivial at all; second, that it's frequency, not intensity, that counts; and third, most of us seem not to know this. If you come to understand which individuals, situations, places, things, or even times of day make you feel happy, and then practice increasing the regularity of such moments, you will gain a hedonic tool that will serve you well in times of crisis, when the doctor delivers bad news, and beyond.

IS IT OKAY TO BE HAPPY AMIDST SUFFERING?

I fully recognize that talk of seeking pleasure during a health crisis makes some people cringe. Indeed, the notion that it's permissible and even desirable to be happy amidst suffering—whether your own or that of others—seems distasteful. You can't—and shouldn't—be truly happy when a close friend is dying of cancer or when you know you will soon lose your ability to hear or see or drive, or when you grasp all too clearly that the world is awash with poverty, war, oppression, and evil. You can't be happy when children are hurting, when many people's lives unfurl in quiet desperation, when dreams are broken and social ills are ubiquitous.

My response to this somewhat self-indulgent question is threefold. First, recognize how much unjust suffering exists in the world and respond by being grateful for your own good fortune. Second, know that deferring your own happiness until all your friends' and the world's problems are solved is not helpful to anyone. Of course, we need to witness and work to redress unhappiness and pain. However, as a great deal of research shows, the happier we are, the better positioned we are to accomplish just that. The happier we are, the more energy, confidence, and motivation we have. The happier we are, the healthier we are, and thus the more productive and creative, more approach-oriented, and more likely to reach out to others. So my final argument is that if we work on and succeed at realizing our own happiness, we will be relatively more likely to help others—and ourselves—as well.

WHAT ABOUT NEGATIVE EMOTIONS?

We know now that positive emotions bring numerous rewards, but are negative emotions ever a good thing? Undeniably, they are.

There are times and situations when we need to feel the anger that motivates us to battle exploitation or injustice, the anxiety that aids us in preparing for a threat or challenge, or the sadness that prompts us to reflect on what is going wrong and to take steps to fix it or accept it. Indeed, in the next section, I describe a theory that suggests that we need to experience the immediate negative emotional aftermath of an upheaval before the positive and healing adjustments can commence. Furthermore, some studies show that, in particular situations, mild negative emotions (like sad mood) can promote better judgments and less stereotyping. Finally, negative experiences can serve as a contrast to the positives in our lives and help us appreciate them. A cherished friend had a close call with death after an infection rendered him paralyzed and unable to eat or breathe on his own for weeks. He recovered, but after the illness, he said that things that used to be only mildly positive—like a sunny day, drinking a Diet Coke, or talking on the phone with one of his grown kids—became intensely positive. Some cultures even deem suffering as a means to an end—for building character or obtaining spiritual salvation—or even as an end in itself. "You can't die yet—you haven't suffered enough!" is a traditional reply in Greece to someone complaining of poor health.

There is value in sadness. There is value in recognizing one's own (and the world's) problems and ills. There is value in learning the lesson that life is not always good or fair. Suffering, however, is never a good thing. Much of the suffering that people endure is agonizing, undeserved, and leads to nothing good.

EVIDENCE-BASED STRATEGIES FOR COPING WITH BAD NEWS

A serious illness can break or splinter many things—our self-esteem, our relationships, our physical body, our religious faith, our hope and optimism, our energy, our stride. How do we put the pieces back together after they have been torn apart? At times this may seem impossibly difficult to accomplish. When a loved one is gone or we have lost the function of something really critical (an arm, a kidney, our sense of smell), we cannot really glue things back together like they were before. The only thing we can hope for is to create a brand-new structure out of what remains. I know this all sounds very abstract, but there is an instructive story that illuminates this notion.[366]

Once upon a time, there lived a painter. He was very good at what he did, but what he really wanted to be successful at was woodworking. One day, the painter's wife said that their family needed a new table, and asked him if he could help. He was very happy, as he loved his wife and wanted to make her happy, and he really wanted to work in wood. He labored many days and nights and fashioned a plain but very strong and solid table. This table became the center of the painter's household. It's where the family gathered for stories, meals, tea, and board games. The painter and his wife kneaded pizza dough on that table and wrote letters to their loved ones and helped their children with their cursive. The table was strong and solid, just like their family.

One day when the family was away, a thief broke into their house and, for reasons they never fathomed, stole one of the table's legs. The artist and his wife were despondent, but they loved that table so much, they decided to make the best of it, even if it now only had three legs. However, the surface of the table had become uneven, so whenever they placed anything on the side with the missing leg, that object would slide right off. So they tried to put a very big and heavy book on the opposite side, to balance the table, but that didn't work out, either. The book took up too much space and the opposite leg started to bow under its weight. The table was in danger of collapsing.

The artist was filled with sorrow. He took the table back to his workshop and worked and worked on it for many nights. He chiseled and etched and molded and sculpted. At last, he emerged from the workshop with a new table. It was quite a bit smaller, but it was lovely and just as strong and functional as the old one had been. This new table had only three legs.

After a health crisis, the new you is like that new three-legged table. Whether your diagnosis is cancer or diabetes, lung disease or infertility, you may have been solid and strong before your life had changed, but now, for reasons you may never know, a part of you has been taken away. At first, you may vainly try to maintain a sense of balance within yourself—striving to balance your work and family and mental health—but you still keep wobbling. You put in Herculean efforts to compensate for what you had lost to keep everything from hurtling to the floor. However, you cannot really put yourself and your life back together again. You must create a new you, which you hope will be just as solid and healthy as the old you, but it will be different. Apparently, a triangle is a stronger geometric figure than a square, which is why triangles are so frequently observed in nature (to make molecules—like proteins and DNA—superstrong), as well as used in construction.[367] Two evidence-based theories I describe below will equip you with some strategies you will need to cope with bad news, such that the new you, like the three-legged table, can be stronger, too.

MOBILIZE-AND-MINIMIZE

Coping is what we all do when we try to respond to, manage, or deal with bad things that happen to us. Researchers have been studying coping for many decades, and they now know a great deal about which types of coping strategies work and which do not, for whom, and in what situations. One of the most powerful approaches comes from UCLA professor Shelley Taylor, who argues that a threatening life event such as a serious illness typically engenders in us two consecutive reactions—a short-term one followed by a long-term one.[368]

Mobilizing. Our first response—which is immediate and fairly short-lived—is to marshal resources to deal with the negative event (e.g., the initial diagnosis, the emergence of new distressing symptoms, or the realization of a deterioration). For example, at the doctor's office, we might instantly become physiologically aroused (e.g., demonstrating increased heart rate and faster breathing—a physical response), start to dwell on how we might have prevented it (which is a cognitive or thought-related response), get depressed (an emotional response), or seek out a shoulder to cry on (a social response).

Minimizing. Our second, more long-term reaction to negative or traumatic experiences involving our health comes when the initial threat of the horrible news has subsided: Our minds and bodies then act to essentially reverse or minimize those initial responses. For example, our body damps down the arousal we may initially have experienced (by slowing heart rate and breathing), our thoughts turn to positive explanations (excusing our own behavior or calling forth pleasant memories to offset the negative ones), our negative emotions of sadness or anxiety turn to relief or relaxation, and our behaviors might involve reciprocating any help we might have obtained earlier.

Taylor's work suggests that we need to recognize our two separate tendencies to respond to a threatening piece of news—the first involving mobilizing ourselves (e.g., crying, heart racing, imagining that our lives are over) and the second, which occurs hours, days, or even months later, involving working to minimize those same responses (e.g., soothing ourselves or thinking more hopeful thoughts). The mobilize-and-minimize theory supports the notion that our first response to a bad situation—while sometimes necessary or inescapable—is not the ultimate or the optimal response. "Time heals all wounds" is a version of the same story.

THE BAD-NEWS RESPONSE MODEL

Another theory of coping, developed by health psychologist Kate Sweeny, attempts to address the specific question: What should we do when the doctor delivers bad news? Sweeny's research points to three possible responses: (1) *watchful waiting* (e.g., staying vigilant, but redirecting our attention to other things), (2) *active change* (e.g., taking action, like doing lots of research on our condition and perhaps signing up for a new, aggressive treatment), and (3) *acceptance* (e.g., making the best of the change in our life and seeking out others for support).[369] Although these three general responses may seem fairly obvious, what is not obvious is which one is best in a given situation. Fortunately, a simple algorithm or formula, illustrated in the flowchart below, can help. First, ask yourself these three questions, and follow the arrows in the chart:

- Is the diagnosis *severe*? (Yes/No)

- Are negative consequences *likely* to occur? (Yes/No)

- Are the consequences *controllable*? (Yes/No)

If the answer is somewhere in between yes and no, choose the one that's closest to the truth.

Studies suggest, for example, that watchful waiting is appropriate in several different situations. One is when the bad news is not severe, the negative repercussions are unlikely, and the situation may or may not be under your control. For example, you have learned that you have a mass in one of your bones. It may be nothing, so you wait and obtain bone scans every six months. Similar advice would be given to someone in the same, but more severe, situation—for example, the bad news is that you are at risk for suffering a blood clot, but this is unlikely to happen and there's nothing you can do anyway, so you take a "wait and see" approach. This is difficult to do. No wonder that patience is a virtue; the word comes from the Latin *pati,* which means "to suffer." Finally, when the bad news you re-

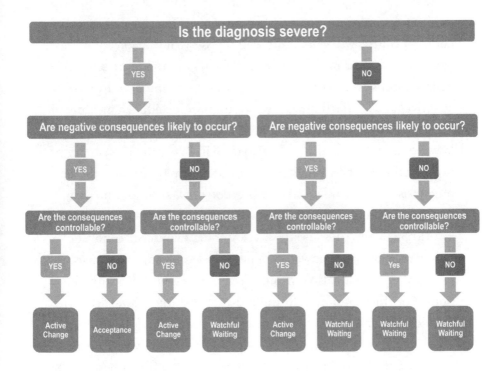

ceive is not severe but very probable (e.g., the tests indicate a likely kidney stone), but there is nothing you can do to prevent it, then again the optimal reaction is to watch and wait.

If your situation is to some extent controllable and it is either severe *or* has a high likelihood of negative consequences, or both, then active change is the optimal option. For example, you have breast cancer, and several efficacious treatment options are available. However, bad news that is severe, with negative and uncontrollable implications, calls for acceptance. Your best bet is to manage your emotional reactions to it (called "emotion-focused coping") rather than doing something to address the problem (called "problem-focused coping").

Research shows that selecting the appropriate response—when done in the thoughtful, systematic way described above—can help guide us toward the most desirable outcome. The nature of that outcome, of course, will vary, but I would posit that it involves the least amount of distress in the long term (distress in the short term, like what happens when we "mobilize," is both common and probably adaptive) and satisfaction with your progress, including a measure of happiness in the present and hope for the future. Finally, if you follow the implications of the chart, you will boost the probability of experiencing the best prognosis for your future health and the best prognosis for your other critical life domains, such as your family relationships and productivity at work.

Although the bad-news response model may seem simplistic at first glance, it is very powerful. The model is meant to apply to the majority of individuals confronting a wide variety of health situations. For this reason, the formula depicted in the flowchart is tremendously versatile and adaptable to many of us. That being so, this is one of the rare situations that I recommend following a general formula rather than identifying the one step that fits us best. To be sure, precisely how we engage in watchful waiting, acceptance, or active change will be influenced by what is right for us, our support systems, and our unique circumstances and goals.

THE CONFIDANTS THAT LIGHTEN YOUR BURDENS

No one can truly ever be prepared for a tragedy, geared up for adversity, or ready for a health crisis. However, much like buying storm windows or carrying a spare tire in the trunk, we can gather and hone the tools that we will need when that dark day inevitably comes. One such tool—an indispensable one at that—is social support. As I discussed in chapter 2, the effects of sharing troubles and obtaining help from a friend, companion, lover, family member, or even a pet are almost magical in their power.

Drawing on decades of research on the importance of relationships, best-selling psychology textbook author David Myers came to the following conclusion: "There are few better remedies for unhappiness than an intimate friendship with someone who cares deeply about you. Confiding is good for soul and body."[370] Indeed, as I alluded earlier, in the presence of social support, our bodies don't react as acutely to stress. For example, a companion—whether a human or a dog—reduces our heart rate and blood pressure when we are doing something really challenging or stressful, like waiting in the doctor's office for the latest test results;[371] and having someone nearby—or simply looking at a photo of a loved one!—renders pain far less excruciating.[372]

The health benefits of social support are particularly important to consider when we have been diagnosed with a grave condition. For example, having one or more close individuals in our lives on whom we can rely has been found to be as important a protective factor with regard to whether or not we develop a chronic disease or die as are well-established risk factors like smoking, having high blood pressure, and being inactive and obese.[373] Women who have good social support live 2.8 years longer than women who don't, and the longevity difference for men is 2.3 years.[374] If that finding still does not impress you, consider the fact that social support insulates us against declines in cognitive functioning that precede dementia,[375] protects us from catching colds, and improves our prognosis after a diagnosis of heart disease or cancer.[376]

In sum, if there ever was a magic pill for health and happiness, social support would be it. Indeed, maintaining close, fulfilling, and emotionally supportive relationships is probably the single best way to prepare for a future fateful diagnosis or any kind of tragedy or crisis. When it happens, they will be there to help you cope— tangibly, emotionally, financially—and you will recover faster and endure with greater strength and courage.

BUILDING A LEGACY, PURPOSE, AND MEANING

Every grim diagnosis suggests an inevitable inching closer to death. With an increased awareness of our mortality, coupled with our instinct for self-preservation, comes unbearable anxiety. Researchers argue that we manage this anxiety by pursuing meaning in our lives.[377] As much as we might fear death, we fear dying insignificant and unloved even more. As a result, we are driven to do something that will make our lives count in the larger picture and leave a lasting mark on the world that persists beyond our individual selves and lifetimes.

How much meaning and purpose do you have in your own life right now? Below are items from two different but related scales—

one that measures our sense of meaningfulness and belongingness (items 1 to 5), and one that measures whether we are undergoing a crisis of meaning, that is, judging our lives as empty and meaningless (items 6 to 10).[378] Determine whether you agree or disagree with, or feel neutral (neither agree nor disagree) about each of these statements.

_____ 1. I think that there is meaning in what I do.

_____ 2. I have a task in life.

_____ 3. I feel part of a bigger whole.

_____ 4. I lead a fulfilled life.

_____ 5. I think my life has a deeper meaning.

_____ 6. When I think about the meaning of my life, I find only emptiness.

_____ 7. My life seems meaningless.

_____ 8. I don't see any sense in life.

_____ 9. I suffer from the fact that I don't see any point in life.

_____ 10. My life seems empty.

The good news is that our sense of meaning rises steadily after we reach adulthood. It appears that meaningfulness is at its nadir when we are teenagers, rises steadily until age thirty-five, remains stable from thirty-five to forty-five, and rises again starting at forty-five and beyond.[379] However, a frightening setback can make us question what we are doing on this earth. If you disagree with any of the first five items and if you agree with any of the last five items, then I would recommend making the pursuit of meaning in life one of your priorities.

There are many ways to find meaning and purpose. One is to establish the metric by which our life will be judged and, from today, to resolve to live each day in such a way that our life will be graded a success. Twelve-year-old Jesse's journey, for example, began with double vision, which turned out to be the first symptom of a brain tumor. In the two months following the diagnosis, she underwent chemotherapy, thirty rounds of radiation, and countless doctor visits. In those early days at the hospital, she would cry for hours, but after a while, she turned to the other patients. Jesse discovered that she found special kinship with the young kids and teens at the hospital who couldn't return home between treatments. Thus, instead of brooding about herself and allowing her illness to define her, she started thinking about others. With her family's and her church's help, she founded a nonprofit foundation, where donors can send "joy jars" to children—containers filled with t-shirts, candy, toys, and other age-appropriate items. Each one sold pays for another that she gives away. Although the final outcome is uncertain, as long as Jesse is alive, she has found meaning by boosting young patients' spirits and encouraging them never to give up as they battle their illnesses.[380]

Like Jesse, for many people, the pursuit of life purpose can be rooted in their desire to help others who are suffering, but it doesn't have to be. Many of us find meaning by linking our existence to something outside ourselves. This "something" may be other people (e.g., imparting our values to our children, who will outlive us, or improving the lives of the less fortunate), institutions (e.g., volunteering for a school or environmental agency), value systems (e.g., blogging about the importance of stem-cell research or auto safety

or whatever cause we care about), or God (e.g., praying or prosely-
tizing our faith). Essentially, we are striving to achieve what researchers call symbolic immortality or a positive personal legacy—for
example, by producing a child or a work of art that will outlive us,
believing in the afterlife, investing in the well-being of future generations (perhaps via community activism), or simply making someone's life better in the future (via mentoring or teaching).

Such personal life meaning can be gained in numerous ways and
will depend on the fit between our preferences and values and the
activities we choose to pursue (e.g., art if we are artistic, worship if
we are religious, community service if we are sociable, and technical
achievement if we are scientific).[381] As a result, no matter how terrified we are of our medical prognosis or our approaching death, feeling that we are part of something larger than ourselves—whether it's
our church, our family, or even our nation—supplies us with a rud-
der to steer the rest of our life course and leads us to feel more cen-
tered and secure.[382]

THE PREPARED MIND

"Your test results were positive" are some of our most dreaded words.
The crossroads we face at that moment involves wallowing in despair versus moving on, living in the present versus poisoning our
future. Once we stop accepting that our situation is the end of happiness, we will be prepared to take action—to embrace, adjust to, or
make the best of each and every day. If moving on or savoring the
present moment seems daunting or even unthinkable today, don't be
concerned. The mobilize-and-minimize theory suggests that our
immediate reactions, which often involve painful thoughts and feel-

ings, will be short-lived, and the healthy, long-term responses will take time to unfold.

So, instead of wallowing, make one or more of the recommendations I described a weekly goal, depending on what feels right to you. For example, you may choose to build and/or reinforce your social support network (e.g., call an old friend and offer your ear) or hone your powers of attention by learning to meditate or simply to be more mindful. Another time, you may resolve to begin setting time each day to enjoy the outdoors (even it means contemplating the clouds outside your window on a frigid day) or learning what situations leave you in a pleasant mood and replicating them on a regular basis. Last but not least, take at least one step each week in the direction that helps you attain purpose in your life and secures your legacy.

CHAPTER 9

I Can't Be Happy When . . . I Know I'll Never Play Shortstop for the Yankees

- I'll never be a doctor or an astronaut.

- I'll never sleep with a lingerie model.

- I'll never be first violin or a prima ballerina.

- I'll never live in Italy.

- I'll never have kids.

- I'll never make as much money as Warren Buffett.

- I'll never be a guest on the *Oprah Winfrey Show.*

- I'll never be thin.

We all have dreams. Some of these dreams we contemplate often and share with others. Other dreams we may have harbored in earlier years or in childhood and have kept them buried in our nether regions. For example, my former classmate Jason, after much early success, gave up on his dream of being an Olympic moving-target shooter, and my old friend Jennifer, after a decade of acting classes, voice lessons, auditions, and rejections, finally relinquished her dream of being a Broadway star. Jennifer and Jason both devoted years of their lives to follow their treasured dreams, and they both failed. But as they look back on the past and acknowledge their regrets, Jennifer is bitter and remorseful, jettisoning all reminders of her acting life, while Jason is gratified and proud of his earlier efforts and achievements. Why do people respond so differently? I believe a great part of the cause lies in our assumptions about whether we can still be happy despite not having realized our dreams. If we strive to change this flawed perspective, then we can learn to approach our life's regrets in the most optimal, mature, and satisfaction-enhancing ways.

When the door to a long-held dream closes, we care deeply, even if we had relinquished that desire long ago, or we never really supposed we would achieve it, or lacked the talent or the dedication to arrive there. If you fear heights, then why regret never being able to fly commercial jets? But, alas, human beings are not always entirely rational. This chapter is about how to thrive and grow in the face of profound disappointment, remorse, and regret.

HOW TO ATTAIN GREATER COMPLEXITY, MATURITY, AND HAPPINESS: EXPLORING YOUR "LOST POSSIBLE SELVES"

Laura King, a professor at the University of Missouri–Columbia, studies our "lost possible selves"—or forsaken goals—and the ways we respond to them.[383] Her work has focused on three groups of people, each of whom possesses a unique set of lost possible selves. The first group is parents who have children with Down syndrome—children who will never be self-supporting, destined never to have their own careers or families. The second is gay men and lesbians, who will never experience the kind of traditional, culturally endorsed family life that their parents have desired for them; they will not be as fully accepted by society as their straight peers. The final group is divorced women of long-established marriages, who are unlikely to grow old with their long-loved partners. As distinctive as these people's situations are, the ways that their life stories play out—and the manner in which they reflect on their lost goals—turn out to have tremendous implications for the rest of us, who have our own unique burdens of personal "lost" selves.

Let's begin with the premise that setbacks, disappointments, missteps, and regrets are inevitable in life.[384] Ninety percent of us, in fact, acknowledge harboring severe regrets.[385] Although reflecting on things that we could have done, but didn't, or things that we did, but shouldn't have, or on awful things that happened to us over which we had no control, makes us feel bad in the present moment, King argues that the capacity to genuinely accept and confront one's regrets—to reflect on what might have been—can only be accomplished by a mature individual. The intriguing twist is that this process of reflecting on regrets can itself accelerate maturity. Thus, having lost possible selves—lost prospects and lost goals—can be seen as an opportunity to develop and mature into a more complex and ultimately happier human being.

How does this happen? After all, relinquishing our cherished goals is extremely difficult. We have to cope with the implications that perhaps our abilities just don't cut it or our resources are not sufficient. It means accepting the possibility that we were wrong to strive for a highly valued goal—whether it was to play in a garage band or to live in a mountain cabin or to have three children. And, of course, it means resigning ourselves to the fact that we will never reap the rewards of attaining that goal. However, psychologists argue that to be truly unburdened by regrets involves freeing ourselves from those lost possible selves—the neurosurgeon self, the grandparent self, the handsome self, the small-business owner self.[386] In a sense, this reckoning moment can be a teachable moment. King describes this process as akin to consulting our life map. In other words, imagine that every year we are moving along a map that includes a timeline, locations, goals, and situations. When a particular goal— say, to make partner in a law firm—becomes untenable, we should refer to that imaginary map, to find that "you are here" spot and ask ourselves, "How did I get here?" and "Where am I heading?"[387]

So if your fantasy was always to play for the Yankees or the Mets,[388] or to visit China, or to be an aunt, revising that fantasy takes psychological work, and this work can prompt newfound understanding and build self-complexity. Indeed, as part of her research, King asks people what is undoubtedly a painful question: "How great would your life have been if only . . . [you hadn't gotten divorced, your child didn't have Down syndrome, you were straight and not gay]?" She has found that the responses people give are incredibly revealing. Analyses of hundreds of people's narratives about their once-hoped-for futures—futures that are no longer possible— suggest ways that we can all achieve the optimal state, namely, that of an individual who has come to terms with legitimate losses in his life *and* whose happiness is grounded in reality. Such a "happy and complex adult," in King's words, is humble, courageous, and has meaning in his life.

If achieving that state seems daunting, we can reassure ourselves that many people have managed it. They have done so by acknowledging that life does not always unfold the way they want it to, that it sometimes genuinely challenges and even flummoxes them, and that even traumatic and distressing events are invaluable for their growth and development. Thus, by reflecting on our lost promises, we gain a new perspective, which enables us to understand ourselves and our lives better and, importantly, to set new priorities and envision new futures for ourselves. In other words, considering our regrets activates us to embark on and strive towards new goals.

But how can we be happy if we are intensely pondering our forsaken goals? Wouldn't all that self-excavation merely make us feel even more miserable and more regretful? In a word, yes. But we must do it—we must admit to ourselves that we have lost a cherished part of ourselves and, at the same time, not be consumed by it. We must acknowledge our regrets and the challenges that we have faced in the past. But there is a critical next step: To move on by committing ourselves to new pursuits, which admittedly may be shaped in part by these past challenges. We must try to focus on the exciting possibilities that lie ahead of us. My classmate Jason was successful at accomplishing this, having faced head-on his regrets about never becoming an Olympian, conceding and accepting them, and resolving to turn in an entirely different direction by playing golf—becoming a weekend warrior rather than a professional. So, instead of construing his life choices as black and white ("Either I'll play professionally or I'll never play again"), he pushed himself toward a new goal that honored his passions and strengths, thus opening himself up to a more complex and satisfying future. Jennifer, by contrast, never even gave herself the chance to acknowledge and move past her regrets about her failed acting career; she threw away all reminders of that past, literally and figuratively. Jennifer thought that examining her regrets would be too painful, but, as the science shows, the profound, elaborate thinking that we must do about "what might have been" is the price we pay—in the temporary unhappiness and regret it generates—for the ultimate benefit of growing into a richer, more complex, more mature, happier self.

King contends that when we acknowledge regret, we make ourselves vulnerable in doing so, and this takes courage. After all, we have admitted to ourselves that it is risky to expect anything from life, yet we continue to commit to new goals. I find this situation similar to that of a person who makes herself vulnerable in a relationship by loving another—whether partner or child—so much that it hurts; that person is being courageous as well. The mother of a child with Down syndrome had this to say about her journey from the time before she had her baby to the months and years after:

> I was on the road to self discovery . . . I was searching for a little more purpose. Being a mother, being a wife, being a nurse was not enough: I wanted to fulfill my destiny. I wanted to continue on the search for self actualization. Well, [my son] came along. Everything was tested—values, beliefs, friendships, wedding vows, etc. Much growth, difficult growth, lots of confusion, but I am on the other side now . . . I am right back on track and could not be happier. I'm stronger—I'm more experienced and, God knows, I'm much more compassionate and humble.[389]

This is a person who has successfully transformed her painful experience into a "new possible self" and has emerged on the other side happier and more mature.

King found in her studies that coming to terms with our regrets can also bolster our sense of humor, strengthen our compassion toward those who have suffered, and imbue us with profound gratitude. So think deeply about how marvelous your life would have been if you had attained the job or relationship or house or body that you always really wanted but now know you'll never get to have. Write about it or talk about it with an intimate other. It'll be painful, but eventually you may truly acknowledge your regret, incorporate it into your identity, and press forward to new, redirected goals—that is, move on to the good that lies ahead.

BUT DON'T RUMINATE!

Many psychological scientists would find something troubling about the above advice to plunge ahead into self-excavating all our deepest regrets and disappointments. After all, a great deal of research—some of it coming out of my very own lab—reveals that dwelling on our negative thoughts and feelings gives rise to a host of unpleasant consequences.[390] Those of us who ruminate, self-focus, and worry are relatively more likely to prolong our distress, to feel pessimistic and out of control, to view ourselves disapprovingly, to lack motivation, to have trouble concentrating, and to get stuck solving our problems. If a compelling recipe exists for creating ever more unhappiness and ever bigger problems, a habit of rumination (or over-thinking) would be an excellent candidate.

So, how can reflecting on our lost possible selves be good for us despite abundant evidence that self-reflection about negative topics is usually toxic? The solution to this apparent contradiction is actually quite simple. It turns out there are different *kinds* of reflection—some beneficial and some detrimental.[391] Certain reflections—when they are deliberate, analytical, philosophical, curious, intellectual, or self-aware—can be thoughtful and insightful. Other kinds of self-reflection—when they are circular, intrusive, neurotic, and uncontrollable—are usually maladaptive and disruptive.

Research on these two types of reflections suggests that when we ponder our lost opportunities, forsaken goals, and deep regrets, we ought to approach them in a systematic, step-by-step, analytical way.

If at all possible, we should use writing as a tool. For example, we might choose to write in a "Dear Diary" format and to describe the facts about our experiences, as well as our thoughts and feelings about them. Alternatively, we could create lists of the pros and cons of what happened or what might have happened.

Above all, we would do well to strive not to sink into rumination. We'll know when this happens when we observe the following two chief signs. First, we find ourselves going over the same material again and again—the same thoughts or feelings—without any increased resolution, insight, or understanding. In other words, we get the sensation that we are looping in circles. Second, we don't feel we have full control over this exercise: Thoughts or images begin to pop up in our minds, even when we don't want them to. If you experience these signs, try to distract yourself by focusing on neutral or pleasant thoughts or absorbing yourself in an engrossing activity, like playing a video game, watching a funny show, or helping someone. Other documented strategies for thwarting harmful rumination include postponing your overthinking to a later time (and then never resuming), talking to a levelheaded friend, praying, and meditating.[392] After trying these approaches, you can return to examining your lost possible selves later—when you're in a neutral or positive mood and, ideally, in a different setting. In one study, researchers followed women over the course of eleven years—from ages thirty-six to forty-seven—and found that those who tended to ruminate about their doubts and inadequacies were unable to convert their regret into positive life changes.[393]

PONDERING YOUR LIFE'S "COUNTERFACTUALS"

The concept of regret has decidedly negative connotations in Western culture. However, research suggests that regret is neither good nor bad, but rather how we think about it makes it so.[394] The same conclusion can be drawn about a related concept, called a *counterfactual*. While regret is really about forever closed-off options ("I'll never do X"), counterfactuals are scientific jargon for the "what-ifs" and "might-have-beens," or life's unexplored possibilities ("Who would I be now if I had done X?"). Instead of neurotically overthinking or passively dwelling on our regrets, researchers suggest that we instead methodically consider our life's counterfactuals. For example, we might wonder how our lives would have turned out differently "if only" we had taken our education more seriously or gotten on that plane to Europe or not said yes on that fateful night. It's important to note that counterfactuals can go either in a positive or negative direction. That is, we could mentally undo something that went right in our pasts (e.g., What if I'd never met my husband?) or something that went wrong (e.g., What if I'd said no to the affair?). Although one would think that reflecting on the "if onlys" would only make us miserable, researchers have recently discovered that doing so actually lends greater meaning—that is, a fuller sense of connectedness, purpose, and growth—to our lives. How would that be? Considering how our lives would have turned out had we not experienced the death of a loved one or had we not gotten that job interview helps us to appreciate our key life transitions and to view the significance of those events in our lives from a big-picture perspective.

I admit that this logic is a bit counterintuitive. After all, contemplating how our lives could have turned out differently seems like a sure formula for making us appreciate the arbitrariness of life. For example, I met my husband rather randomly, at an all-the-Absolut-vodka-you-can-drink benefit for the Museum of Contemporary Art in Los Angeles. The two of us have often observed that had we not met that night, there is zero chance that we would have ever met, as we did not inhabit the same professional or social spheres. From time to time, I consider the fantastic possibility that had one of us ventured several footsteps to the right or the left that evening, my husband, my children, and my home might be subtracted from the life I lead today. However, rather than concluding that my life is arbitrary and random, this counterfactual exercise in considering how much worse off I could be today gives me the sense that our pivotal meeting was somehow predestined or meant to be. Reflections about why and how my husband and I met help me connect the dots and become part of my life story and a piece of my identity—all of which give my life personal meaning. On the other hand, pondering how our lives would have turned out differently had a *misfortune* not occurred is also valuable, as it helps us accept the twists and turns of our life course—however difficult it's been—view it as predestined, and recognize all the good that has issued from it. For example, you were devastated to become a young widow, but now you are caring for three beautiful stepchildren with your second husband.

Thinking about what-ifs and might-have-beens is a ubiquitous part of life. We engage in such counterfactual thinking all the time, and researchers find that doing so is an essential part of healthy functioning.[395] Starting today, review your past and write down at least one dreadful decision that you made, at least one triumph or success that you experienced, at least one foolhardy act, and at least one stroke of good luck and bad luck you experienced. Now mentally undo them.

When we mentally undo and scrutinize a terrible decision, we learn something significant about ourselves, which prepares us to make wiser decisions in the future. And when we mentally undo an instance of good fortune or success, we confer it greater consequence and substance. For example, in a series of studies, participants were asked to mentally undo the fact that they got into the college of their choice, that they had never met a particular close friend, or that a certain critical turning point had not occurred.[396] In all the experiments, relative to a control group, those who engaged in the mental undoing exercise ended up imbuing their college choices, their friendships, and their turning points with greater meaning—in other words, concluding that these were fated or "meant to be" or a "defining moment in their life." Although the logic seems peculiar, these participants appeared to conclude that "Something so improbable could not have possibly happened by chance alone. Therefore, it must have been fated."[397]

ACHIEVING AUTOBIOGRAPHICAL COHERENCE

When we reach adulthood—and especially middle age—we have the opportunity to look back over our lives, review our triumphs and regrets, and contemplate the story that we want to tell. Such stories or "life narratives"—the content and the telling—are important. For the past several decades, psychological scientists have been exploring how the stories that we write about our lives shape the way we think about ourselves, influence our day-to-day behaviors, and impact our happiness. Having a coherent autobiography makes us feel more accepting about our past and less fearful about the future. In other words, we are better off if we are able to construct a life narrative of how we became who we are today and how our future will unfold— for example, by imbuing our life history with a sense of orderliness and significance. For example, instead of regretting that we didn't spend more time with our sister when she was very ill, we come to understand how her battle with cancer propelled us to devote the second half of our career to helping others. We experience greater happiness and life purpose when we are able to construe our lives as more than just a collection of isolated, fleeting moments and can transform those moments into critical pieces of a significant journey. We are better adjusted when we have the capacity to convert an uncertain future into a series of predictable events.

In the 1957 Ingmar Bergman film *Wild Strawberries,* the protagonist, a seemingly benevolent elderly Swedish physician, is haunted by past regrets and images of his own impending death.[398] Forced to reevaluate his life, he undertakes a literal and metaphorical four-hundred-mile journey, during which he visits people and places that remind him of all the key turning points in his life—his admired but actually mean-spirited mother, his childhood on the seaside, the sweetheart he loved who married his brother instead of him, and his bitterly quarrelsome marriage. Recognizing himself in these memories and in the people in his life, the doctor gradually gains a sense of self-acceptance and is able to instill in his life a coherence and significance that it didn't have before.

The Swedish physician achieves something that we should all aim for; researchers call it "autobiographical coherence." Achieving it may require mental time travel—to moments of our earliest youth, for example, finding there the seeds of our present failures and successes as partner, grandparent, worker, and friend. Bergman reportedly got the idea for *Wild Strawberries* during a long car trip across Sweden. After stopping in Uppsala, the town of his birth and childhood, and driving past his grandmother's old home, he imagined what it would be like to open the door and walk back into his childhood. What if we could do that with different periods of our lives? Research shows that by simply writing about the past, people are able to gain a sense of meaning and order about their significant life events, thus affording them the chance to come to terms with these events and reconcile themselves to their regrets. Such writing can help us reconnect to the people, places, and activities from our pasts and give us a sense of autobiographical coherence. Such writing involves not only describing our biographical facts ("I was mistreated," "I lived in Pennsylvania"), but going beyond the facts by selectively appropriating particular memories or aspects of our experiences (e.g., cherished memories or symbolic family traditions) in a way that makes sense to us.[399] In doing so, instead of harping on all the ways we could have acted more virtuously or more wisely, we will make our past life experiences and events come alive and add meaning to our lives.

THE "TAKE ONE RISK PER MONTH SOLUTION": PREVENTING REGRET OVER INACTIONS

What do you typically regret more—the things you haven't done (not pursued that girl across the country, not applied to med school, or not taken that job in Saudi Arabia) or the things you've done (embarrassed yourself at the office Christmas party or experienced a doomed passion)? If you're like the participants of some psychological studies, your answer will be, the things you haven't done.[400] Why is this so?

FIRST, BECAUSE IT'S EASIER TO
RATIONALIZE ACTIONS THAN INACTIONS

Human beings are very good at persuading themselves that blunders or tribulations ultimately did them good. Perhaps we've learned something from the experience—courage, temperance, humor. Perhaps it made us recognize our capacity for love or resilience or tolerance. Perhaps it made us realize who our true friends are or what our biggest priorities in life should be. Perhaps it led to some truly positive consequences (e.g., the wonderful child we acquired from that disastrous one-night stand or the contributions we've made in the job we regret). It is also easier to take action to "fix," undo, or compensate for a blunder than for a failure to act. For example, we can apologize for a hurt we inflicted or we can change jobs. If you regret marrying your wife, you can divorce her, but if you regret not marrying your college sweetheart, you will likely live for the rest of your life with the fact that she is no longer available.

SECOND, BECAUSE REGRETS OVER
INACTIONS MAGNIFY OVER TIME

Although we may be more likely to regret something we did (but wished we hadn't done) immediately afterward, this type of regret, often involving feeling sorry, guilty, angry, etc., fades out pretty quickly, but regret over things we failed to do but wished we had done doesn't dull so fast and can even intensify over time. In other words, regrets over inactions ("I should have studied harder in college," "I wish I had left him then," "I regret that I never left my hometown") are more troubling and painful as time wears on. This happens in part because the original reasons that we *failed* to act become blurry over time. If, for example, we didn't have enough confidence to pursue Mr. Right or to apply to law school, that rationale just seems a lot less compelling many years later.

THIRD, BECAUSE THE CONSEQUENCES OF INACTIONS ARE LIMITLESS

When we consider the things we haven't done, we can conjure up an almost infinite number of possible consequences that could have come to pass had we only done those things. Indeed, this fantasy can be quite unrealistic—like the marital bliss we would have experienced had we married Eric. But when we consider the unwise things we did, the reasons we did it can be compelling (e.g., "But the job seemed perfect at the time—in a lovely city with a great salary"), while the number of consequences of the unwise action are finite and usually not that serious. Indeed, with time, they become pretty unimportant. After failing at something or doing something foolish or even mean, when you ask yourself, "Will this matter in a year?"[401] (or in five years), the answer is very often no.

AND, FINALLY, WE CAN BLAME IT ON ZEIGARNIK

The fact that we are more likely to regret inactions than actions could be related to the Zeigarnik effect—the phenomenon, named after the Soviet psychologist who discovered it, that we are more likely to remember and dwell on unfinished business than on completed tasks.[402] So, when we *don't* do something, or don't finish something that we started, or when we are interrupted, we tend to dwell on that thing for a pretty long time. Why? Probably because regrettable inactions often involve missed opportunities to seize a moment—opportunities for which there are no second chances—and the sense that we had not finished what we started keeps that moment from the past alive much longer. Regrettable actions, on the other hand, are often long finished, belonging entirely to the past: Yes, we messed up, but the deed is done, the story is written, and the case is closed.

THE SOLUTION IS TO TAKE MORE RISKS

The implications of this research are that preventing regret over inactions should be a critical goal for most of us. An obvious route to take is to place effort into shaping our life trajectory in ways that minimize the potential for such regrets. To accomplish this success-fully, I suggest striving to reduce the number of our life's inactions by taking more risks. One risk per month seems a sensible target. So, go forward: Get out of your comfort zone, catch yourself off guard, blunder onward, try something new, or seize an opportunity that may even be a little bit scary. You may spot opportunities that you didn't even know existed. You may unearth a talent, a strength, or a preference that you didn't know you had. An old friend of mine didn't realize how funny she was—and how much she enjoyed it—until she enrolled in a stand-up-comedy class.

The truth is that many paths may lead toward an ultimate goal, but we need to be open to potential surprises, twists, and turns and to possess the flexibility to launch ourselves toward an opportunity that others might miss, or to change our course mid-stride. So, on a walk to the corner grocery, instead of viewing the errand with tun-nel vision (i.e., not noticing our surroundings, seeing nothing be-yond milk and bread), we might anticipate a surprise discovery or an encounter with a new friend or business partner. Taking more risks doesn't mean we drive recklessly or go home with strangers. It may simply mean forgoing our usual coffee shop or route to work and boosting the possibility that we will spy something novel or unexpected. Alternatively, taking more risks may mean breaking the ice with our new neighbor, investigating that new job opportunity, or speaking our minds when others are silent.

There's a saying that holds that all successful people are failures. If you are working at a high level, whether you are an Internet entrepreneur, small-business owner, writer, or politician, you have likely experienced multiple flops, rejections, and disappointments before attaining today's success. If you have difficulty brushing off disappointments and embarking on the next step, make your next goal to take a risk—namely, to say, "What the hell—I'll try it." Even if you fail, you would have begun to change your self-concept to that of someone capable of taking action. And, if things work out, you would have generated an upward spiral, such that a small success boosts your efficacy, optimism, and belief in yourself, which whets your appetite for future risks.

BECOME A SATISFICER AND SURMOUNT THE TYRANNY OF TOO MANY LIFE CHOICES

Although I have covered much of what researchers know about regret, one cause of regret remains to be explored. Regret frequently follows efforts to make the perfect choice, especially in a situation awash with choices. One would think that having choices is desirable and advantageous—and it *is*, when the alternative is *no* choice. But possessing and combing through *too many* choices has now been persuasively shown by scientists to be toxic,[403] because an inability to manage too many choices produces significant regret.

When asked, most people declare that they prefer to have more rather than fewer options, whether they are choosing jobs, romantic partners, radio stations, or ice cream flavors. However, after the act of choosing is over—after we gamble on job A or groom B or sound system C—those of us who had more to choose from are less satisfied and, ultimately, much more likely to experience regret.[404] Swarthmore College professor Barry Schwartz encapsulated this paradox in the title of his book, *The Paradox of Choice* (which he initially, tellingly, called *The Tyranny of Choice*). He further found that there are two kinds of people in the world. The first kind are always hunting for deals and seeking the "best" possible choice (labeled "maximizers"); the second kind are satisfied when they find a choice that is simply "good enough" (labeled "satisficers"). When I tell people about some of my own work on maximizers and satisficers, they instantly recognize themselves (and their loved ones) in one of these two categories.

The problem is that although maximizers are willing to sacrifice their time, energy, and financial resources to do onerous research and to methodically glean all the possible options (I recall one of my undergraduate students spending months on an exhaustive search for the "perfect" doctor to do her laser eye surgery, involving not only weeks of online research but detailed interviews with doctors, their assistants, and their former patients), they are ultimately more dissatisfied with whatever they choose (as this particular student ultimately was). For example, in a study that compared maximizers and satisficers engaged in a job search, maximizers earned objectively superior jobs (with 20 percent higher starting salaries) than did satisficers—their much longer and more intensive searches may have genuinely paid off—but, amazingly, they were less satisfied with the employment outcome than were satisficers.[405]

If you're a maximizer, your endless pursuit of the perfect choice— and the act of scouring through and choosing from many possible alternatives—will leave you relatively more discontented and disappointed. Why? First, because the more decisions you make, the more fatigued you become and the more drained of willpower, which leads you to feel burned out and to make even poorer choices.[406] Second, because the more options there are, and the more research you do, presumably the more likely it is that a satisfactory choice is present among them, and hence the more likely that you'll come to believe that an unacceptable result is your very own fault, the more likely you'll notice that your neighbor's choice is better than yours, and the more reason you'll have for regret. If you spent years exploring every possible career for yourself, and you ultimately chose music, and that didn't work out, then you will blame yourself, feel envious of your college roommate who wisely signed on to hedge fund trading, and wallow in remorse. On the other hand, if you took a shot at the family business without much advance deliberation, and that didn't work out, you will have others (or bad luck) to blame.

Regret is fueled by self-blame and burns brighter under self-doubt. If you're naturally a maximizer, your potential for regret is high, because, as a maximizer, you care not only about a good result, but the best-ever result, and *any* result could be found, on some level, to be lacking. Any result could be deemed to possess some minor flaw or imperfection.

To prepare for the moment when life's regrets start creeping up on us, or hit us out of the blue, we will want to put effort into eliminating all our maximizing tendencies and into making ourselves over as satisficers. This isn't easy, but it's achievable. Schwartz offers the following suggestions.

STOP COMPARING

First, harking back to chapter 5, we should minimize the time we devote to comparing ourselves to others. There will always be someone who is superior to us in some way—more beautiful, more muscular, more prosperous, more knowledgeable, more articulate, funnier, and more artistic. The more we compare ourselves to our peers, friends, neighbors, family members, and celebrities, the more we increase our chances to find out that others have fared better— or chosen better—and the more likely we are to regret that we did not fare as well. Of course, we will also learn that some people have fared worse—and chosen worse—but, as my research shows, learning that someone else is worse off than we are does not somehow compensate for learning that someone is better off.[407]

KEEP A TIME DIARY

Second, we would do well to keep track of how much time and effort we spend making decisions. I have always advocated keeping a time diary for about a week, in which we take stock of each one of the twenty-four hours of each day.[408] People are often surprised at what they find. In any case, if we discover that we squander a great deal of time to making many small or fairly trivial decisions (rather than the weighty ones), we may decide that there are more worthwhile things on which to spend our time, like exercising or hanging out with our kids, or finishing that project. In short, results of the time diary may motivate us to stop "maximizing" every single decision, big and small.

BANK ON EXPERTS

Third, at least in certain domains we should resolve to rely more on experts (like the technically savvy friend) or massed information (like the average ratings for dishwashers or automobiles in *Consumer Reports* or for movie reviews on *Rotten Tomatoes*). But then it's important to give the experts the last word. If we're not careful, consulting expert advice or critics' ratings can become just one stop of many on the path to choosing, and we'll find ourselves staying up half the night reading Amazon reviews from random people with whom we have nothing in common. In short, we should aim to rely on expert reviews, but limit our exposure to such reviews or other kinds of information (much of it now on the Web). Go ahead and look, but limit yourself to a predetermined time or number (e.g., thirty minutes or one expert friend).

AND REMEMBER THAT PERFECTION IS OVERRATED

Finally, we shouldn't expect perfection—not expect always to be right and not dwell on self-blame when a choice is not ideal. Even when we really *are* to blame, worrying about the alternatives that we may have passed up, and feeling sorry for ourselves that what we chose is not all it was cracked up to be, will only make us feel worse; we need to leave the regret behind, accept the consequences, and move on. An antidote to self-blame, as discussed in chapter 1, is to count our blessings—to express gratitude for the good things in our lives.

THE PREPARED MIND

The realization that we may never reach a longed-for goal or that we passed up an unparalleled opportunity is undoubtedly painful. Unfortunately, feeling that we can't be happy if we haven't fulfilled particular dreams—that happiness and regret can't coexist—leads us to an initial response (or "first thoughts") that involves being mired in loops of rumination that are not only fruitless but pernicious. Indeed, pessimistically dwelling on our regrets in passive, circular ways will not only aggravate our sense of pessimism, hopelessness, and loss, but will drive us to feel like giving up on our other—still very much attainable—dreams. Instead of choosing to ruminate mechanically, we can choose to shift our perspective about the harm or danger of regrets. Instead of letting our regrets and might-have-beens poison our happiness, we can choose to examine them in ways that will help us grow into more complex, wiser, and ultimately happier individuals. Psychological theory and research reveals that the healthiest responses to those moments when we are walloped by a what-if, rue a failure to act, or find ourselves paralyzed by choices is to reflect on what the what-ifs or counterfactuals can teach us about our life course and where it's brought us (e.g., a past trauma that ultimately engenders a sense of good fortune that lends richness and meaning to our life), rather than allow them to immobilize us; take tiny (or not so tiny) risks to prevent regret over inactions (e.g., respond to our failure to act yesterday by speaking up forcefully today); and aim for options that are "good enough" rather than perfect.

CHAPTER 10

I Can't Be Happy When . . .
the Best Years of My Life Are Over

For some of us, the first instant of waking is our bleakest and most pessimistic moment. We may realize that those first break-of-day thoughts are not quite rational, but still we cannot help thinking them. The world seems desolate to us, our future barren, our past fruitless, our present only a cluster of worries and aggravations. Later in the day, we might have laughs, and moments of productivity and creativity, and probably affection and amusement, but upon waking those possibilities are not in sight. What hits us hardest in the morning is the knowledge—and, yes, it's something that we feel we *know* the same way we know our parents' names—that the best years of our life are behind us.

Many share these thoughts—if not every morning, then every time our spirits are low from disappointment or fatigue, or every few weeks, or perhaps just once in a while. And although we don't have to be "old" to feel that our best years are over—we don't have to be retired from jobs that once granted us gratification and triumph or to have children who have grown up and moved away—the feeling is undoubtedly most common and most intense in the second half of life.

- I can't be happy when the years in front of me are fewer than the years behind me.

- I can't be happy when I'm past my prime.

The fact that these beliefs are ubiquitous doesn't mean that they are neither harmful nor fallacious. Indeed, not one but two myths underlie our thinking about the second half of life. First is the fallacy that we can judge the best years of our life. Second is the happiness myth—that the younger we are, the happier. My aim is to dismantle both of these false beliefs in turn and then to present some very interesting recent empirical research that illuminates the healthy (and unhealthy) ways to think about our past and future, and that reveals at what ages people are most satisfied and why, and prepares us to make choices that will promote contentment and even joy. Once we revise our assumptions about our life trajectory and our aging, we will feel more liberated to shift our perspective in other areas of life and to make new choices.

THE FALLACY OF JUDGING THE BEST YEARS OF YOUR LIFE

Let us first examine the idea that our best years are over. Is this something we can know? Maybe so, if we assume that it is possible to affix a rating of either goodness and badness to a year, and graph those scores for all the years that we have lived, beginning with the first year from childhood that we can recall and onward through our old age up until our death. As an experimental social psychologist, I would raise a number of methodological problems with this approach, not the least of which is that human beings are profoundly biased in their memories and judgments of their pasts. A phenomenon called *rosy recollection* suggests that we tend to recall past events and periods of our lives more fondly and positively than they really were. A set of three clever studies, for example, tracked people's experiences before, during, and after they went on three different highly anticipated trips.[409] In all three studies, the travelers experienced quite a bit of disappointment, bad weather, gloomy thoughts, distracting hassles, occasional self-doubts, and a sense of little control during their trips. However, almost immediately upon returning, they described the experiences as having been rather idyllic. The same bias rears its head when we try to recall a long-ago romance, those years in film school, or that period after our first promotion. Many of us have fixed theories in our heads about how particular episodes in life should go, and we end up reconstructing, reinterpreting, and selectively forgetting aspects of those episodes so that they fit those pet theories. Try to test this notion for yourself by consulting a diary or datebook you kept during one of those supposedly "rosy" periods in your life; you may be shocked to discover the number of stresses, troubles, and disappointments of life back then.

But what if we were truly capable of appraising our past years honestly and realistically? What if we possessed the accuracy and precision required to evaluate and compare such years? Even if these somewhat dubious assumptions could be held in good faith, a much larger fallacy remains: The problem that we cannot judge what our best years were until we are dead. The fallacy is that simple. So, even if we assume that our judgments are solid and accurate and don't fluctuate across time—after all, how many of us thought that the best years of our lives were our college years or those honeymoon period years, only to revise them in later life, when along came wisdom and hindsight?—we cannot know what our future will bring. Grasping this insight now may take the punch out of such thoughts; it may even forestall the thoughts from striking us in future days.

"WE'LL ALWAYS HAVE PARIS":[410] FILLING UP OUR PSYCHOLOGICAL BANK ACCOUNTS VERSUS COMPARING TO THE GOOD OLD DAYS

Assuming the good old days really were good old days, how should we think about them now so that we can capitalize on having had good fortune, without falling prey to disappointment or painful nostalgia? Along with several colleagues, I published a paper called "Happiness and Memory,"[411] which suggests one path by which this can be achieved, by helping us understand how best to think about our presents and our pasts. This research revolves around the distinction between "endowment effects" and "contrast effects."[412] Consider this example: A fantastic year living abroad could contribute to our "bank account" of experiences, enriching our lives, or it could forever serve as an unfavorable contrast for all future experiences back home, which could never live up to it. The first outcome typifies an endowment effect; the second, a contrast effect. If a positive experience from our past, however great or small, enhances our happiness (and, conversely, if a negative experience detracts from our well-being), this is an endowment effect, because it essentially contributes to a sort of memory "endowment" or experiential bank account. However, when we contrast the present with "the good old days," this can make us feel less happy and limit our experience. A contrast effect also occurs when we compare the present with "the bad old days," making us happier, or at least less *un*happy.

A crucial insight suggested by this notion is that we do not always know what the effect of a particular life event will be. A first love, the birth of a child, or even a fabulous dinner could undoubtedly make us happier—enrich our life, add to it, deepen and improve it. But the joy, thrill, and newfound meaning inherent in those very same experiences from our past could also contrast negatively with the small pleasures and disappointments of our present daily life, thus producing chronic sadness and painful nostalgia.

To test this intriguing idea empirically, my collaborators and I conducted a series of studies in which we asked ethnically diverse U.S. college students to recall events from their youth or childhood, and we asked Israeli adults about events that happened during their military service. In summary, we found that both Americans and Israelis who consider themselves generally happy were more inclined to *endow* positive events from their lifetimes (that is, to extract pleasure and joy from recollecting such experiences as the stirrings of love, the achievement of a long sought-for goal, or the earning of a military honor). However, those who see themselves as generally unhappy revealed themselves to endow negative events—that is, dwell on negative thoughts and feelings involved in pondering past experiences such as illnesses, romantic disappointments, buddies lost at war, or even petty hurts, such that those experiences continued to make them unhappy well into the present day. When it comes to contrast effects, our generally happy participants again were found to adopt the healthier and more adaptive set of strategies. In other words, generally happy people tended to contrast their here and now with particularly negative experiences from their pasts (e.g., "Ha, my life is so much better now"),[413] whereas chronically unhappy ones tended to contrast the present with positive past life events (e.g., "Life used to be so much more exciting").

Because these findings are correlational, we cannot determine whether people's different ways of reflecting on their pasts are a *source* versus a *reflection* of their state of happiness. Nevertheless, they offer us several lessons.

First, the results of this research teach us that the ultimate outcome of a life event isn't knowable.

Second, that that outcome is partially under our control.

Third, that the ways we choose to remember past events can determine both our immediate and our enduring happiness.

When we believe that the best years of our lives are over, we are doing precisely what our chronically unhappy participants did in our studies—contrasting the present with a rosier past. Do you fondly recall your happier days—more youthful, more inspired, more romantic than today—or even times that were less unhappy than now, before the loss of physical vigor or friendship or a loved one? Reflecting on these times by contrasting them with the present would render all of us melancholy and nostalgic. Selectively remembering or exaggerating the joys of earlier days can also drive us to fail to notice or appreciate the joys of our life today.[414]

Imagine standing in the shoes of Humphrey Bogart's Rick Blaine, the protagonist of *Casablanca*, feeling that the best year of your life was the one you spent in Paris with Ingrid Bergman's Ilsa Lund, engrossed in a wildly romantic affair in that most romantic of cities. For reasons beyond your control, the affair had to end, and end wretchedly, and all you have now are the memories. These memories can serve as a source of enduring happiness for you, or they can forever diminish any future happiness, for, as you go about your life, you will always contrast your future relationships, no matter how good, with that idyllic romance. Which perspective and memories will you carry forward? I recommend heeding the advice of Queen Elizabeth II, who said, "Good memories are our second chance at happiness,"[415] and using your memories to *enhance* rather than detract from your well-being. The choice is yours to make.

REPLAY HAPPY MOMENTS, ANALYZE UNHAPPY ONES

The lessons of the "We'll always have Paris" studies are not always easy to apply. They are particularly challenging if endowing, rather than contrasting, positive past events doesn't come naturally to us. A promising strategy, however, is suggested by research in which my students and I asked our participants either to repetitively replay the happiest and unhappiest days of their lives, or to systematically analyze them.[416] We found an intriguing asymmetry in that research—namely, that what makes us happiest when we reflect on happy experiences is precisely what makes us *un*happiest when we reflect on unhappy experiences.

First, our participants became happier after replaying positive events and after analyzing negative ones. In other words, when we recall something wonderful from our past—say, our wedding day or the day we scored the winning goal—we don't want to dissect it, explain it, or break it down into its components. We don't want to ask too many questions ("Why did this happen? How did it make others feel? Would the day have taken a different turn had I acted differently?"). Answers to these questions could take the fun or magic out of the experience—to take something extraordinary and transform it into something ordinary.[417] To the contrary, the most adaptive strategy is to relish and luxuriate in the memory of the positive event—to replay it in our minds the way we might rerun a video clip. This exercise helps us savor the event and extract the maximum possible enjoyment and pleasure from it. To sum up, we should strive to endow (and not contrast) our good old years by re-playing, not analyzing them.

Conversely, when considering our unhappiest—or even our most traumatic—moments, the research suggests that we want to do the exact *opposite* of what I just described. That is, we will be happiest if we systematically analyze our most painful moments—to try to understand them, come to terms with them, extract meaning from them, and thus get past them. My experiments showed that this can be carried out deliberately—for example, by writing step-by-step about why a particular event occurred and how we could grow from it or resolve problems associated with it. As I described in chapter 3, using language to help us with this analyzing process—either via writing or talking with others—helps us comprehend our trials and ordeals, by making it easy to observe connections we might not have observed before and to disentangle causes from effects. In sum, the implication of these findings is that we should strive to savor (and not dissect) our happy times, and we should strive to understand (and not replay) our unhappy times.

Undoubtedly all of us will have moments when we say to ourselves, "I'll never again have an idea (passion, holiday, figure) this good" or "When this trip (job, winning streak, period of my child's life) is over, the only direction for me is down." Two optimal responses to such thoughts can be gleaned from the lessons from above. The first is to deposit the positive in our life—say, our brilliant idea, passion, or career success—into our bank account of experiences so that we can relish it forevermore. The second is to savor the positive by replaying it in our minds, rather than analyzing why it happened and why we believe it'll never reoccur. But wouldn't replaying the good old years drive us to feel even more convinced that we are on the down slope of our lives? Not if we engage in a third equally significant practice. This essentially involves drawing a line from the past positive event into the future via positive and meaningful goal pursuit.

LOOKING TO THE FUTURE:
STRIVE FOR PERSONALLY SIGNIFICANT LIFE GOALS

One of the surest ways to focus on the future rather than dwelling on a seemingly idyllic past is by working toward significant life goals. "There is no happiness without action";[418] there is no happiness without goal pursuit. However, as I mentioned earlier, it is important to choose our goals wisely, and to develop the ability to redirect our goals in ways that can bring us even greater happiness. The goals we select, if you recall, must be intrinsically rather than extrinsically motivated (prompted by our own sense of meaning and enjoyment as opposed to that of our parents or our culture);[419] they must be harmonious (rather than conflicting with one another[420]); they must satisfy innate human needs (such as the need to be an expert at something, to connect with others, and to contribute to our communities, rather than simply desiring to be rich, powerful, beautiful, or famous);[421] they must be aligned with our own authentic values;[422] they must be reachable and flexible;[423] and, ideally, they should focus on attaining something rather than evading or running away from something.[424] The pursuit of all of these types of goals has been found to be associated with greater happiness, fulfillment, and perseverance.

Goal pursuit is a happiness-increasing strategy that is available to all of us, no matter the extent of our opportunities, talents, skills, and resources. Each one of us has something valuable and unique to offer others, learn, cultivate, and strive for. Furthermore, although we can (and should) reach for our loftiest dreams, we need only to begin by breaking the goals down into subgoals and daily aims.

None of these recommendations should be a revelation. Numerous books have been written on how people can achieve their goals—most prominently, business goals (e.g., how to turn your business into a Fortune 500 company, how to win friends and influence people, how to become a millionaire, how to become glamorous and famous, how to get published), relationship goals (how to find your soul mate, how to talk so kids will listen, how to understand the opposite sex, how to turn yourself "from doormat to dreamgirl"), and health goals (how to unleash your "skinnygirl" and lose weight, how to slow aging, etc.). Although much of this literature contains solid advice, I have three quibbles with it. First, a great deal of the advice is rooted in anecdote and opinion rather than scientific research. Second, the authors focus on a particular goal (and how to reach it), and fail to consider whether that goal should be pursued at all. As I just mentioned, a great deal of empirical evidence indicates that the *types* of goals we choose (e.g., finding riches versus finding a soul mate) may be as important as how we fulfill them. Finally, the entire "follow your dreams" oeuvre places a heavy emphasis on goal achievement rather than on goal pursuit. In other words, the authors assume that what readers want above all is to reach a particular goal, and that the attainment of that pinnacle is primary. By contrast, as the "I'll be happy when . . . I'm rich" chapter revealed, research suggests that the realization of goals often fails to boost happiness;[425] in the words of *The Kama Sutra*, "from the moment one has obtained something desired, it is no longer desirable."[426] All of us who have ever experienced an anticlimax after achieving something long-strived for—a date with that cute guy at the gym, a real-estate license, a running distance, a degree—know what I am talking about.

In sum, our goals for the future are worth pursuing if they have the potential to be intrinsic, harmonious, need-satisfying, authentic, flexible, attainable, and approach-oriented. Although our salad days may be long gone, the years ahead can be a time of tremendous growth, passion, and adventure, but we must choose to take forward-thinking steps. Whether we want to improve our relationships, our life skills, or our health, whether we wish to save money to travel to South America or to laugh more, we have the capacity to endow each of these ambitions with meaning and purpose, deflecting our attention and energy from rosy recollections of the past to positive and tenable expectations of the future.

A FINAL CAVEAT

Visualizing and pursuing goals toward a brighter future will help inoculate us against the belief that everything from now on is hedonically downhill and can serve as an antidote (or at least a distraction) to our bemoaning the end of the good old days. But, having said that, I don't want to give the impression that looking forward to the future should be carried out mindlessly or naïvely. British novelist Aldous Huxley is famous for having written *Brave New World,* but he also composed a satire called *Those Barren Leaves.* One of the characters in the book warns people not to "live in the radiant future . . . in a state of permanent intoxication at the thought of what [is] to come, working happily for a gorgeous ideal of happiness."[427] Let that gorgeous ideal inspire and motivate you, but don't lose sight of the bona fide daily toil required in the here and now to get you closer and closer to that ideal.

THE BEST YEARS ARE IN THE SECOND HALF OF LIFE

Whether we are young, middle-aged, or old, the great majority of us believe in the happiness myth regarding aging—namely, that happiness declines with age, falling more and more with every decade until we reach that point at which our lives are characterized by sadness and loss.[428] Thus, we may be surprised to learn what research conclusively confirms—that many of us could not be farther from the truth when we conclude that our finest years are long behind us. Older people are actually happier and more satisfied with their lives than younger people; they experience more positive emotions and fewer negative ones, and their emotional experience is more stable and less sensitive to the vicissitudes of daily negativity and stress.[429] Although exactly when the well-being peak occurs is still unclear, as different investigations find somewhat different results—three recent studies demonstrated that the peak of positive emotional experience occurred at ages sixty-four, sixty-five, and seventy-nine, respectively[430]—what is supremely clear is that youth and emerging adulthood are not the sunniest times of life, but likely the most negative.

For those of us who believe that our best years are over and that absolutely nothing improves with age, this finding is rather baffling. Laura Carstensen, who founded Stanford University's Center on Longevity, has spent over two decades developing and testing a theory to answer the question of why people become happier as they get older.[431] She argues that when we begin to recognize that our years are limited, we fundamentally change our perspective about life. The shorter time horizon motivates us to become more present-oriented and to invest our (relatively limited) time and effort into the things in life that really matter. So, for example, as we age, our most meaningful relationships become much more of a priority than meeting new people or taking risks; we invest more in these relationships and discard those that are not very supportive. Consequently, our emotional experience is more likely to comprise peacefulness and serenity rather than excitement and joy.[432] We also come to a greater appreciation of the positives in our lives and learn how to extract more happiness from them.

Of course, this doesn't mean that after we pass the midpoint of life, we will be happy all the time. As we grow older, we come to recognize more and more that life is fragile—that nothing lasts forever—and feel more gratitude for all the years that we have left. But the longer our life, the more likely we are to encounter and witness losses, which leads us to have relatively more bittersweet or poignant experiences—for example, joy at seeing our sister again mixed with sadness that our brother is no longer alive. This co-occurrence of positive and negative emotions actually may temper our high highs and low lows and render our emotional lives more stable.

The second half of life and beyond is thought to promote happiness in several other ways. Knowing that our time on earth is limited, combined with the increased maturity and social skills that come with every decade, motivates us to maximize our well-being and to control our emotions more successfully. For example, we might do our best to make ourselves feel better when we are feeling down or anxious or angry, and avoid spending time with people or situations that have made us unhappy in the past.[433] Maintaining feelings of contentment, serenity, gladness, or closeness may also come more easily as we get older, because more mature people have been found to show a positivity bias in attention and memory. In other words, the older we are, the more likely we are to focus on and remember the positive features (and overlook the negatives) of our neighborhoods, our relationships, our life histories, and even random bits of information.[434] This positivity bias may be a result of deliberate emotion-regulation strategies (e.g., the older we are, the more consciously we try to turn a blind eye to criticism) or a result of the brain structures associated with the processing of negative emotions experiencing faster atrophy with age.[435] However, the credit for our happiness in later life lies not only with us, but with everyone who interacts with us. A fascinating line of research has documented that the older we are, the more likely we are to be treated with respect and kindness: Others confront and criticize us less, acquiesce to us and forgive us more, and work hard to resolve tensions and de-escalate conflicts.[436] It's no wonder, then, that the best years are in the second half of life.

THE PREPARED MIND

The crossroads we confront as we approach middle age and beyond involves no less a choice than that between decline and flourishing. This is a time when it often dawns on us that the best years of our lives are over. At that point, we have a decision to make—to remain stuck in idealizations of the past, thus deflating and jeopardizing our future goals, or to shift our mind's eye to the future. An important theme of this book is not to heed our first thought or immediate gut response (e.g., "I'm terrified of getting old" or "So be it—I'll be plagued by this feeling forever"), but instead to consider the research described in this chapter that explodes our myths about aging. Then we can begin to practice the healthier, more optimal responses I've described above. Whereas our gut might question the point of us carrying on with sustained enthusiasm, our reasoned "second thoughts" should inform us otherwise. The science spotlights the good news—namely, that the older we are, the happier and emotionally wiser we are, and that the second half of life can be an exciting time of challenge, joy, and growth. Indeed, nearly all the recommendations in this book can be regarded as part of the wisdom and prepared minds that older people already have. Thus, all of us can obtain the benefits of aging before we ourselves actually age.

To accomplish this, we have a range of options—a variety of goals we can pursue and numerous lines we can draw to the future. So, instead of listening to your first thought, listen to the second one: "Sure, I've had joys, passions, and triumphs in the past, but, in the future, so much more awaits." Or perhaps the third one, which might mean accepting a loss in one domain, but transitioning to another: "It's true, my childbearing years (or running years or college years) are over, but a new chapter has begun." Henceforth, we will greet middle and old age with a prepared mind.

Where Happiness Is Really Found

I was midway through completing this book when one June morning, as we were busy preparing our eight-year-old for his first sleep-away camp, I found out—to my great astonishment—that I was pregnant. After much anticipation, anxiety, and morning sickness, Isabella was born on February 12, 2011. I was forty-four, my husband a decade older, and Isabella's siblings nine and almost twelve.

And so it happened that I came face-to-face with my own crisis point right at the time that I was writing about others'. I had viewed my family of four (complete with boy and girl) as perfect and regarded families any larger a bit excessive. I had never imagined having a baby at this stage of my life. My work and home-life balance requires so much energy and creativity to maintain that I was certain a third child—the best predictor of a woman dropping out of the workforce[437]—would upend it all and push the entire family to the limit.

I was wrong.

Life sometimes takes unexpected, peculiar turns. Having an infant is no less demanding or time-consuming the third time around, and balancing the needs of much older kids who are confronting completely different developmental milestones sometimes drives the stress levels very high. But, like the participants in Tim Wilson and Dan Gilbert's affective forecasting studies, I failed to anticipate the efficacy of my own psychological immune system—how effortlessly and swiftly I would justify the miraculousness of a late-in-life baby and the rewards of a bigger family. Likewise, I hadn't foreseen the positive shifts in other areas of life—my older kids' unexpected tangible help and emotional support, my colleagues' deliberately reduced demands on me, and so on. And, of course, with time, my family hedonically adapted to having less leisure time and now acutely appreciate the precious alone time or one-on-one time that we do possess. Finally, I seemed to have forgotten or failed to foresee the bliss of a baby's tiny hand fiercely grasping mine, the joy of seeing her siblings show her a level of affection and care that belies their age, and the magical healing powers of her smile or cuddle when any one of us are sick or blue. The whole family is growing and thriving in ways that would not have been possible without her.

In short, some days it certainly seems that I am playing out many of the predictions and recommendations in this book. I am grateful for having had the experience of scrutinizing the relevant research that challenges our beliefs about what truly makes us happy and unhappy and reveals how very wrong we often are, and I'm glad I took the time to review the healthiest ways to approach our crisis points.

Many of us are waiting for happiness. We fervently believe that, if we're not happy now, we'll be happy when that perfect job and romantic partner come along, when we are well-to-do, with a grand house and two kids—a boy and a girl. Others, by contrast, are dreading turning points that we are sure will usher in great misery—finding the wrong partner or no partner at all, losing our money or our jobs, enduring a worrisome health condition, living with profound regrets, and getting old.

A great deal of research points up the error in these "affective forecasts"—in the myths of happiness that most of us embrace.[438] My goal in these pages was to synthesize this research and highlight its relevance to each specific crisis point in turn—marriage, work, money, aging, health, etc. I also hoped to underscore that believing in the myths of happiness is not innocuous. Not only do our false expectations and misconceptions turn foreseeable life transitions into full-blown crisis points, but, worse, they also steer us to make poor decisions and impair our mental health. If we are convinced, for example, that a certain kind of marriage, job, and prosperity would make us happy (and it doesn't), then misunderstanding the power of hedonic adaptation may compel us to jettison perfectly good marriages and jobs or renounce our worldly belongings to simplify our lives. If we are positive that divorce or singlehood or old age would make us miserable forever, then not recognizing the power of resilience and the rewards of singlehood and aging may lead us to remain in a bad marriage, settle for a poor romantic match, or undergo unnecessary cosmetic surgery. Equally harmful are the repercussions of subscribing to happiness myths for our emotional well-being. Not understanding the universality of our crises, we may suffer surges in depression, anxiety, and low self-esteem. Even the worst-case scenario—suicide—is not unthinkable; if we cannot fathom how we'll ever survive a loss or an ending, we may lose all hope in life.

I cannot stress enough how unfortunate and needless are these deleterious consequences of believing in the happiness myths. We must stop waiting for happiness, and we must stop being terrified of the potential for unhappiness. I am hopeful that knowing what you know now about where happiness truly can be found—and where it can't—will transform your crisis points into straightforward passages of life that are not only unexceptional but growth promoting.

To boot, after appreciating what's fueling your emotional reactions to each crisis point, you will move forward by practicing the recommendations in this book—how to slow adaptation, cope with adversity, pursue new goals, and grow and flourish.

We all experience our crisis points differently and singularly, and the most optimal choices for me may not resemble those for you. However, the healthiest responses to the experience of great fear or great disappointment that such crisis points provoke share some elements in common. Notably, all involve effortful happiness-boosting strategies that spur you to invest in your emotional life, much as you might invest in your body, your money, or your time. The most widely applicable strategies have reappeared throughout this book. When your attention is narrowly focused on something disagreeable or distressing, it may help to consider the bigger picture. When you are overwhelmed and obsessing with particular images and thoughts, you should strive to redirect your attention to something else. Finally, it would serve you well to look on the bright side of negative situations, but to be creative about how you do it; to inject variety and novelty into your life; and to pursue intrinsic, authentic, and flexible goals and make them your own.

In short, after you recognize the extent to which your beliefs about what will make you eternally happy and unhappy have been driving your reactions to life's challenges and transitions, you will be prepared to decide how to behave in ways that promote happiness, flourishing, and growth—to think instead of blink, relying on reasoning rather than instinct. Exploding the myths of happiness means that there's no magic formula for happiness and no sure course toward misery—that nothing in life is as joy producing or as misery inducing as we think it is. Appreciating this truth can not only liberate us, empower us, and broaden our horizons, but it can grant us our best opportunity to choose well, to get it right.

Acknowledgments

During World War II, aviation experts deployed considerable resources and energies to studying military planes that went down. One day, somebody asked, "Why aren't we studying the planes that stay up in the air?" This is an apt metaphor for my field of positive psychology. Instead of focusing on why depressed people are depressed, lonely people are lonely, and divorced people are divorced, we use systematic empirical methodologies to study why happy people are happy and why successful people are successful. In this book, I have tried to draw on the best science (including more than seven hundred scholarly references) to advise all of us on how to shift our perspectives about life's biggest challenges, whether our turning points rise to the occasion, not let negative experiences snowball, and move forward. Accordingly, this book would not have been possible without the support of my department and college at UC Riverside, as well as my terrific collaborators, graduate students, and UC Riverside colleagues, who provided unbounded intellectual stimulation, thought-provoking and lively conversations, ideas, energy, and assistance at all levels. Although I mention a few by name, the contributions of many more are enormously appreciated.

Ken Sheldon has now been my invaluable and tireless research partner for more than a decade. He is owed my biggest thanks. The extraordinary talents, dedication, and hard work of my current and recent graduate students (in alphabetical order)—Katie Bao, Julia Boehm, Joe Chancellor, Matt Della Porta, Kristin Layous, Katie Nelson, and Nancy Sin—never cease to humble and inspire me. Finally, a group of dedicated and detail-oriented research assistants made my work infinitely easier. They are Taher Bhaijee, Matt Dubin, Denise Johnson, William Lee, Thomas Martin, Martin Molinos (who deserves extra thanks), Melissa Monge, Michael Robins, Lucy Serrano, Emily Van Sonnenberg, Zhe Wang, and Ararat Alex Yarijanian.

Several brave individuals read entire drafts of this book, and their many insights and edits are reflected here. Special thanks to Bret Simmons, Aymee Coget, Ran Zilca, and Peter Del Greco.

The team at Penguin Press was fantastic with the *How of Happiness* and have done it again with *The Myths of Happiness*. As before, they pressed me to abide by Albert Einstein's dictum that "The whole of science is nothing more than a refinement of everyday thinking"— that discussions of research need not be dense, boring, or inscrutable. To this end, I owe a huge debt of gratitude to the incomparable Ann Godoff and the hardworking and talented Lindsay Whalen and Tracey Locke. Lindsay Whalen pushed me to reinvent the book from start to finish, and never gave up on making every chapter and every sentence better. Ted Gilley was the best copy editor I ever had. Finally, my literary agent, Richard Pine, is matchless; I hope he ushers me through the literary world forever.

As always, my friends (you know who you are) have made my job—and the challenging balance of family, research, teaching, and book writing—infinitely easier.

Leaving the best for last: My family is the source of my greatest happiness and the wellspring of my gratitude and inspiration. I thank my amazing au pairs, Julia Baune and Annina Sirola, who cared for my children while I was writing; my husband, Pete, who still remains, after three kids, the greatest father and husband of all time, as well as a fount of intellect and humor; and Gabriella, Alexander, and Isabella (aka Belly), for their unconditional affection, unbounded curiosity, and the facility to keep their parents forever young and on their toes.

Notes

NOTE: A searchable PDF of all the references (plus a longer, more complete version) can be downloaded from http://www.faculty.ucr.edu/~sonja/papers.html.

INTRODUCTION: THE MYTHS OF HAPPINESS

1   See this wonderful chapter for a discussion of why human beings overestimate their negative reactions to negative events and their positive reactions to positive events: Gilbert, D. T., Driver-Linn, E., & Wilson, T. D. (2002). The trouble with Vronsky: Impact bias in the forecasting of future affective states. In L. F. Barrett & P. Salovey (Eds.), *The wisdom in feeling* (pp. 114–43). New York: Guilford.

2   (1) Seery, M. D., Holman, E. A., & Silver, R. C. (2010). Whatever does not kill us: Cumulative lifetime adversity, vulnerability, and resilience. *Journal of Personality and Social Psychology (JPSP), 99,* 1025–41. (2) Neff, L. A., & Broady, E. F. (2011). Stress resilience in early marriage: Can practice make perfect? *JPSP, 101,* 1050–67.

3   McAdams, D. P., Josselson, R., & Lieblich, A. (2001). *Turns in the road: Narrative studies of lives in transition.* Washington, DC: APA.

4   Jamie Pennebaker, who has long collected stories of people's best and worst life experiences as part of his research, shares eerily similar examples in his book: Pennebaker, J. W. (1997). *Opening up.* New York: Guilford.

5   For two great reviews of this fascinating literature, which illuminates why we are so off base in our forecasts for how happy or unhappy particular life changes or turning points will make us (or, why the myths of happiness are wrong), see (1) Wilson, T. D., & Gilbert, D. T. (2005). Affective forecasting: Knowing what to want. *Current Directions in Psychological Science (Current Directions), 14,* 131–34. (2) Gilbert, D. T., et al. (2002), op. cit. (See ch. 1, note 1). For several of the best empirical papers, see (1) Gilbert, D. T., et al. (1998). Immune neglect: A source of durability bias in affective forecasting. *JPSP, 75,* 617–38. (2) Gilbert, D. T., et al. (2004). The peculiar longevity of things not so bad. *PsychScience, 15,* 14–19. (3) Wilson, T. D., et al. (2000). Focalism: A source of durability bias in affective forecasting. *JPSP, 78,* 821–36.

6   Luhmann, M., et al. (2012). Subjective well-being and adaptation to life events: A meta-analysis. *JPSP, 102,* 592–615.

7   Salter, J. (1975). *Light years* (p. 36). New York: Random House.

8   Gladwell, M. (2005). *Blink*. New York: Little, Brown.

9   There is a huge literature on these two tracks or systems, and here I offer only some of
the most highly cited papers: (1) Bargh, J. A., & Chartrand, T. L. (1999). The unbearable automaticity of being. *American Psychologist (AmPsych)*, *54*, 462–79. (2) Ep-
stein, S. (2002). Cognitive-experiential self-theory of personality. In T. Millon &
M. J. Lerner, (Eds.), *Comprehensive handbook of psychology, volume 5: Personality and
social psychology* (pp. 159–84). Hoboken, NJ: Wiley. (3) James, W. (1950). *The principles of psychology*. New York: Dover. (Originally published 1890). (4) Kahneman, D.
(2003). A perspective on judgment and choice. *AmPsych*, *58*, 697–720. (5) Sloman,
S. A. (1996). The empirical case for two systems of reasoning. *Psychological Bulletin
(PsychBull)*, *119*, 3–22. (6) Stanovich, K. E., & West, R. F. (2000). Individual differences in reasoning: Implications for the rationality debate? *BBS*, *23*, 645–65.

10   (1) Tversky, A., & Kahneman, D. (1974). Judgment under uncertainty: Heuristics and
biases. *Science*, *185*, 1124–31. (2) Gilovich, T., Griffin, D., & Kahneman, D. (Eds.).
(2002). *Heuristics and biases*. Cambridge, UK: Cambridge University Press. (3) Bazerman, M. H. (2006). *Judgment in managerial decision making*. New York: Wiley.

11   See, for example, work by Michael Norton and Carey Morewedge showing that people who have seemingly spontaneous positive or romantic thoughts about a friend or
colleague weigh those thoughts a great deal.

12   These ideas are adapted from (1) Dane, E., & Pratt, M. G. (2007). Exploring intuition and its role in managerial decision making. *Academy of Management Review*,
32, 33–54. (2) Milkman, K. L., Chugh, D., & Bazerman, M. H. (2009). How
can decision making be improved? *Perspectives on Psychological Science (Perspectives)*,
4, 379–83.

13   (1) Higgins, E. T. (2005). Value from regulatory fit. *Current Directions*, *14*, 209–13.
(2) Chatman, J. (1991). Matching people and organizations: Selection and socializa-
tion in public accounting firms. *Administrative Science Quarterly*, *36*, 459–84.

PART I: CONNECTIONS

CHAPTER 1: I'LL BE HAPPY WHEN . . . I'M MARRIED TO THE RIGHT PERSON

14   I apologize in advance for using only heterosexual examples in the parts of the book
focusing on marriages or committed relationships. Unfortunately, the great majority
of research has been conducted on heterosexual couples. However, I believe that
most, if not all, my recommendations apply to gay and lesbian couples. In addition,
the ideas and advice are just as relevant to committed (unmarried) couples as it is to
married ones.

15   For a review, see Lyubomirsky, S. (2011). Hedonic adaptation to positive and negative experiences. In S. Folkman (Ed.), *The Oxford handbook of stress, health, and coping* (pp. 200–24). New York: Oxford. Note that all my papers can be downloaded
for free from my academic website (www.faculty.ucr.edu/~sonja/papers.html), which
is linked to the book's website (www.themythsofhappiness.org).

16   Some important and relevant papers on hedonic adaptation: (1) Diener, E., Lucas, R. E., & Scollon, C. N. (2006). Beyond the hedonic treadmill: Revising the adaptation theory of well-being. *AmPsych, 61,* 305–14. (2) Easterlin, R. A. (2006). Life cycle happiness and its sources: Intersections of psychology, economics, and demography. *Journal of Economic Psychology, 27,* 463–82. (3) Frederick, S., & Loewenstein, G. (1999). Hedonic adaptation. In D. Kahneman, E. Diener, & N. Schwarz (Eds.), *Well-being* (pp. 302–29). New York: Russell Sage. (4) Lucas, R. E. (2007). Adaptation and the set point model of subjective well-being. *Current Directions, 16,* 75–79. (5) Lyubomirsky, S., Sheldon, K. M., & Schkade, D. (2005). Pursuing happiness: The architecture of sustainable change. *Review of General Psychology (RGP), 9,* 111–31. (6) Wilson, T. D., & Gilbert, D. T. (2008). Explaining away: A model of affective adaptation. *Perspectives, 3,* 370–86.

17   The phrase comes from Elizabeth Kolbert.

18   Lucas, R. E., et al. (2003). Reexamining adaptation and the set point model of happiness: Reactions to changes in marital status. *JPSP, 84,* 527–39. See also (1) Lucas, R. E., & Clark, A. E. (2006). Do people really adapt to marriage? *Journal of Happiness Studies (JoHS), 7,* 405–26. (2) Stutzer, A., & Frey, B. S. (2006). Does marriage make people happy or do happy people get married? *Journal of Socio-Economics, 35,* 326–47.

19   (1) Glenn, N. D. (1990). Quantitative research on marital quality in the 1980s: A critical review. *Journal of Marriage and the Family (JMF), 52,* 818–31. (2) Rollins, B., & Feldman, H. (1970). Marriage satisfaction over the family life cycle. *JMF, 32,* 20–28. (3) Tucker, P., & Aron, A. (1993). Passionate love and marital satisfaction at key transition points in the family life cycle. *JSCP, 12,* 135–47. (4) Huston, T. L., et al. (2001). The connubial crucible: Newlywed years as predictors of marital delight, distress, and divorce. *JPSP, 80,* 237–52. (5) Karney, B. R., & Bradbury, T. N. (1997). Neuroticism, marital interaction, and the trajectory of marital satisfaction. *JPSP, 72,* 1075–92.

20   (1) Sternberg, R. J. (1986). A triangular theory of love. *Psychological Review (Psych-Review), 93,* 119–35. (2) Hatfield, E., & Walster, G. W. (1978). *A new look at love.* Lanham, MD: University Press of America. (3) Hatfield, E., et al. (2008). The endurance of love: Passionate and companionate love in newlywed and long-term marriages. *Interpersona, 2,* 35–64.

21   (1) Hatfield, E., & Sprecher, S. (1986). Measuring passionate love in intimate relations. *Journal of Adolescence, 9,* 383–410. (2) Berscheid, E., & Walster, E. H. (1978). *Interpersonal attraction* (2nd ed.). Reading, MA: Addison-Wesley. (3) Hatfield, E., & Rapson, R. (1996). *Love and sex.* Needham Heights, MA: Allyn & Bacon.

22   Linklater, R. (Producer/Director). (2004). *Before sunset* [Motion picture]. Burbank, CA: Warner Independent Pictures.

23   For a scholarly reference, see Fisher, H. (1998). Lust, attraction, and attachment in mammalian relationships. *Human Nature, 9,* 23–52. For a trade book extremely accessible to the nonscientist, see Fisher, H. (2004). *Why we love.* New York: Holt.

24   In stop-and-start relationships (i.e., you repeatedly break up and get back together) and in highly unstable, conflictual, abusive, and even battering relationships, passionate love can sometimes be sustained—at an immense cost.

25   (1) Murray, S. L., et al. (2011). Tempting fate or inviting happiness? Unrealistic realization prevents the decline of marital satisfaction. *PsychScience, 22,* 619–26. (2) Huston, T. L., McHale, S. M., & Crouter, A. C. (1986). When the honeymoon's over: Changes in the marriage relationship over the first year. In R. Gilmour & S. Duck (Eds.), *The emerging field of personal relationships* (pp. 109–32). Hillsdale, NJ: Erlbaum. (3) Huston et al. (2001), op. cit. (See ch. 1, note 19).

26   Names, identifying information, and details about interviews have been changed for some of the examples offered in this book.

27   (1) Lyubomirsky (2011), op. cit. (See ch. 1, note 15). (2) Sheldon, K. M., Boehm, J. K., & Lyubomirsky, S. (in press). Variety is the spice of happiness: The hedonic adaptation prevention (HAP) model. In J. Boniwell & S. David (Eds.), *Oxford handbook of happiness.* Oxford: Oxford University Press. (2) Sheldon, K. M., & Lyubomirsky, S. (2012). The challenge of staying happier: Testing the Hedonic Adaptation Prevention (HAP) model. *Personality and Social Psychology Bulletin (PSPB), 38,* 670–80.

28   Kahneman, D., & Thaler, R. H. (2006). Anomalies: Utility maximization and experienced utility. *Journal of Economic Perspectives, 20,* 221–34.

29   Sheldon, K. M., & Lyubomirsky, S. (2009). Change your actions, not your circumstances: An experimental test of the Sustainable Happiness Model. In A. K. Dutt & B. Radcliff (Eds.), *Happiness, economics, and politics* (pp. 324–42). Cheltenham, UK: Edward Elgar. See also Sheldon & Lyubomirsky (2012), op cit. (See ch. 1, note 27).

30   For reviews, see (1) Emmons, R. A. (2007). *THANKS!* New York: Houghton Mifflin. (2) Bryant, F. B., & Veroff, J. (2006). *Savoring.* Mahwah, NJ: Erlbaum.

31   Kubacka, K. E., et al. (2011). Maintaining close relationships: Gratitude as a motivator and a detector of relationship maintenance. *PSPB, 37,* 1362–75.

32   Much of this research, and its implications, is discussed in chapter 4 of Lyubomirsky, S. (2008). *The how of happiness.* New York: Penguin Press. For a sample of relevant empirical papers, see: (1) Emmons, R. A., & McCullough, M. E. (2003). Counting blessings versus burdens: An experimental investigation of gratitude and subjective well-being in daily life. *JPSP, 84,* 377–89. (2) Lyubomirsky, Sheldon, et al. (2005), op. cit. (See ch. 1, note 16). (3) Boehm, J. K., Lyubomirsky, S., & Sheldon, K. M. (2011). A longitudinal experimental study comparing the effectiveness of happiness-enhancing strategies in Anglo Americans and Asian Americans. *Cognition & Emotion 25,* 1263–72. (4) Lyubomirsky, S., et al. (2011). Becoming happier takes both a will and a proper way: An experimental longitudinal intervention to boost well-being. *Emotion, 11,* 391–402. (5) Seligman, M. E., et al. (2005). Positive psychology progress: Empirical validation of interventions. *AmPsych, 60,* 410–21. (6) Froh, J. J., Sefick, W. J., & Emmons, R. A. (2008). Counting blessings in early adolescents: An experimental study of gratitude and subjective well-being. *Journal of School Psychology, 46,* 213–33. (7) King, L. A. (2001). The health benefits of writing about life goals. *PSPB, 27,* 798–807. (8) Bryant, F. B., Smart, C. M., & King, S. P. (2005). Using the past to enhance the present: Boosting happiness through positive reminiscence. *JoHS, 6,* 227–60.

33   Koo, M., et al. (2008). It's a wonderful life: Mentally subtracting positive events improves people's affective states, contrary to their affective forecasts. *JPSP, 95,* 1217–24.

34   Ibid.

35   Sheldon, K. M., & Lyubomirsky, S. (2006). Achieving sustainable gains in happiness: Change your actions, not your circumstances. *JoHS, 7,* 55–86.

36   (1) Sheldon & Lyubomirsky (2006), ibid. (2) Sheldon, K. M., & Lyubomirsky, S. (2009). Change your actions, not your circumstances. In Dutt & Radcliff (Eds.), op. cit. (See ch. 1, note 29). (3) Sheldon & Lyubomirsky (2012), op. cit. (See ch. 1, note 27).

37   (1) Frederick & Loewenstein (1999), op. cit. (See ch. 1, note 16). (2) Helson, H. (1964). Current trends and issues in adaptation-level theory. *AmPsych, 19,* 26–38. (3) Parducci, A. (1995). *Happiness, pleasure, and judgment.* Mahwah, NJ: Erlbaum.

38   (1) Berlyne, D. E. (1970). Novelty, complexity, and hedonic value. *Perception and Psychophysics, 8,* 279–86. (2) Ratner, R. K., Kahn, B. E., & Kahneman, D. (1999). Choosing less-preferred experiences for the sake of variety. *Journal of Consumer Research (JCR), 26,* 1–15. (3) Leventhal, A. M., et al. (2007). Investigating the dynamics of affect: Psychological mechanisms of affective habituation to pleasurable stimuli. *Motivation and Emotion, 31,* 145–57.

39   (1) Rebec, G. V., et al. (1997). Regional and temporal differences in real-time dopamine efflux in the nucleus accumbens during free-choice novelty. *Brain Research, 776,* 61–67. (2) Suhara, T., et al. (2001). Dopamine D2 receptor in the insular cortex and the personality trait of novelty seeking. *NeuroImage, 13,* 891–95.

40   (1) Arias-Carrión, O., & Pöppel, E. (2007). Dopamine, learning, and reward-seeking behavior. *Acta Neurobiologiae Experimentalis, 67,* 481–88. (2) Ashby, F. G., Isen, A. M., & Turken, U. (1999). A neurobiological theory of positive affect and its influence on cognition. *PsychReview, 106,* 529–50.

41   Sheldon et al. (in press), op. cit. (See ch. 1, note 27).

42   Norton, M. I., Frost, J. H., & Ariely, D. (2007). Less is more: The lure of ambiguity, or why familiarity breeds contempt. *JPSP, 92,* 97–105.

43   Wilson & Gilbert (2008), op. cit. See ch. 1, note 16.

44   Wilson, T. D., et al. (2005). The pleasures of uncertainty: Prolonging positive moods in ways people do not anticipate. *JPSP, 88,* 5–21.

45   Berns, G. S., et al. (2001). Predictability modulates human brain response to reward. *The Journal of Neuroscience, 21,* 2793–98.

46   Langer, E. (2005). *On becoming an artist.* New York: Ballantine.

47   (1) Nelson, L. D., & Meyvis, T. (2008). Interrupted consumption: Disrupting adaptation to hedonic experiences. *Journal of Marketing Research, XLV,* 654–64. (2) Nelson, L. D., Meyvis, T., & Galak, J. (2008). Enhancing the television viewing experience through commercial interruptions. *JCR, 36,* 160–72.

48   Ibid.

49   James, W. (1899). *Talks to teachers on psychology* (p. 105). Boston: George H. Ellis.

50   Reissman, C., Aron, A., & Bergen, M. R. (1993). Shared activities and marital satisfaction: Causal direction and self-expansion versus boredom. *Journal of Social and Personal Relationships, 10,* 243–54.

51   Aron, A., et al. (2000). Couples' shared participation in novel and arousing activities and experienced relationship quality. *JPSP, 78,* 273–84.

52   Graham, J. M. (2008). Self-expansion and flow in couples' momentary experiences: An experience sampling study. *JPSP, 95,* 679-94.

53   Dutton, D. G., & Aron, A. (1974). Some evidence for heightened sexual attraction under conditions of high anxiety. *JPSP, 30,* 510–17.

54   Slatcher, R. B. (2008, January). *Effects of couple friendships on relationship closeness.* Talk presented at the annual SPSP meeting, Albuquerque, NM.

55   Groening, M. (1994). "Warning signs your lover is bored: 1. Passionless kisses. 2. Frequent sighing. 3. Moved, left no forwarding address." From *Love is hell.* New York: Pantheon.

56   (1) O'Donohue, W. T., & Geer, J. H. (1985). The habituation of sexual arousal. *Archives of Sexual Behavior, 14,* 233–46. (2) Koukounas, E., & Over, R. (1993). Habituation and dishabituation of male sexual arousal. *Behaviour Research and Therapy, 31,* 575–85. (3) Meuwissen, I., & Over, R. (1990). Habituation and dishabituation of female sexual arousal. *Behaviour Research and Therapy, 28,* 217–26.

57   Chandler, R. (1953/1988). *The long goodbye* (p. 23). New York: Vintage.

58   Bermant, G. (1976). Sexual behavior: Hard times with the Coolidge effect. In M. H. Siegel & H. P. Zeigler (Eds.), *Psychological research* (pp. 76–103). New York: Harper.

59   Ryan, C., & Jethá, C. (2010). *Sex at dawn.* New York: Harper.

60   For a revealing study of the reasons that married women believe that they have lost sexual desire in their marriages, see this paper describing women's responses to in-depth open-ended interviews: Sims, K. E., & Meana, M. (2010). Why did passion wane? A qualitative study of married women's attributions for declines in sexual desire. *Journal of Sex & Marital Therapy, 36,* 360–80. Three major themes emerged in these interviews. First, the married women blamed marriage for stripping sex of its sense of sexiness and turning it into an obligation. Second, they blamed "overfamiliarity," and sex becoming more mechanical, scripted, and results oriented. Finally, they complained that their roles as mothers, homemakers, or career women made it difficult for them to perceive themselves as sexual.

61   (1) Laumann, E. O., et al. (1994). *The social organization of sexuality.* Chicago: University of Chicago Press. (2) Klusmann, D. (2002). Sexual motivation and the duration of partnership. *Archives of Sexual Behavior, 31,* 275–87. (3) Levine, S. B. (2003). The nature of sexual desire: A clinician's perspective. *Archives of Sexual Behavior, 32,* 279–85. (4) Sprecher, S. (2002). Sexual satisfaction in premarital relationships: Associations with satisfaction, love, commitment, and stability. *Journal of Sex Research, 39,* 190–96. For a review, see Baumeister, R. F., & Bratslavsky, E. (1999). Passion, intimacy, and time: Passionate love as a function of change in intimacy. *Personality and Social Psychology Review (PSPR), 3,* 49–68.

62   (1) McCabe, M. P. (1997). Intimacy and quality of life among sexually dysfunctional men and women. *Journal of Sex and Marital Therapy, 23,* 276–90. (2) Trudel, G., Landry, L., & Larose, Y. (1997). Low sexual desire: The role of anxiety, depression, and marital adjustment. *Sexual and Marital Therapy, 12,* 95–99.

63   For an excellent review of this research, see Baumeister, R. F., Catanese, K. R., & Vohs, K. D. (2001). Is there a gender difference in strength of sex drive? Theoretical views, conceptual distinctions, and a review of relevant evidence. *PSPR, 5,* 242–73. For studies of sexual fantasies in particular, see also Leitenberg, H., & Henning, K. (1995). Sexual fantasy. *PsychBull, 117,* 469–96.

64 (1) Thompson, A. P. (1983). Extramarital sex: A review of the research literature. *Journal of Sex Research, 19,* 1–22. (2) Hunt, M. (1974). *Sexual behavior in the 70's.* Chicago: Playboy Press. (3) Kinsey, A., et al. (1953). *Sexual behavior in the human female.* Philadelphia: Saunders.

65 Blow, A. J., & Hartnett, K. (2005). Infidelity in committed relationships II: A substantive review. *Journal of Marital and Family Therapy, 31,* 217–33.

66 Tiger divorce secrets: 121 women while married to Elin (2010, April). *National Enquirer.*

67 For example, Klusmann, D. (2002). Sexual motivation and the duration of partnership. *Archives of Sexual Behavior, 31,* 275–87.

68 Chivers, M. L., & Bailey, J. M. (2005). A sex difference in features that elicit genital response. *Biological Psychology, 70,* 115–20.

69 Chivers, M. L. (2010, June). *The puzzle of women's sexual orientation: Measurement issues in research on sexual orientation.* Paper presented at the Puzzle of Sexual Orientation Workshop, Lethbridge, Alberta, Canada.

70 Meana, M. (2010). Elucidating women's (hetero)sexual desire: Definitional challenges and content expansion. *Journal of Sex Research, 47,* 104–22.

71 Bergner, D. (2009, January 22). What do women want? *New York Times Magazine.*

72 Acevedo, B. P., & Aron, A. (2009). Does a long-term relationship kill romantic love? *RGP, 13,* 59–65.

73 Gable, S. L. (2006). Approach and avoidance social motives and goals. *Journal of Personality, 74,* 175–222. See also Elliot, A. J., & McGregor, H. A. (2001). A 2 X 2 achievement goal framework. *JPSP, 80,* 501–19.

74 (1) Gable (2006), op. cit. (See ch. 1, note 73). (2) Impett, E. A., Gable, S. L., & Peplau, L. A. (2005). Giving up and giving in: The costs and benefits of daily sacrifice in intimate relationships. *JPSP, 89,* 327–44.

75 Impett, E. A., et al. (2008). Maintaining sexual desire in intimate relationships: The importance of approach goals. *JPSP, 94,* 808–23.

76 To my mind, the best example of such work is Gottman, J. M., & Silver, N. (1999). *The seven principles for making marriage work.* New York: Three Rivers.

77 Gable, S. L., et al. (2004). What do you do when things go right? The intrapersonal and interpersonal benefits of sharing positive events. *JPSP, 87,* 228–45.

78 Ibid.

79 Schueller, S. M., & Seligman, M. E. P. (2007, May). *Personality fit and positive interventions: Is extraversion important?* Poster presented at 19th Annual APS Convention, Washington, DC.

80 Rusbult, C. E., & Van Lange, P. A. M. (2003). Interdependence, interaction, and relationships. *Annual Review of Psychology, 54,* 351–75.

81 Stone, I. (1961). *The agony and the ecstasy.* New York: Collins.

82 Rusbult, C. E., Finkel, E. J., & Kumashiro, M. (2009). The Michelangelo phenomenon. *Current Directions, 18,* 305–09.

83 (1) Drigotas, S. M., et al. (1999). Close partner as sculptor of the ideal self: Behavioral affirmation and the Michelangelo phenomenon. *JPSP, 77,* 293–323. (2) Drigotas, S. M. (2002). The Michelangelo phenomenon and personal well-being. *Journal of Personality, 70,* 59–77. (3) Kumashiro, M., et al. (2007). To think or to do: The

impact of assessment and locomotion orientation on the Michelangelo phenomenon. *Journal of Social and Personal Relationships, 24,* 591–611.

84   (1) Sheldon et al. (in press), op. cit. (See ch. 1, note 27). (2) Lyubomirsky, Sheldon, et al. (2005), op. cit. (See ch. 1, note 16). (3) Dunn, E. W., Aknin, L. B., & Norton, M. I. (2008). Spending money on others promotes happiness. *Science, 319,* 1687–88. (4) Williamson, G. M., & Clark, M. S. (1989). Providing help and desired relationship type as determinants of changes in moods and self-evaluations. *JPSP, 56,* 722–34. (5) Piliavin, J. A. (2003). Doing well by doing good: Benefits for the benefactor. In C. L. M. Keyes & J. Haidt (Eds.), *Flourishing* (pp. 227–47). Washington, DC: APA.

85   (1) Eibl-Eibesfeldt, I. (1989). *Human ethology.* New York: De Gruyter. (2) Hertenstein, M. J., et al. (2009). The communication of emotion via touch. *Emotion, 9,* 566–73.

86   Hertenstein, M. J. (2002). Touch: Its communicative functions in infancy. *Human Development, 45,* 70–94.

87   Korner, A. F. (1990). The many faces of touch. In K. E. Barnard & T. B. Brazelton (Eds.), *Touch* (pp. 269–97). Madison, CT: International Universities Press.

88   (1) Bowlby, J. (1951). *Maternal care and mental health.* New York: Schocken. (2) Harlow, H. F. (1958). The nature of love. *AmPsych, 13,* 673–85.

89   (1) Harlow (1958), op. cit. (See ch. 1, note 88). (2) Ainsworth, M. D. S., et al. (1978). *Patterns of attachment.* Hillsdale, NJ: Erlbaum.

90   Punzo, F., & Alvarez, J. (2002). Effects of early contact with maternal parent on locomotor activity and exploratory behavior in spiderlings of *Hogna carolinensis* (Araneae: Lycosidae). *Journal of Insect Behavior, 15,* 455–65.

91   Remland, M. S., Jones, T. S., & Brinkman, H. (1995). Interpersonal distance, body orientation, and touch: Effects of culture, gender, and age. *The Journal of Social Psychology, 135,* 281–97.

92   In order of mention in the text: (1) Rolls, E. T. (2000). The orbitofrontal cortex and reward. *Cerebral Cortex, 10,* 284–94. (2) Francis, D., & Meaney, M. J. (1999). Maternal care and the development of stress responses. *Development, 9,* 128–34. (3) Coan, J. A., Schaefer, H. S., & Davidson, R. J. (2006). Lending a hand: Social regulation of the neural response to threat. *PsychScience, 17,* 1032–39.

93   Hertenstein, M. J., et al. (2006). Touch communicates distinct emotions. *Emotion, 6,* 528–33.

94   Hertenstein et al. (2009), op. cit. (See ch. 1, note 85).

95   Levav, J., & Argo, J. J. (2010). Physical contact and financial risk taking. *PsychScience, 21,* 804–10.

96   Noller, P., & Ruzzene, M. (1991). Communication in marriage: The influence of affect and cognition. In G. J. O. Fletcher & F. D. Fincham (Eds.), *Cognition in close relationships* (pp. 203–33). Hillsdale, NJ: Erlbaum.

CHAPTER 2: I CAN'T BE HAPPY WHEN . . . MY RELATIONSHIP HAS FALLEN APART

97   Hollon, S. D., Haman, K. L., & Brown, L. L. (2002). Cognitive-behavioral treatment of depression. In I. H. Gotlib & C. L. Hammen (Eds.), *Handbook of depression* (pp. 383–403). New York: Guilford.

98 (1) Fredrickson, B. L., & Levenson, R. W. (1998). Positive emotions speed recovery from the cardiovascular sequelae of negative emotions. *Cognition and Emotion, 12,* 191–220. (2) Fredrickson, B. L., et al. (2000). The undoing effect of positive emotions. *Motivation and Emotion, 24,* 237–58. (3) Fredrickson, B. L. (2001). The role of positive emotions in positive psychology: The broaden-and-build theory of positive emotions. *AmPsych, 56,* 218–26. (4) Keltner, D., & Bonnano, G. A. (1997). A study of laughter and dissociation: Distinct correlates of laughter and smiling during bereavement. *JPSP, 73,* 687–702. (5) Ong, A. D., et al. (2006). Psychological resilience, positive emotions, and successful adaptation to stress in later life. *JPSP, 91,* 730–49.

99 (1) Fredrickson, B. L., & Branigan, C. (2005). Positive emotions broaden the scope of attention and thought–action repertoires. *Cognition and Emotion, 19,* 313–32. (2) Isen, A. M., Daubman, K. A., & Nowicki, G. P. (1987). Positive affect facilitates creative problem solving. *JPSP, 52,* 1122–31. (3) Waugh, C. E., & Fredrickson, B. L. (2006). Nice to know you: Positive emotions, self-other overlap, and complex understanding in the formation of a new relationship. *The Journal of Positive Psychology, 1,* 93–106. (4) Dunn, J. R., & Schweitzer, M. E. (2005). Feeling and believing: The influence of emotion on trust. *JPSP, 88,* 736–48. (5) Fredrickson, B. L., et al. (2008). Open hearts build lives: Positive emotions, induced through loving-kindness meditation, build consequential personal resources. *JPSP, 95,* 1045–62. (6) King, L. A., et al. (2006). Positive affect and the experience of meaning in life. *JPSP, 90,* 179–96.

100 Algoe, S. B., Fredrickson, B. L., & Chow, S-M. (2011). The future of emotions research within positive psychology. In K. M. Sheldon, T. B. Kashdan, & M. F. Steger (Eds.), *Designing positive psychology* (pp. 115–32). Oxford: Oxford University Press.

101 Fredrickson, B. L., & Losada, M. F. (2005). Positive affect and the complex dynamics of human flourishing. *AmPsych, 60,* 678–86. For a terrific and accessible description of this research, and its implications for your own life, see Fredrickson, B. L. (2009). *Positivity.* New York: Crown.

102 The actual ratio is 2.7 to 1. (1) Gottman, J. M. (1994). *What predicts divorce?* Hillsdale, NJ: Erlbaum. (2) Losada, M. (1999). The complex dynamics of high performance teams. *Mathematical and Computer Modeling, 30,* 179–92. (3) David, J. P., Green, P. J., Martin, R., & Suls, J. (1997). Differential roles of neuroticism, extraversion, and event desirability for mood in daily life: An integrative model of top-down and bottom-up influences. *JPSP, 73,* 149–59.

103 (1) Gottman (1994), op. cit. (See ch. 2, note 102). For a critique of this work, however, see Abraham, L. (2010, March 8). Can you really predict the success of a marriage in 15 minutes? *Slate.*

104 For a nice review, see Lambert, N. M., et al. (2011). Positive relationship science: A new frontier for positive psychology. In Sheldon et al. (Eds.), op. cit., pp. 280–92. (See ch. 2, note 100).

105 Gottman, J. M. (2002). *The relationship cure.* New York: Three Rivers.

106 Jacobson, N. S., & Addis, M. E. (1993). Research on couples and couple therapy: What do we know? Where are we going? *Journal of Consulting and Clinical Psychology (JCCP), 61,* 85–93.

107 For two reviews of this very interesting and very recent literature, see (1) McNulty, J. K. (2010). When positive processes hurt relationships. *Current Directions, 19,*

167–71. (2) McNulty, J. K., & Fincham, F. D. (2012). Beyond positive psychology? Toward a contextual view of psychological processes and well-being. *AmPsych, 67,* 101–10.

108 Ireland, M. E., et al. (2011). Language style matching predicts relationship initiation and stability. *PsychScience, 22,* 39–44.

109 (1) Karremans, J. C., & Verwijmeren, T. (2008). Mimicking attractive opposite-sex others: The role of romantic relationship status. *PSPB, 34,* 939–50. (2) Chartrand, T. L., & Van Baaren, R. (2009). Human mimicry. *Advances in Experimental Social Psychology, 41,* 219–74.

110 Ireland, M. E., & Pennebaker, J. W. (2010). Language style matching in writing: Synchrony in essays, correspondence, and poetry. *JPSP, 99,* 549–71.

111 Hall, J. A. (1984). *Nonverbal sex differences.* Baltimore, MD: The Johns Hopkins University Press.

112 See, for example, Pasupathi, M., & Rich, B. (2005). Inattentive listening undermines self-verification in personal storytelling. *Journal of Personality, 73,* 1051–86.

113 (1) Baumeister, R. F., & Leary, M. R. (1995). The need to belong: Desire for inter-personal attachments as a fundamental human motivation. *PsychBull, 117,* 497–529. (2) Caporeal, L. R. (1997). The evolution of truly social cognition: The core config-uration model. *PSPR, 1,* 276–98. (3) Dunbar, R. (1996). *Grooming, gossip, and the evolution of language.* Cambridge, MA: Harvard University Press.

114 (1) Allen, K. M., et al. (1991). Presence of human friends and pet dogs as moderators of autonomic responses to stress in women. *JPSP, 61,* 582–89. (2) McConnell, A. R., et al. (1991). Friends with benefits: On the positive consequences of pet ownership. *JPSP, 101,* 1239–52.

115 Schnall, S., et al. (2008). Social support and the perception of geographical slant. *Journal of Experimental Social Psychology, 44,* 1246–55.

116 (1) Eisenberger, N. I., et al. (2007). Neural pathways link social support to attenu-ated neuroendocrine stress responses. *NeuroImage, 35,* 1601–12. (2) Pressman, S. D., et al. (2005). Loneliness, social network size, and immune response to influenza vaccination in college freshmen. *Health Psychology, 24,* 297–306. (3) Lepore, S. J. (1998). Problems and prospects for the social support-reactivity hypothesis. *Annals of Behavioral Medicine, 20,* 257–69.

117 Anik, L., & Norton, M. I. (2010, January). *Egotistically resourceful social capitalists: The well-being benefits of bridging social actors and building network connections.* Paper presented at the annual SPSP meeting, Las Vegas, NV.

118 Langner, T., & Michael, S. (1960). *Life stress and mental health.* New York: Free Press.

119 For reviews of the literature on rumination and its toxic consequences, see (1) Lyu-bomirsky, S., & Tkach, C. (2004). The consequences of dysphoric rumination. In C. Papageorgiou & A. Wells (Eds.), *Rumination* (pp. 21–41). Chichester, UK: John Wiley & Sons. (2) Nolen-Hoeksema, S., Wisco, B. E., & Lyubomirsky, S. (2008). Rethinking rumination. *Perspectives, 3,* 400–24.

120 (1) Nolen-Hoeksema, S. (2003). *Women who think too much.* New York: Holt. (2) Lyubomirsky, S. (2008). *The how of happiness.* New York: Penguin Press. (3) Carlson, R. (1997). *Don't sweat the small stuff: And it's all small stuff.* New York: Hyperion.

121   For a review of this work, see Kross, E., & Ayduk, Ö. (2011). Making meaning out of negative experiences by self-distancing. *Current Directions, 20*, 187–91.

122   Ayduk, Ö., & Kross, E. (2010). From a distance: Implications of spontaneous self-distancing for adaptive self-reflection. *JPSP, 98*, 809–29.

123   See, for example, Kross, E., Ayduk, Ö., & Mischel, W. (2005). When asking "why" doesn't hurt: Distinguishing reflective processing of negative emotions from rumination. *PsychScience, 16*, 709–15.

124   Ayduk, Ö., & Kross, E. (2008). Enhancing the pace of recovery: Self-distanced analysis of negative experiences reduces blood pressure reactivity. *PsychScience, 19*, 229–31.

125   (1) Ayduk & Kross (2010), op. cit. (See ch. 2, note 122). (2) Kross et al. (2005), op. cit. (See ch. 2, note 123).

126   Li, X., Wei, L., & Soman, D. (2010). Sealing the emotions genie: The effects of physical enclosure on psychological closure. *PsychScience, 21*, 1047–50.

127   In the published studies, participants chose from a variety of deep regrets or hurts to think about, or else were instructed to mull over a news story of a baby's tragic death.

128   Harris, A. H. S., et al. (2006). Effects of a group forgiveness intervention on forgiveness, perceived stress, and trait-anger. *Journal of Clinical Psychology, 62*, 715–33.

129   Kang, C. (2005, October 14). On Yom Kippur, forgiveness is divine. *Los Angeles Times*.

130   Pope, A. (1711/1962). Essay on criticism. In D. J. Enright & E. DeChickera (Eds.), *English critical texts* (pp. 111–30). Oxford: Oxford University Press.

131   (1) McCullough, M. E., et al. (1998). Interpersonal forgiving in close relationships: II. Theoretical elaboration and measurement. *JPSP, 75*, 1586–1603. (2) Karremans, J. C., Van Lange, P. A. M., & Holland, R. W. (2005). Forgiveness and its associations with prosocial thinking, feeling, and doing beyond the relationship with the offender. *PSPB, 31*, 1315–26.

132   (1) Baskin, T., & Enright, R. (2004). Intervention studies on forgiveness: A meta-analysis. *Journal of Counseling and Development, 82*, 79–90. (2) Harris et al. (2006), op. cit. (See ch. 2, note 128). (3) Karremans, J. C., et al. (2003). When forgiving enhances psychological well-being: The role of interpersonal commitment. *JPSP, 84*, 1011–26. (4) Fincham, F. D., Beach, S. R. H., & Davila, J. (2007). Longitudinal relations between forgiveness and conflict resolution in marriage. *Journal of Family Psychology (JFP), 21*, 542–45. (5) Harris, A. H. S., & Thoresen, C. E. (2005). Forgiveness, unforgiveness, health, and disease. In E. L. Worthington Jr. (Ed.), *Handbook of forgiveness* (pp. 321–33). New York: Brunner–Routledge. (6) Witvliet, C. V. O., Ludwig, T. E., & Vander Laan, K. L. (2001). Granting forgiveness or harboring grudges: Implications for emotion, physiology, and health. *PsychScience, 12*, 117–23. (7) Luskin, F., Aberman, R., & DeLorenzo, A. (2003). The training of emotional competency in financial advisers. *Issues and Recent Developments in Emotional Intelligence, 1(3)*.

133   (1) Ripley, J. S., & Worthington, E. L., Jr. (2002). Hope-focused and forgiveness-based group interventions to promote marital enrichment. *Journal of Counseling and Development, 80*, 452–63. (2) Freedman, S. R., & Enright, R. D. (1996). Forgiveness as an intervention goal with incest survivors. *JCCP, 64*, 983–92. (3) Al-Mabuk,

R. H., & Downs, W. R. (1996). Forgiveness therapy with parents of adolescent sui-cide victims. *Journal of Family Psychotherapy, 7,* 21–39. (4) Coyle, C. T., & Enright, R. D. (1997). Forgiveness intervention with post abortion men. *JCCP, 65,* 1042–46. (5) Hui, E. K. P., & Chau, T. S. (2009). The impact of a forgiveness intervention with Hong Kong Chinese children hurt in interpersonal relationships. *British Journal of Guidance and Counseling, 37,* 141–56. (6) Bonach, K. (2009). Empirical support for the application of the Forgiveness Intervention Model to postdivorce coparenting. *Journal of Divorce and Remarriage, 50,* 38–54.

134 Karremans et al. (2005), op. cit. (See ch. 2, note 131).

135 McCullough, M. E. (2008). *Beyond revenge.* San Francisco: Jossey–Bass.

136 1) Murphy, J. G. (2005). Forgiveness, self-integrity, and the value of resentment. In Worthington (Ed.), op. cit. pp. 33–40. (See ch. 2, note 132). (2) Baumeister, R. F., Exline, J. J., & Sommer, K. L. (1998). The victim role, grudge theory, and two di-mensions of forgiveness. In E. L. Worthington Jr. (Ed.), *Dimensions of forgiveness* (pp. 79–104). Philadelphia: Templeton Foundation Press. (3) McNulty (2010), op. cit. (See ch. 2, note 107). (4) McNulty, J. K. (2011). The dark side of forgiveness: The tendency to forgive predicts continued psychological and physical aggression in marriage. *PSPB, 37,* 770–83. (4) McNulty & Fincham (2012), op. cit. (See ch. 2, note 107).

137 McNulty, J. K. (2008). Forgiveness in marriage: Putting the benefits into context. *JFP, 22,* 171–75.

138 Luchies, L. B., et al. (2010). The doormat effect: When forgiving erodes self-respect and self-concept clarity. *JPSP, 98,* 734–49.

139 This story comes from Michael Neill (www.geniuscatalyst.com).

140 Bramlett, M. D., & Mosher, W. D. (2002). *Cohabitation, marriage, divorce, and re-marriage in the United States.* Hyattsville, MD: National Center for Health Statistics.

141 Luhmann et al. (2012), op. cit. (See introduction, note 6). Other studies that present evidence of people's resilience following divorce include: (1) Amato, P. R. (2010). Research on divorce: Continuing trends and new developments. *JMF, 72,* 650–66; (2) Mancini, A. D., Bonanno, G. A., & Clark, G. E. (2011). Stepping off the hedonic treadmill: Individual differences in response to major life events. *Journal of Individual Differences, 32,* 144–52.

142 Masten, A. S. (2001). Ordinary magic: Resilience processes in development. *Am-Psych, 56,* 227–38.

143 For examples of eight such resources, see Fazio, R. J. (2009). Growth consulting: Practical methods of facilitating growth through loss and adversity. *Journal of Clinical Psychology: In Session, 65,* 532–43.

144 Lacey, H. P., Smith, D. M., & Ubel, P. A. (2006). Hope I die before I get old: Mis-predicting happiness across the adult lifespan. *JoHS, 7,* 167–82.

145 The concept of emotional intelligence was developed by Peter Salovey and John Mayer and popularized by Daniel Goleman: (1) Salovey, P., & Mayer, J. D. (1990). Emo-tional intelligence. *Imagination, Cognition, and Personality, 9,* 185–211. (2) Gole-man, D. (1995). *Emotional intelligence.* New York: Bantam.

146 This is the most commonly used self-esteem scale. The reference is Rosenberg, M. (1965). *Society and the adolescent self-image.* Princeton, NJ: Princeton University

Press. © 1965 Princeton University Press. Reprinted with permission from Princeton University Press.

147 In a pioneering paper, psychologist Jennifer Crocker quotes researchers who assert that recent findings "do not support continued widespread efforts to boost self-esteem" (p. 395). Countering their conclusion, Crocker's research suggests that a counterintuitive way to raise self-esteem is by supporting others rather than by controlling one's self-image. Pursuing compassionate goals leads a person to become more responsive to others, which leads others to view her more positively, which, in turn, bolsters her own self-esteem. See Crocker, J. (2011). Self-image and compassionate goals and construction of the social self: Implications for social and personality psychology. *PSPR, 15,* 394–407.

148 Booth, A., & Amato, P. (1991). Divorce and psychological stress. *Journal of Health and Social Behavior, 32,* 396–407.

149 Gilbert et al. (1998), op. cit. See introduction, note 5.

150 (1) Gilbert et al. (2002), op. cit. (See introduction, note 1) (2) Gilbert et al. (1998), op. cit. (See introduction, note 5).

151 Wilson et al. (2000), op. cit. (See introduction, note 5).

152 Cohen, L. H. (2007). *House lights* (p. 299). New York: Norton.

153 Hetherington, M., & Kelly, J. (2002). *For better or worse.* New York: Norton.

154 Lansford, J. E. (2009). Parental divorce and children's adjustment. *Perspectives, 4,* 140–52. Many of the studies described in this section are cited in this very nice paper.

155 Amato, P. R. (2001). Children of divorce in the 1990s: An update of the Amato and Keith (1991) meta-analysis. *JFP, 15,* 355–70.

156 (1) Hetherington & Kelly (2002), op. cit. (See ch. 2, note 153). (2) Allison, P. D., & Furstenberg, F. F. Jr. (1989). How marital dissolution affects children: Variations by age and sex. *Developmental Psychology, 25,* 540–49.

157 (1) Amato, P. R., & DeBoer, D. D. (2001). The transmission of marital instability across generations: Relationship skills or commitment to marriage? *JMF, 63,* 1038–51. Tucker, J. S., et al. (1997). Parental divorce: Effects on individual behavior and longevity. *JPSP, 73,* 381–91.

158 (1) Lykken, D. T. (2002). How relationships begin and end: A genetic perspective. In A. L. Vangelisti, H. T. Reis, & M. A. Fitzpatrick (Eds.), *Stability and change in relationships* (pp. 83–102). New York: Cambridge University Press. (2) Jocklin, V., McGue, M., & Lykken, D. T. (1996). Personality and divorce: A genetic analysis. *JPSP, 71,* 288–99.

159 Umberson, D., et al. (2005). As good as it gets? A life course perspective on marital quality. *Social Forces, 84,* 593–611.

160 (1) Kiecolt-Glaser, J. K., et al. (1987). Marital quality, marital disruption, and immune function. *Psychosomatic Medicine, 49,* 13–34. (2) Hughes, M. E., & Waite, L. J. (2009). Marital biography and health at mid-life. *Journal of Health and Social Behavior, 50,* 344–58. (3) Sprehn, G. C., et al. (2009). Decreased cancer survival in individuals separated at time of diagnosis—critical period for cancer pathophysiology? *Cancer, 115,* 5108–16.

161 Orth-Gomér, K., et al. (2000). Marital stress worsens prognosis in women with coro-

nary heart disease: The Stockholm Female Coronary Risk Study. *Journal of the AMA, 284,* 3008–14.

162 (1) Malarkey, W. B., et al. (1994). Hostile behavior during marital conflict alters pituitary and adrenal hormones. *Psychosomatic Medicine, 56,* 41–51. (2) Kiecolt-Glaser, J. K., et al. (2005). Hostile marital interactions, proinflammatory cytokine production, and wound healing. *Archives of General Psychiatry, 62,* 1377–84. (3) Holt-Lundstad, J., Smith, T. B., & Layton, J. B. (2010). Social relationships and mortality risk: A meta-analytic review. *PLoS Medicine, 7,* e100316.

163 Timothy, B. Smith.

164 Amato, P. R., Loomis, L. S., & Booth, A. (1995). Parental divorce, marital conflict, and offspring well-being during early adulthood. *Social Forces, 73,* 895–915.

CHAPTER 3: I'LL BE HAPPY WHEN . . . I HAVE KIDS

165 Luhmann et al. (2012), op. cit. (See introduction, note 6).

166 Nelson, S. K., English, T., Kushlev, K., Dunn, E. W., & Lyubomirsky, S. (in press). In defense of parenthood: Children are associated with more joy than misery. *Psych-Science.* (2) Nelson, S. K., Kushlev, K., & Lybomirsky, S. (2012). *When and why are parents happy or unhappy? A review of the association between parenthood and well-being.* Manuscript under review.

167 (1) Clark, A. E., et al. (2008). Lags and leads in life satisfaction: A test of baseline hypotheses. *The Economic Journal, 118,* F222–F243. (2) Umberson et al. (2005), op. cit. (See ch. 2, note 159).

168 Gorchoff, S. M., John, O. P., & Helson, R. (2008). Contextualizing change in marital satisfaction during middle age. *PsychScience, 19,* 1194–1200.

169 For just a couple of examples, see (1) Twenge, J. M., Campbell, W. K., & Foster, C. A. (2003). Parenthood and marital satisfaction: A meta-analytic review. *JMF, 65,* 574–83. (2) Glenn, N. D., & Weaver, C. N. (1979). A note on family situation and global happiness. *Social Forces, 57,* 960–67. For an exception, see Nelson et al. (in press), op. cit. (See ch. 3, note 166). For a review, see Lyubomirsky, S., & Boehm, J. K. (2010). Human motives, happiness, and the puzzle of parenthood: Commentary on Kenrick et al. (2010). *Perspectives, 5,* 327–34.

170 Kahneman, D., et al. (2004). A survey method for characterizing daily life experience: The day reconstruction method. *Science, 306,* 1776–80. However, we recently failed to replicate this result, finding that parents actually experience more happiness when interacting with their children during the day and more daily positive emotions in general: Nelson et al. (in press), op. cit. (See ch. 3, note 166).

171 Compton, W. C. (2004). *Introduction to positive psychology.* New York: Wadsworth.

172 Papp, L. M., Cummings, E. M., & Goeke-Morey, M. C. (2009). For richer, for poorer: Money as a topic of marital conflict in the home. *Family Relations, 58,* 91–103.

173 Senior, J. (2010, July 4). All joy and no fun: Why parents hate parenting. *New York Magazine.*

174 Nelson et al. (in press), op. cit. (See ch. 3, note 166).

175 Loewenstein, G., & Ubel, P. A. (2006, September). *Hedonic adaptation and the role of*

decision and experience utility in public policy. Paper presented at the Conference on Happiness and Public Economics, London.

176 (1) Baumeister, R. F., et al. (2001). Bad is stronger than good. *RGP, 5,* 323–70. (2) Birditt, K. S., Fingerman, K. L., & Zarit, S. (2010). Adult children's problems and successes: Implications for intergenerational ambivalence. *Journal of Gerontology, 65,* 145–53.

177 Martinez, G. M., et al. (2006). Fertility, contraception, and fatherhood: Data on men and women from cycle 6 (2002) of the 2002 National Survey of Family Growth. *Vital Health Statistics,* 1–142.

178 Hattiangadi, N., Medvec, V. H., & Gilovich, T. (1995). Failing to act: Regrets of Terman's geniuses. *International Journal of Aging and Human Development, 40,* 175–85.

179 Kanner, A. D., et al. (1981). Comparison of two modes of stress measurement: Daily hassles and uplifts versus major life events. *Journal of Behavioral Medicine, 4,* 1–39.

180 Bosson, J. K., et al. (2009). *Inaccuracies in folk wisdom: Evidence of a spilled milk fallacy.* Unpublished manuscript, Department of Psychology, University of South Florida, Tampa, FL.

181 Gilbert et al. (2004), op. cit. See introduction, note 5.

182 Bosson et al. (2009), op. cit., p. 34. (See ch. 3, note 180).

183 Gilbert et al. (2004), op. cit. See introduction, note 5.

184 Aumann, K., Galinsky, E., & Matos, K. (2011). The new male mystique (National Study of the Changing Workforce). New York: Families and Work Institute.

185 (1) Crouter, A. C., & Bumpus, M. F. (2001). Linking parents' work stress to children's and adolescents' psychological adjustment. *Current Directions, 10,* 156–59. (2) Repetti, R. L., & Wood, J. (1997). The effects of daily stress at work on mothers' interactions with preschoolers. *JFP, 11,* 90–108. (3) Repetti, R. L. (1989). Effects of daily workload on subsequent behavior during marital interaction: The roles of social withdrawal and spouse support. *JPSP, 57,* 651–59.

186 (1) Niederhoffer, K. G., & Pennebaker, J. W. (2009). Sharing one's story: On the benefits of writing or talking about emotional experience. In S. J. Lopez (Ed.), *Oxford handbook of positive psychology* (2nd ed; pp. 621–32). New York: Oxford University Press. (2) Frattaroli, J. (2006). Experimental disclosure and its moderators: A meta-analysis. *PsychBull, 132,* 823–65. (3) Pennebaker, J. W., & Seagal, J. D. (1999). Forming a story: The health benefits of narrative. *Journal of Clinical Psychology, 55,* 1243–54. (4) Finally, for a terrific introduction to Jamie Pennebaker's work, buy a copy of Pennebaker (1997). op. cit. (See ch. 1, note 4).

187 Many of these studies are reviewed in the following excellent article, by one of my former students and collaborators: Frattaroli (2006), op. cit. (See ch. 3, note 186).

188 (1) Umberson, D. (1989). Relationships with children: Explaining parents' psychological well-being. *JMF, 51,* 999–1012. (2) Hansen, T., Slagsvold, B., & Moum, T. (2009). Childlessness and psychological well-being in midlife and old age: An examination of parental status effects across a range of outcomes. *Social Indicators Research (SIR), 94,* 343–62. (3) Spitze, G., & Logan, J. (1990). Sons, daughters, and intergenerational social support. *JMF, 52,* 420–30. (4) Robertson, J. F. (1977). Grandmotherhood: A study of role conceptions. *JMF, 39,* 165–74.

189 (1) U.S. Government Printing Office (2009). *CIA World Factbook*. (2) De Marco, A. C. (2008). The influence of family economic status on home-leaving patterns during emerging adulthood. *Families in Society, 89*, 208–18. (3) Koo, H. P., Suchindran, C. M., & Griffith, J. D. (1987). The completion of childbearing: Change and variation in timing. *JMF, 49*, 281–93. (4) Matthews, T. J., & Hamilton, B. E. (2009). Delayed childbearing: More women are having their first child later in life. *NCHS Data Brief, 21*, 1–8. (5) Sonfield, A. (2002). Looking at men's sexual and reproductive health needs. *The Guttmacher Report on Public Policy, 5*, 7–9.

190 Pillemer, K. (2011). *30 lessons for living* (p. 117). New York: Hudson Street.

191 Bianchi, S. M. (2000). Maternal employment and time with children: Dramatic change or surprising continuity? *Demography, 4*, 401–14.

192 Milkie, M. A., Raley, S., & Bianchi, S. M. (2009). Taking on the second shift: Time allocations and time pressures of U.S. parents of preschoolers. *Social Forces, 88*, 487–517.

193 (1) Warner, J. (2005). *Perfect madness*. New York: Riverhead. (2) Furedi, F. (2002). *Paranoid parenting*. Chicago: Chicago Review Press.

194 Clinton, H. (1996). *It takes a village*. New York: Simon & Schuster.

195 It's worth mentioning that my mom is no parenting slacker, but the epitome of the sacrificial parent.

196 This quote is from Brandi Snyder.

CHAPTER 4: I CAN'T BE HAPPY WHEN . . . I DON'T HAVE A PARTNER

197 This reader had been using a smartphone application that tracks users' well-being and prompts them to do eight different exercises designed to make them happier. The application, designed for the iPhone, is called Live Happy (www.livehappyapp.com). I don't have a financial interest in it, but it generates fascinating research data for my lab about how people pursue happiness in the real world, and what is most successful. See Parks, A., Della Porta, M. D., Pierce, R. S., Zilca, R., & Lyubomirsky, S. (in press). Pursuing happiness in everyday life: A naturalistic investigation of online happiness seekers. *Emotion*.

198 (1) Rainie, L., & Madden M. (2006). Not looking for love. *Pew Research Center Publications*. (2) U.S Census Bureau (2010). America's families and living arrangements: 2010. *Families and Living Arrangements*. (3) Connidis, I. A. (2001). *Family ties and aging*. Thousand Oaks, CA: Sage.

199 If you are interested in the topic of singles, read Bella DePaulo's engaging and unique book and Kate Bolick's excellent article: (1) DePaulo, B. (2007). *Singled out*. New York: St. Martin's Griffin. (2) Bolick, K. (2011, November). All the single ladies. *The Atlantic*.

200 Krueger, A. B., et al. (2009). Time use and subjective well-being in France and the U.S. *SIR, 93*, 7–18.

201 (1) Haring-Hidore, M., et al. (1985). Marital status and subjective well-being: A research synthesis. *JMF, 47*, 947–53. (2) Gove, W. R., & Shin, H. (1989). The psychological well-being of divorced and widowed men and women. *Journal of Family Issues, 10*, 122–44.

202 Lucas et al. (2003), op. cit. (See ch. 1, note 18).

203 (1) Hughes & Waite (2009), op. cit. (See ch. 2, note 160). (2) Tucker, J. S., et al. (1996). Marital history at midlife as a predictor of longevity: Alternative explanations to the protective effect of marriage. *Health Psychology, 15,* 94–101.

204 DePaulo, B. M., & Morris, W. L. (2005). Singles in society and in science. *Psychological Inquiry, 16,* 57–83.

205 Ibid.

206 For reviews, see: (1) Baumeister & Leary (1995), op. cit. (See ch. 2, note 113). (2) Berscheid, E., & Reis, H. T. (1998). Attraction and close relationships. In D. T. Gilbert, S. T. Fiske, & G. Lindzey (Eds.), *The handbook of social psychology* (4th ed., vol. 2, pp. 193–281). New York: McGraw-Hill. (3) Stack, S., & Eshleman, J. R. (1998). Marital status and happiness: A 17-nation study. *JMF, 60,* 527–36.

207 For a review of the literature examining the associations of positive traits to people's trait judgments, likability, marital status, and marital satisfaction, see Lyubomirsky, S., King, L. A., & Diener, E. (2005). The benefits of frequent positive affect: Does happiness lead to success? *PsychBull, 131,* 803–55.

208 Harker, L., & Keltner, D. (2001). Expressions of positive emotions in women's college yearbook pictures and their relationship to personality and life outcomes across adulthood. *JPSP, 80,* 112–24.

209 Voltaire, F. (1759/1957). *Candide.* New York: Fine Editions.

210 Hornby, N. (2009). *Slam* (p. 227). New York : Riverhead.

211 (1) King (2001), op. cit. (See ch. 1, note 32). (2) Burton, C. M., & King, L. A. (2008). Effects of (very) brief writing on health: The two-minute miracle. *British Journal of Health Psychology, 13,* 9–14. (3) Lyubomirsky, Sheldon, et al. (2005), op. cit. (See ch. 1, note 16). (4) Sheldon & Lyubomirsky (2006b), op. cit. (See ch. 1, note 32). (5) Boehm et al. (2011), op. cit. (See ch. 1, note 32). (6) Lyubomirsky, Dickerhoof, et al. (2011), op. cit. (See ch. 1, note 32.).

212 (1) Carver, C. S., Scheier, M. F., & Segerstrom, S. C. (Feb 1, 2010). Optimism. *Clinical Psychology Review.* (2) Segerstrom, S. C. (2001). Optimism, goal conflict, and stressor-related immune change. *Journal of Behavioral Medicine, 24,* 441–67. (3) Snyder, C. R., et al. (1991). The will and the ways: Development and validation of an individual-differences measure of hope. *JPSP, 60,* 570–85. (4) Lyubomirsky, S., Tkach, C., & DiMatteo, M. R. (2006). What are the differences between happiness and self-esteem? *SIR, 78,* 363–404.

213 (1) Wrosch, C., & Scheier, M. F. (2003). Personality and quality of life: The importance of optimism and goal adjustment. *Quality of Life Research, 12 (Suppl. 1),* 59–72. (2) Scheier, M. F., Weintraub, J. K., & Carver, C. S. (1986). Coping with stress: Divergent strategies of optimists and pessimists. *JPSP, 51,* 1257–64.

214 Winston Churchill said, "A pessimist sees difficulty in every opportunity. But an optimist sees the opportunity in every difficulty."

215 (1) Wrosch & Scheier (2003), op. cit. (See ch. 4, note 213). (2) Wrosch, C., et al. (2003). The importance of goal disengagement in adaptive self-regulation: When giving up is beneficial. *Self-Identity, 2,* 1–20.

216 (1) Klinger, E. (1975). Consequences of commitment to and disengagement from incentives. *PsychReview, 82,* 1–25. (2) Wrosch et al. (2003), op. cit. (See ch. 4, note 215).

217 Sprangers, M. A. G., & Schwartz, C. E. (1999). Integrating response into health related quality of life research: A theoretical model. *Social Science & Medicine, 48,* 1507–15.

218 (1) U.S. Census Bureau (2010). *America's families and living arrangements: 2010.* (2) Bolick (2011), op. cit. (See ch. 4, note 199).

219 (1) Moskowitz, J. T., et al. (1996). Coping and mood during AIDS-related caregiving and bereavement. *Annals of Behavioral Medicine, 18,* 49–57. (2) Tunali, B., & Power, T. G. (1993). Creating satisfaction: A psychological perspective on stress and coping in families of handicapped children. *Journal of Child Psychology and Psychiatry, 34,* 945–57.

220 Wrosch, C., & Heckhausen, J. (1999). Control processes before and after passing a developmental deadline: Activation and deactivation of intimate relationship goals. *JPSP, 77,* 415–27.

221 Winnicott, D. (1953). Transitional objects and transitional phenomena. *International Journal of Psychoanalysis, 34,* 89–97.

PART II: WORK AND MONEY

222 (1) United States Bureau of Labor Statistics. (2010). *American Time Use Survey—2009 Results* [Data file]. (2) National Sleep Foundation. (2008, March 3). *Longer work days leave Americans nodding off on the job.* (3) Mandel, M. (2005, October 3). The real reasons you're working so hard . . . and what you can do about it. *Business Week.*

223 Harper, H. (2011). *The wealth cure.* New York: Gotham.

CHAPTER 5: I'LL BE HAPPY WHEN . . . I FIND THE RIGHT JOB

224 Gallup-Healthways. (2010). Gallup-Healthways Well-being Index.

225 Sigmund Freud reportedly once stated in a conversation with Carl Jung that *lieben und arbeiten*—to love and to work—are what a "normal" person should be able to perform well.

226 Boswell, W. R., Boudreau, J. W., & Tichy, J. (2005). The relationship between employee job change and job satisfaction: The honeymoon-hangover effect. *Journal of Applied Psychology, 90,* 882–92.

227 (1) Schkade, D. A., & Kahneman, D. (1998). Does living in California make people happy? A focusing illusion in judgments of life satisfaction. *PsychScience, 9,* 340–46. (2) Galak, J., Kruger, J., & Loewenstein, G. (2011). Is variety the spice of life? It all depends on rate of consumption. *Judgment & Decision Making, 6,* 230–38. (3) Frey, B., & Stutzer, A. (2002). *Happiness and economics.* Princeton, NJ: Princeton University Press. (4) Lucas et al. (2003), op. cit. (See ch. 1, note 18). (5) O'Donohue & Geer (1985), op. cit. (See ch. 1, note 56).

228 (1) Lyubomirsky (2011), op. cit. (See ch. 1, note 15). (2) Sheldon et al. (in press), op. cit. (See ch. 1, note 27). (3) Wilson & Gilbert (2008), op. cit. (See ch. 1, note 16). (4) Wilson et al. (2000), op. cit. (See introduction, note 5).

229 Ferrante, F. (2009). Education, aspirations, and life satisfaction. *Kyklos, 62,* 542–62.

230 As the philosopher Aristotle advised, "Bring your desires down to your present means. Increase them only when your increased means permit."

231 Liberman, V., Boehm, J. K., Lyubomirsky, S., & Ross, L. (2009). Happiness and memory: Affective significance of endowment and contrast. *Emotion, 9,* 666–80.

232 Like the Live Happy application for the iPhone (www.livehappyapp.com) based on my book, *The How of Happiness* (Penguin Press, 2007), or the many others springing up every month.

233 The benefits of gratitude, as well as specific recommendations for practicing it, are described in an accessible way in Emmons (2007), op. cit. (See ch. 1, note 30) and in chapter 4 of Lyubomirsky (2008), op. cit. (See introduction, note 32).

234 20 incredible dream jobs that really do exist (2010, May 5). Retrieved from http://www.careeroverview.com/blog/2010/20-incredible-dream-jobs-that-really-do-exist/.

235 Starr, K. (2007, July 11). Testing video games can't possibly be harder than an afternoon with Xbox, right? *Seattle Weekly.*

236 Ensor, D. (2005, January 12). Moran: "It's dirty business." *CNN.*

237 Kurtz, J. L. (2008). Looking to the future to appreciate the present: The benefits of perceived temporal scarcity. *PsychScience, 19,* 1238–41.

238 There are hundreds of studies in this area, but, for a review, see Locke, E. A., & Latham, G. P. (1991). Self-regulation through goal setting. *Organizational Behavior and Human Decision Processes, 50,* 212–47. Examples of self-fulfilling prophecies include placebo effects, Pygmalion effects, and stereotype threat.

239 See this engaging and invaluable book by one of my new colleagues: Mednick, S., & Ehrman, M., (2006). *Take a nap! Change your life.* New York: Workman.

240 (1) Rossi, E. L. (1991). *The 20-minute break.* Los Angeles: J. P. Tarcher. (2) Loehr, J., & Schwartz, T. (2003). *The power of full engagement.* New York: Free Press. (3) Schwartz, T., Gomes, J., & McCarthy, C. (2010). *The way we're working isn't working.* New York: Free Press.

241 Schwartz, T., & McCarthy, C. (2007, October). Manage your energy, not your time. *Harvard Business Review,* 1–10.

242 Reeve, C. (1999). *Still me* (p. 161). New York: Arrow.

243 Top executives carry titles like chief executive officer, chief operating officer, general manager, president, vice president, school superintendent, county administrator, and mayor. U. S. Department of Labor, Bureau of Labor and Statistics. *Occupational Outlook Handbook, 2010-11 Edition, Top Executives.*

244 (1) Buunk, B. P., et al. (1990). The affective consequences of social comparison: Either direction has its ups and downs. *JPSP, 59,* 1238–49. (2) Major, B., Testa, M., & Bylsma, W. H. (1991). Responses to upward and downward social comparisons: The impact of esteem-relevance and perceived control. In J. Suls & T. A. Wills (Eds.), *Social comparison* (pp. 237–60). Hillsdale, NJ: Erlbaum.

245 This notion stems from a quote attributed to a fantastically well-compensated Wall Street bond salesman: "You don't get rich in this business. You only attain new levels of relative poverty." From Lewis, M. (1989). *Liar's poker* (p. 251). New York: W. W. Norton.

246 (1) Lyubomirsky, S., & Ross, L. (1997). Hedonic consequences of social comparison:

A contrast of happy and unhappy people. *JPSP, 73,* 1141–57. (2) Lyubomirsky, S., Tucker, K. L., & Kasri, F. (2001). Responses to hedonically conflicting social comparisons: Comparing happy and unhappy people. *European Journal of Social Psychology, 31,* 511–35. (3) Lyubomirsky, S., et al. (2011). The cognitive and hedonic costs of dwelling on achievement-related negative experiences: Implications for enduring happiness and unhappiness. *Emotion, 11,* 1152–67.

247 Lyubomirsky & Ross (1997), op. cit. (See ch. 5, note 246).

248 Brosnan, S. F., & de Waal, F. B. M. (2003). Monkeys reject unequal pay. *Nature, 425,* 297–99.

249 Because unfavorable comparisons are more painful than favorable comparisons are pleasurable, even if half our friends are better off and half are worse off, we will generally suffer when comparing with others. See chapter 2 ("Aim for a three-to-one ratio"), as well as the following: (1) Baumeister, Bratslavsky, et al. (2001), op. cit. (See ch. 3, note 176). (2) Senik, C. (2009). Direct evidence on income comparisons and their welfare effects. *Journal of Economic Behavior & Organization, 72,* 408–24.

250 Sullivan, H. S. (1955, reprinted 2001). *The interpersonal theory of psychiatry* (p. 309). London: Routledge.

251 (1) Kasser, T., & Ryan, R. M. (1996). Further examining the American dream: Differential correlates of intrinsic and extrinsic goals. *PSPB, 22,* 280–87. (2) McGregor, I., & Little, B. R. (1998). Personal projects, happiness, and meaning: On doing well and being yourself. *JPSP, 74,* 494–512. (3) Cantor, N., & Sanderson, C. A. (1999). Life task participation and well-being: The importance of taking part in daily life. In Kahneman et al. (Eds.), op. cit. pp. 230–43. (See ch. 1, note 16). (4) Sheldon, K. M., & Elliot, A. J. (1999). Goal striving, need-satisfaction, and longitudinal well-being: The Self-Concordance Model. *JPSP, 76,* 482–97. (5) Emmons, R. A., & King, L. A. (1988). Conflict among personal strivings: Immediate and long-term implications for psychological and physical well-being. *JPSP, 54,* 1040–48.

252 (1) Csikszentmihalyi, M. (1990). *Flow.* New York: Harper. (2) Kruglanski, A. W. (1996). Goals as knowledge structures. In P. M. Golwitzer & J. A. Bargh (Eds.), *The psychology of action* (pp. 599–618). New York: Guilford. (3) Lyubomirsky (2011), op. cit. (See ch. 1, note 15).

253 Thomas, E. (2009, April 6). Obama's Nobel headache. *Newsweek.*

254 (1) Carver, C. S., & Scheier, M. F. (1990). Origins and functions of positive and negative affect: A control-process view. *PsychReview, 97,* 19–35. (2) Emmons, R. A., et al. (1996). Goal orientation and emotional well-being: Linking goals and affect through the self. *Striving and feeling* (pp. 79–98). Hillsdale, NJ: Lawrence Erlbaum Associates, Inc.

255 (1) Ericsson, K. A., & Ward, P. (2007). Capturing the naturally occurring superior performance of experts in the laboratory. *Current Directions, 16,* 346–50. (2) Simonton, D. K. (2009). *Genius 101.* New York: Springer. (3) Gladwell, M. (2008). *Outliers.* New York: Little, Brown.

256 The classic paper on deliberate practice is Ericsson, K. A., Krampe, R. T., & Tesch-Römer, C. (1993). The role of deliberate practice in the acquisition of expert performance. *PsychReview, 100,* 363–406. We should not overlook, however, some equally persuasive evidence on the role of heritable abilities. See for example, (1) Meinz, E. J.,

& Hambrick, D. Z. (2010). Deliberate practice is necessary but not sufficient to explain individual differences in piano sight-reading skill: The role of working memory capacity. *PsychScience, 21,* 914–19. (2) Simonton, D. K. (2008). Scientific talent, training, and performance: Intellect, personality, and genetic endowment. *RGP, 12,* 28–46.

257 See Angela Duckworth's compelling recent work. For example, Duckworth, A. L., et al. (2011). Deliberate practice spells success: Why grittier competitors triumph at the National Spelling Bee. *Social Psychological and Personality Science, 2,* 174–81.

258 For a recent example, see Chua, A. (2011). *Battle hymn of the tiger mother.* New York: Penguin Press.

259 To be more precise, the first type of motivation (i.e., striving toward a goal because it is fundamentally engaging and enjoyable) is called "intrinsic," and the second type of motivation (i.e., working toward a goal that expresses our deepest values) is called "identified." For simplicity, I use the term intrinsic to refer to both. (1) Deci, E. L., & Ryan, R. M. (2000). The "what" and "why" of goal pursuits: Human needs and the self-determination of behavior. *Psychological Inquiry, 4,* 227–68. (2) Sheldon & Elliot (1999), op. cit. (See ch. 5, note 251). (3) Sheldon, K. M., & Kasser, T. (1995). Coherence and congruence: Two aspects of personality integration. *JPSP, 68,* 531–43.

260 (1) Deci & Ryan (2000), op. cit. (See ch. 5, note 259). (2) Kasser, T. (2002). *The high price of materialism.* Cambridge, MA: MIT Press. (3) Kasser, T., & Ryan, R. M. (1993). A dark side of the American dream: Correlates of financial success as a central life aspiration. *JPSP, 65,* 410–22. (4) Niemiec, C. P., Ryan, R. M., & Deci, E. L. (2009). The path taken: Consequences of attaining intrinsic and extrinsic aspirations in postcollege life. *Journal of Research in Personality, 43,* 291–306.

261 Quinn, M. (2007, November 24). The iPod lecture circuits. *Los Angeles Times.*

262 Norcross, J. C., Mrykalo, M. S., & Blagys, M. D. (2002). Auld lang syne: Success predictors, change processes, and self-reported outcomes of New Year's resolvers and nonresolvers. *Journal of Clinical Psychology, 58,* 397–405.

263 (1) Brunstein, J. C., Dangelmayer, G., & Schultheiss, O. C. (1996). Personal goals and social support in close relationships: Effects on relationship mood and marital satisfaction. *JPSP, 71,* 1006–19. (2) Rusbult et al. (2009), op. cit. (See ch. 1, note 82).

264 (1) Maslow, A. H. (1943). A theory of human motivation. *PsychReview, 50,* 370–96. (2) Maslow, A. H. (1970). *Motivation and personality* (2nd ed.). New York: Harper. (3) William Compton, Department of Psychology, Middle Tennessee University. Personal communication, 2007.

CHAPTER 6: I CAN'T BE HAPPY WHEN . . . I'M BROKE

265 (1) Easterbrook, G. (2009). *Sonic boom.* New York: Random House. (2) Gosselin, P. (2008). *High wire.* New York: Basic Books.

266 For a review of this vast literature, see Diener, E., & Biswas-Diener, R. (2002). Will money increase subjective well-being? A literature review and guide to needed research. *SIR, 57,* 119–69.

267 (1) Diener, E., et al. (2010). Wealth and happiness across the world: Material prosperity predicts life evaluation, whereas psychosocial prosperity predicts positive feel-

ing. *JPSP, 99,* 52–61. (2) Kahneman, D., & Deaton, A. (2010). High income improves evaluation of life but not emotional well-being. *PNAS, 107,* 16489–93. (3) Luhmann, M., Schimmack, U., & Eid, M. (2011). Stability and variability in the relationship between subjective well-being and income. *Journal of Research in Personality, 45,* 186–97.

268 Kahneman & Deaton (2010). op. cit. (See ch. 6, note 267).

269 Diener, E., et al. (2002). Dispositional affect and job outcomes. *SIR, 59,* 229–59. For a review, see Lyubomirsky, King, et al. (2005), op. cit. (See ch. 4, note 207).

270 (1) Deaton, A. (2008). Income, health and well-being around the world: Evidence from the Gallup World Poll. *Journal of Economic Perspectives, 22,* 53–72. (2) Diener et al. (2010), op. cit. (See ch. 6, note 267). (3) Eckersley, R. (2005). *Well and good* (2nd ed.). Melbourne, Australia: Text Publishing. (4) Howell, H., & Howell, C. (2008). The relation of economic status to subjective well-being in developing countries: A meta-analysis. *PsychBull, 134,* 536–60. (5) Inglehart, R. (2000). Globalization and postmodern values. *The Washington Quarterly, 23,* 215–28.

271 For an interesting study showing that wealth buffers well-being after experiencing a disabling health condition, see Smith, D. M., et al. (2005). Health, wealth, and happiness: Financial resources buffer subjective well-being after the onset of a disability. *PsychScience, 16,* 663–66.

272 (1) Kristof, K. M. (2005, January 14). Study: Money can't buy happiness, security either. *Los Angeles Times,* C1. (2) Levine, R., & Norenzayan, A. (1999). The pace of life in 31 countries. *Journal of Cross-Cultural Psychology, 30,* 178–205. (3) Ng, W., et al. (2008). Affluence, feelings of stress, and well-being. *SIR, 57,* 119–69.

273 Quoidbach, J., et al. (2010). Money giveth, money taketh away: The dual effect of wealth on happiness. *PsychScience, 21,* 759–63.

274 (1) Diener & Biswas-Diener (2002). op. cit. (See ch. 6, note 266). (2) Inglehart, R., & Klingemann, H.-D. (2000). Genes, culture, democracy, and happiness. In E. Diener & E. M. Suh (Eds.), *Subjective well-being across cultures* (pp. 165–83). Cambridge, MA: MIT Press. (3) Stevenson, B., & Wolfers, J. (2008). Economic growth and happiness: Reassessing the Easterlin paradox. *Brookings Papers on Economic Activity,* 1–87.

275 This finding is at the heart of the so-called Easterlin paradox: (1) Easterlin, R. A. (1974). Does economic growth improve the human lot? Some empirical evidence. In P. A. David & M. W. Reder (Eds.), *Nations and households in economic growth* (pp. 89–125). New York: Academic Press. (2) Easterlin, R. A., et al. (2010). The happiness-income paradox revisited. *PNAS, 107,* 22463–68. (3) Diener, E., Oishi, S., & Tay, L. (2011). *Easterlin is wrong—and right: Income, psychosocial factors, and the changing happiness of nations.* Manuscript under review. (4) Diener & Biswas-Diener (2002). op. cit. (See ch. 6, note 266). (5) Oswald, A. J. (1997). Happiness and economic performance. *The Economic Journal, 108,* 1815–31. For a recent challenge to these findings, see Stevenson & Wolfers (2008). op. cit. (See ch. 6, note 274).

276 Myers, D. G. (2000). The funds, friends, and faith of happy people. *AmPsych, 55,* 56–67.

277 (1) Boyce, C. J., Brown, G. D. A., & Moore, S. C. (2010). Money and happiness: Rank of income, not income, affects life satisfaction. *PsychScience, 21,* 471–75.

(2) Clark, A. E., Frijters, P., & Shields, M. A. (2008). Relative income, happiness, and utility: An explanation for the Easterlin paradox and other puzzles. *Journal of Economic Literature, 46*, 95–144. (3) Clark, A. E., & Oswald, A. J. (1996). Satisfaction and comparison income. *Journal of Public Economics, 61*, 359–81. (4) Ferrer-i-Carbonell, A. (2005). Income and well-being: An empirical analysis of the comparison income effect. *Journal of Public Economics, 89*, 997–1019. (5) Luttmer, E. F. P. (2005). Neighbors as negatives: Relative earnings and well-being. *Quarterly Journal of Economics, 120*, 963–1002.

278   For examples of this fascinating research, see: (1) Mischel, W., Shoda, Y., & Rodriguez, M. L. (1989). Delay of gratification in children. *Science, 244*, 933–38. (2) Mischel, W., Shoda, Y., & Peake, P. L. (1988). The nature of adolescent competencies predicted by preschool delay of gratification. *JPSP, 54*, 687–96. (3) Eigsti, I-M., et al. (2006). Predicting cognitive control from preschool to late adolescence and young adulthood. *PsychScience, 17*, 478–84.

279   Baumeister, Bratslavsky, et al. (2001), op. cit. (See ch. 3, note 176).

280   (1) Boswell et al. (2005), op. cit. (See ch. 5, note 226). (2) Lucas, R. E. (2005). Time does not heal all wounds: A longitudinal study of reaction and adaptation to divorce. *PsychScience, 16*, 945–50. (3) Lucas et al. (2003), op. cit. (See ch. 1, note 18). (4) Lucas, R. E., et al. (2004). Unemployment alters the set point for life satisfaction. *PsychScience, 15*, 8–13. (5) Nezlek, J. B., & Gable, S. L. (2001). Depression as a moderator of relationships between positive daily events and day-to-day psychological adjustment. *PSPB, 27*, 1692–1704. (6) Sheldon, K. M., Ryan, R., & Reis, H. T. (1996). What makes for a good day? Competence and autonomy in the day and in the person. *PSPB, 22*, 1270–79.

281   (1) U.S. Federal Reserve (2010). *Balance sheet of households and nonprofit organizations* (Flow of Funds Accounts of the United States No. B.100). Board of Governors of the Federal Reserve System [Data file]. (2) GfK Roper Public Affairs & Media, & Associated Press. (2010). *AP-GfK poll finances topline* [Data file].

282   (1) David et al. (1997), op. cit. (See ch. 2, note 102). (2) Fredrickson & Losada (2005), op. cit. (See ch. 2, note 101). (3) Gottman (1994), op. cit. (See ch. 2, note 102).

283   (1) Van Boven, L., & Gilovich, T. (2003). To do or to have? That is the question. *JPSP, 85*, 1193–1202. (2) Van Boven, L. (2005). Experientialism, materialism, and the pursuit of happiness. *RGP, 9*, 132–42. (3) Carter, T., & Gilovich, T. (2010). The relative relativity of experiential and material purchases. *JPSP, 98*, 146–59. An interesting exception, however, is materialism in people: Nicolao, L., Irwin, J. R., & Goodman, J. K. (2009). Happiness for sale: Do experiential purchases make consumers happier than material purchases? *JCR, 36*, 188–98.

284   Carter & Gilovich (2010), op. cit. (See ch. 6, note 283).

285   (1) Mitchell, T. R., et al. (1997). Temporal adjustments in the evaluation of events: The "rosy view." *Journal of Experimental Social Psychology, 33*, 421–48. (2) Wirtz, D., et al. (2003). What to do on spring break? The role of predicted, on-line, and remembered experience in future choice. *PsychScience, 14*, 520–24.

286   Van Boven & Gilovich (2003), op. cit. (See ch. 6, note 283).

287   Ibid. See also Carter, T. J., & Gilovich, T. (2012). I am what I do, not what I have. *JPSP, 102*, 1304–17.

288 (1) Kasser (2002), op. cit. (See ch. 5, note 260). (2) Belk, R. W. (1985). Materialism: Trait aspects of living in the material world. *JCR, 12,* 265–80. (3) Richins, M. L., & Dawson, S. (1992). A consumer values orientation for materialism and its measurement: Scale development and validation. *JCR, 19,* 303–16. (4) Kashdan, T. B., & Breen, W. E. (2007). Materialism and diminished well-being: Experiential avoidance as a mediating mechanism. *Journal of Social and Clinical Psychology, 26,* 521–53. (5) Van Boven, L., Campbell, M. C., & Gilovich, T. (2010). Stigmatizing materialism: On stereotypes and impressions of materialistic and experiential pursuits. *PSPB, 36,* 551–63.

289 Diener, E., Sandvik, E., & Pavot, W. (1991). Happiness is the frequency, not the intensity, of positive versus negative affect. In F. Strack, M. Argyle, & N. Schwarz (Eds.) (1991). *Subjective well-being: An interdisciplinary perspective* (pp. 119–40). Oxford: Pergamon.

290 (1) Linville, P. W., & Fischer, G. W. (1991). Preferences for separating or combining events. *JPSP, 60,* 5–23. (2) Nelson, L. D., Meyvis, T., & Galak, J. (2009). Enhancing the television-viewing experience through commercial interruptions. *JCR, 36,* 160–72. (3) Nelson & Meyvis (2008), op. cit. (See ch. 1, note 47). (4) Zhong, J. Y., & Mitchell, V. W. (2010). A mechanism model of the effect of hedonic product consumption on well-being. *Journal of Consumer Psychology, 20,* 152–62.

291 Pollan, M. (2009). *Food rules* (p. 111). New York: Penguin.

292 Zhong & Mitchell (2010), op. cit. (See ch. 6, note 290).

293 This research was done by Richard Tunney (University of Nottingham).

294 Mochon, D., Norton, M. I., & Ariely, D. (2008). Getting off the hedonic treadmill, one step at a time: The impact of regular religious practice and exercise on well-being. *Journal of Economic Psychology, 29,* 632–42.

295 (1) Berlyne (1970), op. cit. (See ch. 1, note 38). (2) Ratner et al. (1999), op. cit. (See ch. 1, note 38).

296 Ginsberg, A. (2000). Letter to the *Wall Street Journal*. In B. Morgan (Ed.), *Deliberate prose* (pp. 145–46). New York: Harper Perennial.

297 (1) Havighurst, R. J., & Glasser, R. (1972). An exploratory study of reminiscence. *Journal of Gerontology,* 245–53. (2) Pasupathi, M., & Carstensen, L. L. (2003). Age and emotional experience during mutual reminiscing. *Psychology and Aging, 18,* 430–42.

298 Kahneman, D., Knetsch, J. L., & Thaler, R. H. (1991). Anomalies: The endowment effect, loss aversion, and status quo bias. *Journal of Economic Perspectives, 5,* 193–206.

299 Bucchianeri, G. W. (2009). *The American dream or the American delusion? The private and external benefits of homeownership*. Working paper, The Wharton School of Business, Philadelphia, PA.

300 Lyubomirsky (2011), op. cit. (See ch. 1, note 15).

301 (1) Senior, J. (2009, May 10). Recession culture: No money changes everything, from murder rates to museum attendance, from career choices to what you eat for dinner. And not all of it for the worse. *Los Angeles Times*. (2) Gorman, A., & Becerra, H. (2009, April 11). Garage sales are a win-win in this economy. *Los Angeles Times*.

CHAPTER 7: I'LL BE HAPPY WHEN . . . I'M RICH

302 Important identifying information has been changed. I am deeply grateful to Thomas Martin.

303 I could cite many empirical articles to back this up, but one eminently readable and laugh-out-loud funny source is Gilbert, D. (2006). *Stumbling on happiness*. New York: Knopf.

304 Shakespeare, W. (1594/2010). "The rape of Lucrece." In C. Brown (Ed.), *Venus and Adonis* (p. 109). New York: Nabu.

305 For a fascinating anecdote about Walker Percy's musings about hurricanes, see the following passage from the gifted Walter Isaacson: Isaacson, W. (2009). *American sketches* (pp. 269–70). New York: Simon & Schuster.

306 Ben-Shahar, T. (2009). *The pursuit of perfect*. New York: McGraw-Hill.

307 Ridley, M. (2010). *The rational optimist*. New York: Harper.

308 (1) Quoidbach et al. (2010), op. cit. (See ch. 6, note 273). (2) Parducci, A. (1984). Value judgments: Toward a relational theory of happiness. In J. R. Eiser (Ed.), *Attitudinal judgment* (pp. 3–21). New York: Springer-Verlag. (3) Oishi, S., et al. (2007). The dynamics of daily events and well-being across cultures: When less is more. *JPSP, 93*, 685–98. (4) Brickman, P., Coates, D., & Janoff-Bulman, R. (1978). Lottery winners and accident victims: Is happiness relative? *JPSP, 36*, 917–27.

309 See for example, (1) Sapolsky, R. M. (2004). *Why zebras don't get ulcers*. New York: Holt. (2) Justice, B. (1988). *Who gets sick*. New York: Tarcher. (3) Overbeek, G., et al. (2010). Positive life events and mood disorders: Longitudinal evidence for an erratic lifecourse hypothesis. *Journal of Psychiatric Research, 44*, 1095–1100. (4) Brown, D. B., & McGill, K. L. (1989). The cost of good fortune: When positive life events produce negative health consequences. *JPSP, 57*, 1103–10.

310 Pryor, J. H., et al. (2010). *The American freshman: National norms fall 2010*. Los Angeles: Higher Education Research Institute, UCLA.

311 (1) Stutzer, A. (2004). The role of income aspirations in individual happiness. *Journal of Economic Behaviour and Organization, 54*, 89–109. (2) Van Praag, B. M. S., & Ferrer-i-Carbonell, A. (2004). *Happiness quantified*. Oxford: Oxford University Press.

312 See, for example, Krueger et al. (2009), op. cit. (See ch. 4, note 200).

313 Loewenstein, G., & Schkade, D. (1999). Wouldn't it be nice? Predicting future feelings. In Diener et al. (Eds.), op. cit., pp. 85–105. (See ch. 1, note 16).

314 Dutt, A. K. (2009). Happiness and the relative consumption hypothesis. In Dutt & Radcliff (Eds.), op. cit., pp. 127. (See ch. 1, note 29).

315 1) Solnick, S. J., & Hemenway, D. (1998). Is more always better? A survey on positional concerns. *Journal of Economic Behavior and Organization, 37*, 373–83. (2) Zizzo, D. J., & Oswald, A. J. (2001). Are people willing to pay to reduce others' incomes? *Annales d'Economie et de Statistique, 63/64*, 39–65.

316 Richins, M. L. (2004). The Material Values Scale: Measurement properties and development of a short form. *JCR, 31*, 209–19.

317 Ibid.

318 (1) Brown, K. W., & Kasser, T. (2005). Are psychological and ecological well-being compatible? The role of values, mindfulness, and lifestyle. *SIR, 74*, 349–68.

(2) Kasser & Ryan (1993), op. cit. (See ch. 5, note 260). (3) Nickerson, C., Schwarz, N., Diener, E., & Kahneman, D. (2003). Zeroing in on the dark side of the American dream: A closer look at the negative consequences of the goal for financial success. *PsychScience, 14,* 531–36. (4) Kasser (2002), op. cit. (See ch. 5, note 260).

319 (1) Brown & Kasser (2005), op. cit. (See ch. 7, note 318). (2) Richins & Dawson (1992), op. cit. (See ch. 6, note 288).

320 (1) Belk (1985), op. cit. (See ch. 6, note 288). (2) Richins & Dawson (1992), op. cit. (See ch. 6, note 288). (3) Kashdan & Breen (2007), op. cit. (See ch. 6, note 288). (4) Kasser & Ryan (1993), op. cit. (See ch. 5, note 260). (5) Solberg, E. G., Diener, E., & Robinson, M. D. (2004). Why are materialists less satisfied? In T. Kasser & A. D. Kanner (Eds.), *Psychology and consumer culture* (pp. 29–48). Washington, DC: APA.

321 James, O. (2007). *Affluenza.* New York: Vermillion.

322 Csikszentmihalyi, M. (1999). If we are so rich, why aren't we happy? *AmPsych, 54,* 821–27.

323 Adams, J. T. (2001). *The epic of America.* New York: Simon. (Originally published 1931.)

324 On the other hand, my other favorite quote, from Bo Derek, is "Those who say money can't buy happiness just don't know where to shop."

325 I discovered that at least four of these six principles are also described in the following eloquent and persuasive paper: Dunn, E. W., Gilbert, D. T., & Wilson, T. D. (2011). If money doesn't make you happy then you probably aren't spending it right. *Journal of Consumer Psychology, 21,* 115–25. My graduate student Joe Chancellor's and my response to these ideas is contained in Chancellor, J., & Lyubomirsky, S. (2011). Happiness and thrift: When (spending) less is (hedonically) more. *Journal of Consumer Psychology, 21,* 131–38.

326 (1) Kasser & Ryan (1993), op. cit. (See ch. 5, note 260). (2) Kasser & Ryan (1996), op. cit. (See ch. 5, note 251). (3) Ryan, R. M., & Deci, E. L. (2000). Self-determination theory and the facilitation of intrinsic motivation, social development, and well-being. *AmPsych, 55,* 68–78.

327 (1) Koob, G. F., & Le Moal, M. (2001). Drug addiction, dysregulation of reward, and allostasis. *Neuropsychopharmacology, 24,* 97–129. (2) Myers (2000), op. cit. (See ch. 6, note 276).

328 (1) Lyubomirsky, King, et al. (2005), op. cit. (See ch. 4, note 207). (2) Norton, M. I., et al. (2009). *From wealth to well-being: Spending money on others promotes happiness.* Paper presented at the SPSP annual meeting, Tampa, FL. (3) Otake, K., et al. (2006). Happy people become happier through kindness: A counting kindnesses intervention. *JoHS, 7,* 361–75.

329 (1) Havens, J. J. (2006). Charitable giving: How much, by whom, to what, and how? In W. W. Powell & R. Steinberg (Eds.) *The non-profit sector.* New Haven, CT: Yale University Press. (2) Easterbrook, G. (2007, March 18). A wealth of cheapskates. *Los Angeles Times.* (3) James, R. N., III, & Sharpe, D. L. (2007). The nature and causes of the U-shaped charitable giving profile. *Nonprofit and Volunteer Sector Quarterly, 36,* 218–38. See also Piff, P. K., et al. (2010). Having less, giving more: The influence of social class on prosocial behavior. *JPSP, 99,* 771–84.

330 Dunn et al. (2008), op. cit. (See ch. 1, note 84).

331 Aknin, L., et al. (2010). *Prosocial spending and well-being: Cross-cultural evidence for a psychological universal.* Manuscript under review.

332 A chapter devoted to the subject of why acts of kindness make us happy and how to practice them is in Lyubomirsky (2008), op. cit. (See introduction, note 32).

333 (1) Lyubomirsky, Sheldon, et al. (2005), op. cit. (See ch. 1, note 16). (2) Sheldon et al. (in press), op. cit. (See ch. 1, note 27).

334 Layard, R. (2005). *Happiness.* London: Penguin Press.

335 Loewenstein, G. (1999). Because it is there: The challenge of mountaineering . . . for utility theory. *KYKLOS, 52,* 315–44.

336 Loewenstein, G. (1987). Anticipation and the valuation of delayed consumption. *The Economic Journal, 97,* 666–84.

337 Mitchell et al. (1997), op. cit. (See ch. 6, note 285).

338 Nawijn, J., et al. (2010). Vacationers happier, but most not happier after a holiday. *Applied Research in Quality of Life, 5,* 35–47. See also Van Boven, L., & Ashworth, L. (2007). Looking forward, looking back: Anticipation is more evocative than retrospection. *Journal of Experimental Psychology: General, 136,* 289–300.

339 The chef was Thomas Keller of the French Laundry, and despite the fact that we ended up having that unlikely future child (Isabella), we bailed on the pledge.

340 But the remaining three—wrath, pride, and envy—aren't far behind.

341 (1) Read, D., Loewenstein, G., & Kalyanaraman, S. (1999). Mixing virtue and vice: Combining the immediacy effect and the diversification heuristic. *Journal of Behavioral Decision Making, 12,* 257–73. (2) Read, D., & Van Leeuwen, B. (1998). Predicting hunger: The effects of appetite and delay on choice. *Organizational Behavior and Human Decision Processes, 76,* 189–205.

342 Hawn, G. (2005). *Goldie: A lotus grows in the mud* (p. 163). New York: Putnam.

PART III: LOOKING BACK

CHAPTER 8: I CAN'T BE HAPPY WHEN . . . THE TEST RESULTS WERE POSITIVE

343 Edwards, E. (2009). *Resilience* (p. 129 and p. 133). New York: Broadway.

344 Ibid. (p. 141).

345 My friend Sarah Stroud, a professor of philosophy at McGill University, picked up on the leap in logic I am making here. If we accept as true that our experience is what we agree to attend to, this statement doesn't mean that we can *control* what we attend to. I acknowledge the lapse, but argue that research supports the notion that we have power over much of our attention and thought processes.

346 William James was credited with the statement that "man can alter his life simply by altering his attitude of mind."

347 William, J. (1890). *Principles of psychology* (p. 402). New York: Holt.

348 Calloway, E., & Naghdi, S. (1982). An information processing model for schizophrenia. *Archives of General Psychiatry, 39,* 339–47.

349 Jacobson, N. S., & Moore, D. (1981). Spouses as observers of the events in their relationship. *JCCP, 49,* 269–77.

350 Psychological scientists from William James to the present day have presented evidence for two kinds of attention—voluntary attention (the kind that I am talking about in this section and the kind we can control) and involuntary attention (the kind that is "captured" by important or exciting events or objects in our environments, like the sound of a gunshot or a beautiful sunset). Not only are these two types of attention experienced differently, but they appear to rely on different parts of the brain. To learn more, see Kaplan, S., & Berman, M. G. (2010). Directed attention as a common resource for executive function and self-regulation. *Perspectives, 5,* 43–57.

351 Frank, R. H. (2009). The Easterlin paradox revisited. In Dutt & Radcliff (Eds.), op. cit., p. 156. (See ch. 1, note 29).

352 Kaplan & Berman (2010), op. cit. (See ch. 8, note 350).

353 (1) Kaplan, S. (1995). The restorative benefits of nature: Toward an integrative framework. *Journal of Environmental Psychology, 15,* 169–82. (2) Kaplan & Berman (2010), op. cit. (See ch. 8, note 350).

354 (1) Kaplan, S., & Talbot, J. F. (1983). Psychological benefits of a wilderness experience. In I. Altman & J. F. Wohlwill (Eds.), *Behavior and the natural environment* (pp. 163–203). New York: Plenum. (2). Ulrich, R. S., et al. (1991). Stress recovery during exposure to natural and urban environments. *Journal of Environmental Psychology, 11,* 201–30. (3) Nisbet, E. K., & Zelenski, J. M. (2011). Underestimating nearby nature: Affective forecasting errors obscure the happy path to sustainability. *PsychScience, 22,* 1101–6.

355 Berman, M. G., Jonides, J., & Kaplan, S. (2008). The cognitive benefits of interacting with nature. *PsychScience, 19,* 1207–12.

356 Mayer, F. S., et al. (2009). Why is nature beneficial? The role of connectedness to nature. *Environment and Behavior, 41,* 607–43.

357 (3) Much of this fascinating research is reviewed in Kabat-Zinn, J. (2003). Mindfulness-based interventions in context: Past, present, and future. *Clinical Psychology: Science and Practice, 10,* 144–56. See also (1) Lutz, A., et al. (2008). Regulation of the neural circuitry of emotion by compassion meditation: Effects of meditative expertise. *PLoS ONE, 3,* e1897. (2) Fredrickson et al. (2008), op. cit. (See ch. 2, note 99). (3) Davidson, R. J., et al. (2003). Alterations in brain and immune function produced by mindfulness meditation. *Psychosomatic Medicine, 65,* 564–70.

358 (1) Tang, Y.-Y., et al. (2007). Short-term meditation training improves attention and self-regulation. *PNAS, 104,* 17152–56. (2) Slagter, H. A., et al. (2007). Mental training affects use of limited brain resources. *PLoS Biology, 5,* e138. (3) MacLean, K. A., et al. (2010). Intensive meditation training improves perceptual discrimination and sustained attention. *PsychScience, 21,* 829–39.

359 (1) Fredrickson (2001), op. cit. (See ch. 2, note 98). (2) Fredrickson, B. L. (2009). *Positivity.* New York: Crown.

360 For reviews and evidence for these points, see (1) Lyubomirsky, King, et al. (2005), op. cit. (See ch. 4, note 207). (2) King et al. (2006), op. cit. (See ch. 2, note 99). (3) Cohn, M. A., et al. (2009). Happiness unpacked: Positive emotions increase life satisfaction by building resilience. *Emotion, 9,* 361–68.

361 For example, see Merton, R. K. (1968). The Matthew effect in science. *Science, 159(3810),* 56–63.

362 Matthew 25:29. New Revised Standard Version.

363 (1) Diener et al. (1991), op. cit. (See ch. 6, note 289). (2) Larsen, R. J., Diener, E., & Cropanzano, R. (1987). Cognitive operations associated with individual differences in affect intensity. *JPSP, 53,* 767–74.

364 Carstensen, L. L., et al. (2011). Emotional experience improves with age: Evidence based on over 10 years of experience sampling. *Psychology and Aging, 26,* 21–33.

365 Mochon et al. (2008), op. cit. (See ch. 6, note 294).

366 I borrowed this lovely story from Edwards (2009), op. cit. (See ch. 8, note 343).

367 Herzog, D. (2007). *Math you can use–everyday.* Hoboken, NJ: Wiley.

368 Taylor, S. E. (1991). Asymmetrical effects of positive and negative events: The mobilization-minimization hypothesis. *PsychBull, 110,* 67–85.

369 Sweeny, K., & Shepperd, J. A. (2007). Being the best bearer of bad tidings. *RGP, 11,* 235–57.

370 This quote comes from the wisdom of David Myers.

371 Allen, K., Blascovich, J., & Mendes, W. B. (2002). Cardiovascular reactivity in the presence of pets, friends, and spouses: The truth about cats and dogs. *Psychosomatic Medicine, 64,* 727–39.

372 (1) Brown, J. L., et al. (2003). Social support and experimental pain. *Psychosomatic Medicine, 65,* 276–83. (2) Master, S. L., et al. (2009). A picture's worth: Partner photographs reduce experimentally induced pain. *PsychScience, 20,* 1316–18.

373 House, J. S., Landis, K. R., & Umberson, D. (1988). Social relationships and health. *Science, 241,* 540–45.

374 Berkman, L. F., & Syme, S. L. (1979). Social networks, host resistance, and mortality: A nine-year follow-up study of Alameda County residents. *American Journal of Epidemiology, 109,* 186–204.

375 Seeman, T. E., et al. (2001). Social relationships, social support, and patterns of cognitive aging in healthy, high-functioning older adults: MacArthur Studies of Successful Aging. *Health Psychology, 20,* 243–55.

376 For three good reviews of the social support and health literature, see (1) Cohen, S., & Janicki-Deverts, D. (2009). Can we improve our physical health by altering our social networks? *Perspectives, 4,* 375–78. (2) Uchino, B. N. (2009). Understanding the links between social support and physical health: A life-span perspective with emphasis on the separability of perceived and received support. *Perspectives, 4,* 236–55. (3) Seeman, T. E. (2000). Health promoting effects of friends and family on health outcomes in older adults. *American Journal of Health Promotion, 14,* 362–70.

377 Grant, A. M., & Wade-Benzoni, K. A. (2009). The hot and cool of death awareness at work: Mortality cues, aging, and self-protective and prosocial motivations. *Academy of Management Review, 34,* 600–622.

378 Schnell, T. (2009). The Sources of Meaning and Meaning in Life Questionnaire (SoMe): Relations to demographics and well-being. *The Journal of Positive Psychology, 4,* 483–99. Reprinted by permission of the publisher (Taylor & Francis Ltd, www.tandfonline.com).

379 Ibid.

380 http://losangeles.cbslocal.com/2011/05/18/girl-spreads-joy-to-others-while-battling-cancer/

381 Wade-Benzoni, K. A., & Tost, L. P. (2009). The egoism and altruism of intergenerational behavior. *PSPR, 13,* 165–93.

382 Pyszczynski, T., Greenberg, J., & Solomon, S. (1999). A dual-process model of defense against conscious and unconscious death-related thoughts: An extension of terror management theory. *PsychReview, 106,* 835–45.

CHAPTER 9: I CAN'T BE HAPPY WHEN . . . I KNOW I'LL
NEVER PLAY SHORTSTOP FOR THE YANKEES

383 King, L. A., & Hicks, J. A. (2007). Whatever happened to "What might have been"? Regrets, happiness, and maturity. *AmPsych, 62,* 625–36.

384 Stewart, A. J., & Vandewater, E. A. (1999). "If I had it to do over again.": Midlife review, midcourse corrections, and women's well-being in midlife. *JPSP, 76,* 270–83.

385 Wrosch, C., Bauer, I., & Scheier, M. F. (2005). Regret and quality of life across the adult life span: The influence of disengagement and available future goals. *Psychology and Aging, 20,* 657–70.

386 Ibid.

387 King & Hicks (2007), op. cit., p. 626. (See ch. 9, note 383).

388 My husband and son, lifelong Mets fans, were aghast at the title of this chapter.

389 King & Hicks (2007), op. cit., p. 630. (See ch. 9, note 383).

390 (1) Nolen-Hoeksema et al. (2008), op. cit. (See ch. 2, note 119). (2) Lyubomirsky & Tkach (2004), op. cit. (See ch. 2, note 119). For a well-researched, highly accessible, and engaging review of this work, see Nolen-Hoeksema (2003), op. cit. (See ch. 2, note 120).

391 (1) McFarland, C., & Buehler, R. (1998). The impact of negative affect on autobiographical memory: The role of self-focused attention to moods. *JPSP, 75,* 1424–40. (2) Trapnell, P. D., & Campbell, J. D. (1999). Private self-consciousness and the five-factor model of personality: Distinguishing rumination from reflection. *JPSP, 76,* 284–304. (3) Segerstrom, S. C., et al. (2003). A multidimensional structure for repetitive thought: What's on your mind, and how, and how much? *JPSP, 85,* 909–21. (4) Lyubomirsky et al. (2011), op. cit. (See ch. 5, note 246).

392 For exhaustive and excellent advice, see Nolen-Hoeksema (2003), op. cit. (See ch. 2, note 120).

393 Stewart & Vandewater (1999), op. cit. (See ch. 9, note 384).

394 My apologies for paraphrasing Shakespeare's Hamlet, who famously said, "Nothing is good or bad but thinking makes it so."

395 (1) Summerville, A., & Roese, N. J. (2008). Dare to compare: Fact-based versus simulation-based comparison in daily life. *Journal of Experimental Social Psychology, 44,* 664–71. (2) Summerville, A. (2011). Counterfactual seeking: The scenic overlook of the road not taken. *PSPB, 37,* 1522–33.

396 Kray, L. J., et al. (2010). From what *might* have been to what *must* have been: Counterfactual thinking creates meaning. *JPSP, 98,* 106–18.

397 Ibid. (p. 109).

398 I am grateful to Landau, Greenberg, and Sullivan (2009) for this example.

399 Routledge, C., et al. (2011). The past makes the present meaningful: Nostalgia as an existential resource. *JPSP, 101,* 638–52.

400 (1) Gilovich, T., & Medvec, V. H. (1995). The experience of regret: What, when, and why. *PsychReview, 102,* 379–95. (2) Gilovich, T., et al. (2003). Regrets of action and inaction across cultures. *Journal of Cross-Cultural Psychology, 34,* 61–71.

401 Carlson (1997), op. cit. (See ch. 2, note 120).

402 Zeigarnik, B. (1935). On finished and unfinished tasks. In K. Lewin (Ed.), *A dynamic theory of personality* (pp. 300–14). New York: McGraw-Hill.

403 Schwartz, B. (2004). *The paradox of choice.* New York: HarperCollins.

404 Schwartz, B., et al. (2002). Maximizing versus satisficing: Happiness is a matter of choice. *JPSP, 83,* 1178–97.

405 Iyengar, S. S., Wells, R. E., & Schwartz, B. (2006). Doing better but feeling worse: Looking for the "best" job undermines satisfaction. *PsychScience, 17,* 143–50.

406 (1) Danziger, S., Levav, J., & Avnaim-Pesso, L. (2011). Extraneous factors in judicial decisions. *PNAS, 108,* 6889–92. (2) Vohs, K. D., et al. (2008). Making choices impairs subsequent self-control: A limited-resource account of decision making, self-regulation, and active initiative. *JPSP, 94,* 883–98. (3) Levav, J., et al. (2010). Order in product customization decisions: Evidence from field experiments. *Journal of Political Economy,* 118, 274–99.

407 Lyubomirsky & Ross (1997), op. cit. (See ch. 5, note 246).

408 An excellent book that advocates time diaries is Vanderkam, L. (2010). *168 hours.* New York: Portfolio.

CHAPTER 10: I CAN'T BE HAPPY WHEN . . . THE BEST YEARS OF MY LIFE ARE OVER

409 Mitchell et al. (1997), op. cit. (See ch. 6, note 285).

410 Humphrey Bogart (as Rick Blaine) to Ingrid Bergman (as Ilsa Lund) in the film *Casablanca.*

411 To read the full paper, see: Liberman et al. (2009), op. cit. (See ch. 5, note 231).

412 This distinction was first described by the late Amos Tversky, a brilliant scientist who collaborated with Daniel Kahneman on groundbreaking work in the field of judgment and decision making. The ideas I describe here were first published in a chapter: Tversky, A., & Griffin, D. (1991). Endowment and contrast in judgments of well-being. In Strack, Argyle, & Schwarz (Eds.), op. cit. (See ch. 6, note 289).

413 Just this one finding was evident only among the Americans surveyed, not the Israelis.

414 Lacey et al. (2006), op. cit. (See ch. 2, note 144).

415 However, as my husband puts it, our *first* chance at happiness is apparently being born to royalty!

416 Lyubomirsky, S., Sousa, L., & Dickerhoof, R. (2006). The costs and benefits of writing, talking, and thinking about life's triumphs and defeats. *JPSP, 90,* 692–708.

417 Timothy Wilson and Daniel Gilbert call this process "ordinizing": (1) Wilson, T. D.,

& Gilbert, D. T. (2003). Affective forecasting. *Advances in Experimental Social Psychology, 35,* 345–411. (2) Wilson et al. (2005), op. cit. (See ch. 1, note 44).

418   From English statesman Benjamin Disraeli: Disraeli, B. (2000). *Lothair* (vol. III) (p. 206). Cambridge, UK: Chadwyck-Healey Ltd.

419   For a review, see Ryan & Deci (2000), op. cit. (See ch. 7, note 326).

420   (1) Emmons & King (1988), op. cit. (See ch. 5, note 251). (2) Sheldon & Kasser (1995), op. cit. (See ch. 5, note 259).

421   For example, see Kasser & Ryan (1996), op. cit. (See chapter 5, note 251).

422   (1) Sheldon, K. M., & Elliot, A. J. (1999). Goal striving, need satisfaction, and longitudinal well-being: The self-concordance model. *JPSP, 76,* 546–57. (2) Sheldon, K. M. (2002). The self-concordance model of healthy goal-striving: When personal goals correctly represent the person. In E. L. Deci & R. M. Ryan (Eds.), *Handbook of self-determination theory* (pp. 65–86). Rochester, NY: University of Rochester Press.

423   (1) King, L. A. (1996). Who is regulating what and why? Motivational context of self-regulation. *Psychological Inquiry, 7,* 57–60. (2) Emmons, R. A. (1986). Personal strivings: An approach to personality and subjective well-being. *JPSP, 51,* 1058–68.

424   (1) Elliot, A. J., & Sheldon, K. M. (1998). Avoidance personal goals and the personality–illness relationship. *JPSP, 75,* 1282–99. (2) Elliot, A. J., Sheldon, K. M., & Church, M. A. (1997). Avoidance personal goals and subjective well-being. *PSPB, 23,* 915–27. (3) Elliot, A. J., & McGregor, H. A. (2001). A 2 X 2 achievement goal framework. *JPSP, 80,* 501–19.

425   Kruglanski (1996), op. cit. (See ch. 5, note 252).

426   Vatsyayana. (2005). *The Kama Sutra.* (S. R. Burton & F. F. Arbuthont, Trans.). London: Elibron Classics. (Originally published 1883).

427   Huxley, A. (1925). *Those barren leaves* (p. 79). Normal, IL: Dalkey Archive Press.

428   (1) Lacey et al. (2006), op. cit. (See ch. 2, note 144). (2) Hummert, M. L., et al. (1994). Stereotypes of the elderly held by young, middle-aged, and elderly adults. *Journals of Gerontology, 49,* 240. (3) Nosek, B. A., Banaji, M., & Greenwald, A. G. (2002). Harvesting implicit group attitudes and beliefs from a demonstration Web site. *Group Dynamics: Theory, Research, and Practice, 6,* 101–15.

429   The empirical evidence is incredibly strong; here are a few examples: (1) Carstensen et al. (2011), op. cit. (See ch. 8, note 364). (2) Carstensen, L. L., et al. (2000). Emotional experience in everyday life across the adult life span. *JPSP, 79,* 644–55. (3) Charles, S. T., Reynolds, C. A., & Gatz, M. (2001). Age-related differences and change in positive and negative affect over 23 years. *JPSP, 80,* 136–51. (4) Mroczek, D. K., & Spiro, A., III. (2005). Change in life satisfaction during adulthood: Findings from the Veterans Affairs Normative Aging Study. *JPSP, 88,* 189–202. (5) Williams, L. M., et al. (2006). The mellow years? Neural basis of improving emotional stability over age. *The Journal of Neuroscience, 26,* 6422–30. (6) Vaillant, G. E. (1994). "Successful aging" and psychosocial well-being: Evidence from a 45-year study. In E. H. Thompson (Ed.), *Older men's lives* (pp. 22–41). Thousand Oaks, CA: Sage.

430   (1) Carstensen et al. (2011), op. cit. (See ch. 8, note 364). (2) Mroczek & Spiro (2005), op. cit. (See ch. 10, note 430). (3) Williams et al. (2006), op. cit. (See ch. 10, note 430).

431 For an excellent and accessible introduction to this literature, see Carstensen, S. (2009). *A long bright future*. New York: Broadway. For scholarly articles, see (1) Carstensen, L. L. (2006). The influence of a sense of time on human development. *Science, 312,* 1913–15. (2) Carstensen, L. L., Isaacowitz, D. M., & Charles, S. T. (1999). Taking time seriously: a theory of socioemotional selectivity. *AmPsych, 54,* 165–81.

432 Mogilner, C., Kamvar, S. D., & Aaker, J. (2011). The shifting meaning of happiness. *Social Psychological and Personality Science, 2,* 395–402.

433 (1) Riediger, M., et al. (2009). Seeking pleasure and seeking pain: Differences in prohedonic and contra-hedonic motivation from adolescence to old age. *PsychScience, 20,* 1529–35. (2) Carstensen, L. L., Fung, H. H., & Charles, S. T. (2003). Socioemotional selectivity theory and the regulation of emotion in the second half of life. *Motivation and Emotion, 27,* 103–23. (3) Urry, H. L., & Gross, J. J. (2010). Emotion regulation in older age. *Current Directions, 19,* 352–57. (4) Labouvie-Vief, G., & DeVoe, M. (1991). Emotional regulation in adulthood and later life: a developmental view. *Annual Review of Gerontology and Geriatrics, 11,* 172–94. (5) Fingerman, K. L., & Charles, S. T. (2010). It takes two to tango: Why older people have the best relationships. *Current Directions, 19,* 172–76.

434 For reviews, see (1) Carstensen, L. L., & Mikels, J. A. (2005). At the intersection of emotion and cognition: Aging and the positivity effect. *Current Directions, 14,* 117–21. (2) Charles, S. T. (2010). Strength and vulnerability integration: A model of emotional well-being across adulthood. *PsychBull, 136,* 1068–91.

435 Calder, A. J., et al. (2003). Facial expression recognition across the adult life span. *Neuropsychologia, 4,* 195–202.

436 (1) Fingerman & Charles (2010), op. cit. (See ch. 10, note 434). (2) Fingerman, K. L., Miller, L., & Charles, S. T. (2008). Saving the best for last: How adults treat social partners of different ages. *Psychology and Aging, 23,* 399–409. (3) Miller, L. M., Charles, S. T., & Fingerman, K. L. (2009). Perceptions of social transgressions in adulthood: Does age make a difference? *Journal of Gerontology, 64B,* 551–59.

CONCLUSION: WHERE HAPPINESS IS REALLY FOUND

437 Cohany, S. R., & Sok, E. (2007, February). Trends in labor force participation of married mothers of infants. *Monthly Labor Review,* 9–16.

438 See the references in the introduction (notes 1 and 5).

Index

About the Author

SONJA LYUBOMIRSKY is a professor of psychology at the University of California, Riverside. Her research on the possibility of permanently increasing happiness has been honored with a Science of Generosity grant, a John Templeton Foundation grant, a Templeton Positive Psychology Prize, and a grant from the National Institute of Mental Health. Lyubomirsky's 2008 book, *The How of Happiness,* has been translated into nineteen languages. She lives in Santa Monica, California, with her family. For more information, please visit www.drsonja.net.